# ON THE ASHES

Gideon Haigh was born in England and lives in Australia, with a parent from each. He was eight when he attended his first Ashes Test, twenty-four when he reported his first Ashes series. Gideon has written about cricket in *The Australian*, *The Times*, *The Guardian*, the *Financial Times* and in more than thirty books.

# GIDEON HAIGH
# ON THE ASHES

ALLEN&UNWIN

Published in hardback in Great Britain in 2023 by Allen & Unwin,
an imprint of Atlantic Books Ltd.

10 9 8 7 6 5 4 3 2 1

A CIP catalogue record for this book is available from the British Library.

Hardback ISBN: 978 1 83895 997 5
E-book ISBN: 978 1 83895 998 2

Printed and bound by CPI (UK) Ltd, Croydon CR0 4YY

Allen & Unwin
An imprint of Atlantic Books Ltd
Ormond House
26–27 Boswell Street
London
WC1N 3JZ

www.atlantic-books.co.uk

*For Cee*

# Contents

Foreword . . . . . . . . . . 1

Golden Age, Darker Lining . . . . 5

Bodyline and Other Lines . . . . 77

Cricket's Cold War . . . . . . 141

The Instant Age . . . . . . . 207

Ashes Eyewitness . . . . . . 265

Index . . . . . . . . . . 397

# Foreword

## AN ASHES LIFE

The Ashes may have been in my stars. I was born in England, live in Australia, with a parent from each. I was eight when I attended my first Ashes Test, twenty-four when I reported my first Ashes series. I never intended becoming a cricket journalist, and would rather be considered a journalist who sometimes writes about cricket. But this collection, I'm bound to admit, makes an opposite case, collaging writings that cover almost a century and a half of Anglo-Australian cricket, people and places, news and olds.

Nothing compares to the Ashes, which in some respects is a shame, as this results from the lamentable abeyance in bilateral competition between India and Pakistan. But it is surely remarkable. After all, how many ideas endure from 1882, when creationism and phrenology flourished, nobody had heard of viruses or dreamed of X-rays, dreams of universal suffrage and a universal eight-hour day seemed fanciful, and cremation, of course, was a subject ripe for jokes? As the Empire sprawled mightily, the Australian continent was a mere patchwork of colonies reporting individually to faraway masters.

The Ashes has benefited hugely since by continuity, interrupted only by world wars, adulterated only by greedy administrators – I'm looking at those who inflicted ten consecutive Tests on us in 2013–14. The Ashes is always coming, even when it is finished. Especially in England, the intervening years are concerned with either soul-searching or brainstorming. There are, to be sure, bigger games in town. Indian visits line the vaults; World Cups gleam in the trophy cabinet. But the Ashes is where hope, expectation, magic and chagrin flourish in equal measure, and performance is permanently burnished. Ben Stokes at Headingley 2019 would have been a marvel against any opposition; its additional gilding is that it came at Australia's expense.

Ahead of the Ashes of 2023, we find ourselves in a very particular period, where home advantage is bordering on the unassailable: Australia has not won a series in England since 2001, England not won a Test in Australia since 2011. But in a rivalry so long, everything can be deemed a phase. Even Bradman retired. Even Warne could be worked around. The Ashes, moreover, still connects. There is in marketing an established taxonomy of brands: the 'ritual' brand, identified with special occasions; the 'symbolic' brand, identified with a recognized logo; the 'heritage of good' brand, established as according a special benefit; the 'aloof snob' brand, nourishing a sense of superiority; the 'belonging' brand, which binds a self-perceived special group; and the 'legend' brand, which derives from an epic story. If it be possible, Ashes cricket works on all six levels.

But the Ashes is, of course, also more than a brand. Within it is the dynamic of rivalry, about which it is impossible to be neutral. I am not a particular patriot or partisan, except in barracking for Test matches: nothing so disappoints me as cricket that fails to rise to the occasion (such as, sad to say, the Ashes of 2021–22). But from my tangle of DNA and my hope for a worthy contest, I confess, arises a modest but unreducing satisfaction when England fares well. Australia is always competitive. They fight; they strike back. Since 1977, only once has Australia not won at least one Test in a series, and then, in 2013, they were about to whitewash England on home soil. This it is only possible to respect. It is England's measuring up to and every so often exceeding Australia's standard that completes the Ashes: their worst moments resonate uneasily with senses of national masochism and post-imperial marginalization. When these countries meet, in fact, there is always something slightly more at stake than cricket supremacy. They are saying something of themselves to the world.

What am I saying of myself? I grew up on anthologies of cricket writing: Pollard's *Six and Out*, Ross's *The Cricketer's Companion*, compilations from sundry mastheads and about particular series, and particularly the canonical treasuries of Cardus, Robertson-Glasgow, Arlott, Swanton, Kilburn, Robinson and Fingleton. To curate my own collection is a happy act of homage, as well as an attempt to cover the full arc of history, from Charles Bannerman, the first Australian century-maker against England, to Joe Root, England's most recent Ashes captain. I've had a press box vantage on the last three decades; by profiles, interviews, reviews and obituaries I've sought a communion with the past. I hope that the partialities of *On The Ashes* will be pardoned, that the gaps will be overlooked, and that the forthcoming cricket compels an updated edition.

GIDEON HAIGH
Melbourne 2023

# GOLDEN AGE, DARKER LINING

*Records are proverbially made to be broken; firsts stand for all time. Before the First World War, the Ashes was a blank tablet to carve feats into. So here are some of the carvers: the first scorer of a century, Charles Bannerman; the first taker of a five-for, William Midwinter; the first Ashes diarist, Tom Horan; the first giant series, 1894–95. The achievements have lasted as long as the lives associated proved short and benighted: Midwinter and captain extraordinaire Harry Trott became asylum inmates; Drewy Stoddart and Arthur Shrewsbury were suicides; Victor Trumper and Tip Foster, top scorers in the grand Sydney Test of 1903, were prematurely slain by illness; the whole belle époque would be drowned in mud, blood and disillusionment. But by 1914, the Ashes were established enough to survive, and nothing short of war has been equal to stopping them since.*

# The Ashes

## SACRED SOOT (2017)

The Ashes fails almost every test as a modern sporting trophy. It confers no number one status, involves no massive cash prize and plods along in a slow-moving format widely considered obsolete. The small, frail urn would not catch your eye in a bric-a-brac shop, embodying the rivalry of a distant time, and riffing on a forgotten joke – about, for heaven's sake, cremation. Although, considering what else was in vogue in 1882, England and Australia are lucky not to be playing for a trophy in the shape of Jumbo the elephant or the Eddystone Lighthouse.

In uniqueness, of course, lies the Ashes' success. Aslant the priorities of contemporary sport, it occupies a universe of one. Its history can be exposited at voluminous length, or in a shorthand that summons legends by a name, by a year, or even by a single delivery, whether it's Bradman b Hollies or Gatting b Warne. Better yet, success has exhibited a gratifying cyclicality: of seventy-two series, Australia have won thirty-four, England thirty-two, with six series drawn.

*

The totem's origins are improbable – the fruit of youthful high spirits. When the fifth Anglo-Australian Test ended in a breathless seven-run victory for the visitors at The Oval, twenty-seven-year-old journalist Reginald Shirley Brooks secured immortality of a sort by inserting a death notice in London's *Sporting Times* 'in affectionate memory of English cricket', with the addendum: 'The body will be cremated and the ashes taken to Australia.'

Some months later in Australia, a twenty-three-year-old nob, The Hon. Ivo Walter Francis Bligh, who had come as captain of an English touring XI, referred jestingly to his objective as 'recovery of the ashes'. The notion so captivated some Melbourne society belles, one of who became his bride, that they subsequently awarded Bligh a dark red pottery urn containing something sooty, popularly a burned bail, of which the Marylebone Cricket Club has been custodian since 1927. By then, the Ashes had gained a capital letter, thanks to the title of Pelham Warner's journal of his team's 1903–04 tour: *How We Recovered the Ashes.*

From the first, then, the Ashes has echoed and reinforced the relationship of the countries, playing out their differences in such a way as to emphasize their closeness. Perhaps only rivals with so much in common could afford such unbridled competition; at the same time, empire's bonds never sat so heavily on the colonized because of cricket's free play.

On a per capita basis, the Ashes has probably always meant more to Australians. 'Cricket was the great way out of Australian cultural ignominy,' wrote the novelist and re-publican gadfly Thomas Keneally. 'No Australian had written *Paradise Lost*, but Bradman had made 100 before lunch at Lord's.' England's frequent underdog status since the

1960s has also resonated with popular sensations of global decline, while also offering, every now and again, the salve of sporting superiority.

In the history of the Ashes, the decisive figure is Sir Donald Bradman, not merely because of his prowess, or his fame, or his statistics, but more generally the intensity his presence lent the contest. In piling up nineteen hundreds against England, he scaled the greatest heights; in provoking Bodyline, he engendered the most controversial counter-measures; in being knighted, he raised the cricketer to the level of imperial statesman. It helped universalize his popularity that Bradman was himself a conservative man, deeply respectful of the English institutions and assumptions he challenged. 'We want him to do well,' noted R. C. Robertson-Glasgow. 'We feel we have a share in him. He is more than Australian. He is a world batsman.'

In our own generation, Richie Benaud and Shane Warne have achieved something like the same warm regard, Benaud by blending perfectly into the English media landscape, Warne by standing out from it with a certain irrepressibly comedic Aussieness. In the shadow of the unforgettable 2005 Ashes, a crowd at The Oval serenaded Warne with choruses of 'We wish you were English.' No sunhat has been so ceremoniously doffed as Warne did in acknowledgement.

Although it has been easier for Australians to win English admiration than the other way round, the panache of Ian Botham and Andrew Flintoff made them favourites. Some unexpected accommodations have also been reached. Grim Douglas Jardine and saturnine Harold Larwood were vilified through the Antipodes in 1932–33 as England rained bouncers on Australian batsmen. But the former returned as a tourist, remarking drily: 'Though they may not hail me as Uncle Doug, I am no longer the bogeyman. Just an old so-and-so who got away with it.' The latter was by then comfortably settled in Sydney, rather as if Mitchell Johnson was to become an English market town's friendly greengrocer.

Issues have run the gamut, of course: from chucking to sledging, from doctoring pitches to conniving substitutes. The decisive weapon more often than not has been fast bowling, which tends to make blood pump and tempers flare. Yet it's worth a small prayer of thanks for the extremities of competition being all in the one direction. There has never been an Ashes fix; there has never even been the thought of one. The cricket has been good and bad, exciting and dull, even-tempered and one-sided. But the only object has ever been winning or, failing that, avoiding defeat.

In this century, cricket has also been bent out of shape by economics, demographics and geopolitics; it has veered towards bigger markets and shorter attention spans, brighter colours and louder noises. Yet it remains the case that the biggest verified crowd for a day's Test cricket anywhere, 91,112, was for the 2013 Boxing Day Ashes, on the same patch of earth where English and colonial teams met as far back as 1862. Bigger purses and greater prestige may be available elsewhere, but one joins no continuous cricket lineage longer or more meaningful. Bring it on.

# Charles Bannerman

## STANDARD SETTER (2016)[*]

C harles Bannerman is known today by a feat and an image. The feat, of course, is that of having faced Test cricket's first ball and scored its first run before peeling off its maiden century, a match-winning 165 from an Australian all out score of 245 at the MCG in March 1877. The image is a widely published photograph taken nearly fifty-three years later of an elderly Bannerman, in hat and coat, laying a gently approving hand on the shoulder of Donald Bradman at the SCG, when the twenty-one-year-old was about to commence his near-vertical ascent through cricket's hierarchy of records.

The time lapse between feat and image is perhaps just as evocative. Bannerman's cricket peak was brief and lonely: you can almost argue that it was confined to that innings, when he took toll of an English bowling attack still queasy from a

---

[*] Review of *Charles Bannerman: Australia's Premier Batsman* by Alfred James (Cricket Publishing Company), 2016.

stormy crossing of the Tasman, for it was almost exactly twice his next best first-class score, and he played only two further Test matches. But a first can never be busted to second. Bannerman's feat afforded him such imperishable status that he could, as it were, induct Bradman in an Australian batting lineage, with the additional prophecy: 'This boy will clip all the records.'

The big gap is also an enigma, both enticing and off-putting to a potential biographer. Bannerman has probably waited as long as any cricketer for a historian to go searching for him, and Alfred James, a studious classicist, reveals the pressure of the years in *Australia's Premier Batsman*: the traces are scant, limited and ambiguous. There are no photographs of Bannerman in action. The written accounts of his batting are disappointingly short of detail. James deems him a pioneer of 'forward play', but a mental image of his batting is hard to summon. Likewise a personal image. When James quotes a fond 1923 memoir of Bannerman from the journalist Jack Worrall – 'May he long remain with us, with his big blue eyes and his lisp' – the intimacy of the observation is powerful because it is so exceptional. Otherwise James is lumbered with reciting a great many scores, including some lengthy thread-bare sequences, which seem a little redundant seeing that they're recapitulated in statistical appendices.

Yet there is something here, and if the writing is mainly serviceable, with the occasional Latinate flourish, an intriguing story is hinted. Born in Woolwich, Bannerman was two years old when his family arrived in Sydney, his mother heavily pregnant with his brother Alick, himself destined to play twenty-eight Tests. Their father worked at Sydney's Mint, whose deputy master was an accomplished round-arm bowler: the boys walked in, then, on an evolving game.

It was also the unruly game of an unruly people, and

Charles Bannerman was no exception. James reveals that nineteen-year-old Bannerman lost his own Mint job for 'insolence to his superior officer and general insubordination', and went through a period in his early twenties when he alienated many contemporaries by his cocky club and colony hopping. 'The colt was considered a bright particular star while he lasted,' said a censorious columnist in the *Sydney Mail* in March 1874, 'but a good many people have come to the conclusion that for some time he has been on the wane, and that if common sense does not come to his aid he will be snuffed out for ever.' David Warner, then, has a distinguished antecedent. Although not even David Warner had three children with his first wife and two children with a mistress ten years his junior.

Bannerman's crowded hour of glorious batting life came when he was twenty-five. After the subsequent Australian tour of England, he dropped away precipitously, in a way strangely foretold. And although James has been unable to establish any satisfactory explanation, writers seemed uncannily aware that the process was irreversible. By 1879, the *Sydney Morning Herald* was calling him 'only the ghost of himself', *Australian Town and Country Journal* 'only the ghost of the player we used to know', and the *Sydney Mail* was asserting that there was 'no prospect of improvement'. Whatever they meant, they were right: for the next five years, Bannerman averaged less than 15 in first-class cricket. 'Drink and gambling, it is reputed, was his downfall,' wrote a contemporary many years later, although James shies from this 'far-fetched conclusion on the slight evidence available'.

James being a reluctant interpreter, the reader is left in a way to build their own story. My own was this. Bannerman was unusual in his Australian era in playing openly as a 'professional'. After losing his Mint job, he seems to have had only fragmentary employment outside the game: instead he relied on playing, touring, coaching and umpiring. His only other fallback, bookmaking, was a constraint. Not only did it eat into his Saturdays, but the England team of 1882–83 refused to accept him as an umpire – not surprising, really, given the betting-related cricket riot four years earlier when the SCG crowd stormed the field in protest at an umpiring decision against NSW's Billy Murdoch during a game with Lord Harris's Englishmen.

Bannerman was a 'professional', in other words, long before there was anything like a professional cricket structure. And for it he, and others, paid a price. Probably the most moving passages in James's book are from a news story in Sydney's *Evening News*, 27 May 1891, headlined 'A Cricketer in Low Circumstances': Bannerman had been arraigned to answer charges of desertion of his wife, and failure to provide for her. An exchange is recorded:

JUDGE: Your family is in destitute circumstances. How do you get your living?

BANNERMAN: By cricketing, your Worship.

JUDGE: But it's the off season now, and there's not much doing in that line.

BANNERMAN: I've nothing to say against my wife, your worship, at all. If you will give me a week to try and get the money, I might get some of it.

*By cricketing, your Worship*: four desperate words to encapsulate the precariousness of the professional cricket life, for the player, and for their financial dependents. Blessedly it was not to be the end. Cricket biography reserves a special place for the tragic figure. Bannerman ends up being a rarer figure in biography – a subject who flirted with tragedy and survived.

When his wife died in 1895, he was able to marry his mistress, and he benefited by testimonial matches in 1899 and 1922; his prudent brother, meanwhile, grew wealthy.

In that 1930 photograph with bashful Bradman, Bannerman strikes a pose of solemn dignity befitting the prestige of his achievement – with maybe just a hint of the character he had been in his playing days. For is that a cigarette in his hand?

# Tom Horan

## FELIX ON THE BAT (2006)

I n the last few weeks I have exchanged a number of emails
with a young Indian, eagerly immersing himself in a dis-
sertation on Australian cricket writing and full of questions.
What did I think of Ray Robinson? Jack Fingleton? Peter
Roebuck? (Peter will be gratified to know that he's now seen as
one of us.) I answered these enquiries as best I was able, then
made my own modest proposal: if he was a serious scholar in
the field, he should probably acquaint himself with Tom
Horan.

When answer came there none, I was not especially
surprised. If Horan rings a bell at all today, it is as a name in
the very first Test in 1877, and on the Australians' inaugural
tour of England a year later, where he enjoyed the signal
honour of the winning hit in their rout of Marylebone.

Born in County Cork on 8 March 1855 and brought to
Melbourne as a boy, Horan became a steady top order
batsman, worth 4027 first-class runs at 23, and considered
good enough to captain Australia at a pinch in 1884–85
when more uppity teammates decided to hold out for a

few extra shillings. By then, however, he had commenced a greater contribution to cricket's common weal: the 'Cricket Chatter' columns in *The Australasian*, the weekly sister paper of Melbourne's *Argus*, which he would compose for an extraordinary thirty-seven years. This transition was in its time highly unusual; in fact, distinguishing. Australian cricket was well supplied with competent scribes before the First World War, notably J. C. Davis and A. H. Gregory in Sydney, and Donald McDonald and Harry Hedley in Melbourne. Only Horan, however, had represented Australia, at home and abroad. There was no television to apparently drop the fan into the middle of the game; on the writer fell the entire responsibility for bringing the game to the fan, and no one in their time was on such intimate terms with cricket at the top level. It wasn't merely out of Hibernian loyalty that Bill O'Reilly described Horan as 'the cricket writer par excellence'; it was, he explained, because Horan was 'a writer who really did know what he was writing about'.

'Felix', as he was pseudonymously known, was not an adventurous stylist: he wrote, instead, with his ears and eyes, with a sense of the telling remark and the evocative detail, such as in his recollection of his first encounter with Victor Trumper in 1897:

> While on the Melbourne Ground the veteran Harry Hilliard introduced me to him and I was struck by the frank, engaging facial expression of the young Sydneyite. After a few words he went away and old Harry said to me: 'That lad will have to be reckoned with later on.' My word! But do you know what particularly attracted my attention when I first saw Victor fielding? You wouldn't guess in three. It was the remarkably neat way in which his shirt sleeves were folded. No loose, dangling down,

and folding back again after a run for the ball, but always trim and artistic.

I have never failed since to note this detail in Beldam's famous image of Trumper jumping out to drive.

My own acquaintance with Horan dates from the early 1990s, thanks to Australia's grand old man of cricket bibliophilia, Brisbane's Pat Mullins. Horan was Pat's great favourite, for his other great enthusiasm was all things Irish, and he had dedicated years of effort to compiling voluminous scrapbooks of Horaniana. When he foisted these on me at our first meeting, I accepted them with some reticence: seldom have I been so completely converted.

Horan knew everyone, and reported their deeds in a prose as breezy and inviting as his personality. When he is recounting the experiences of the English team of 1884–85 on tour, for instance, it is as though you have a seat at their table:

Barnes says that at Narrabri the heat was simply awful,
and immediately up in the ranges at Armidale he had to
wear a top coat and sit by the fire to keep himself
warm . . . It would do one good to hear Ulyett, little
Briggs or Attewell laugh as they detail some of their
Australian experiences; how Flowers was frightened of
the native bears on the banks of the Broken River at
Benalla; how Ulyett jumped from the steamer on a hot
afternoon on his way down from Clarence; and how
little Briggs came to grief on a backjumper at Armidale.
Briggs to this day maintains that the horse had nothing
to do with unseating him, it was simply the saddle. His
comrades, however, will not believe him . . . Briggs gives
a graphic description of a murderous raid he made one
night upon the mosquitos in Gympie, and how, when

that proved futile, he quenched the light and pulled his bed into another corner of the room to dodge them.

In January 1893, *The Australasian* commissioned from 'Felix' a regular supplementary column called `Round the Ground'. Horan's preferred vantage point at the MCG was under an elm tree near the sight board opposite the pavilion; from here he would embark on long peregrinations round the arena and through his memory, each personal encounter bringing forth a fund of reminiscences. It was during one of these ambles, in January 1902, that he committed to print perhaps his most famous passages, which concern the dying moments of the inaugural Ashes Test at The Oval in 1882 in which he had played.

Subsequently cited by H. S. Altham in *A History of Cricket*, these lines have been unconsciously paraphrased by scores of writers since:

> . . . the strain even for the spectators was so severe, that one onlooker dropped down dead, and another with his teeth gnawed out pieces of his umbrella handle. That was the match in which for the final half-hour you could have heard a pin drop, while the celebrated batsmen, A. P. Lucas and Alfred Lyttelton, were together, and Spofforth and Boyle bowling at them as they never bowled before. That was the match in which the last English batsman had to screw his courage to the sticking place by the aid of champagne, when one man's lips were ashen grey and his throat so parched that he could hardly speak as he strode by me to the crease; when the scorer's hand shook so that he wrote Peate's name like 'geese', and when in the wild tumult at the fall of the last wicket, the crowd in one tremendous roar cried 'bravo Australia'.

That inaugural Ashes Test had, I suspect, another impact on Horan's writing. He was not the last Australian journalist to be struck by the vehemence of the local criticisms of his English opponents:

> The very papers which, in dealing with the first day's play, said, in effect, that the English cricketers were the noblest, the bravest and the best; that, like the old guard of Napoleon, they would never know they are beaten, now turn completely around, and, with very questionable taste, designate these same cricketers as a weak-kneed and pusillanimous lot, who shaped worse than eleven schoolboys.

So even after his active cricketing days were over, Horan remained at heart a player: 'Felix' rejoiced in successes, and sympathized with failures, understanding sensitivities and susceptibilities as only one who has been there can. If he felt a point of order worth making, he did so with utmost even-handedness, the lightest touch and a peculiarly Victorian circumlocution.

'All this should be enough, indeed, to make one long to be in possession of Cagliostro's famous secret, so that one might have everlasting youth to enjoy to the full and for ever the glorious life of a first-class Australian cricketer,' he wrote of the frequency of cricket tours in the 1880s. 'Though, to be sure, one must not forget that the thing might pall upon the taste in the long run, for does not the sonnet tell us that "sweets grown common lose their dear delight".'

No danger of that with Horan's writing today; its sweetness remains well worth savouring.

# Billy Midwinter

## LOST SOUL (2015)

William Midwinter's cricket career was full of firsts. He was the first bowler to take five wickets in an innings in a Test match. He was the first and remains the only cricketer to play for Australia against England and for England against Australia. But the first whose 125th anniversary falls today [3 December 2015] is that he was the first Australian Test cricketer to die, aged only thirty-nine, and in circumstances that caused Arthur Haygarth to remark in *Cricket Scores and Biographies*: 'May the death of no other cricketer who has taken part in great matches be like his!'

Like the first Test centurion, Charles Bannerman, and the first number three, Tom Horan, Midwinter was an adopted Australian born in the UK. He was nine when his gamekeeper father brought the family from the Forest of Dean to California Gully, near Sandhurst, where he formed a lasting association with Harry Boyle, a precocious teenage medium-pace bowler who had organized a local team. He grew into a sandy-haired six-footer with a physique testifying to work as a miner and butcher. In the 1971 *Wisden*, the secretary of Gloucestershire

CCC, Grahame Parker, published a superbly thorough account of Midwinter's wanderings: how he came to the attention of his fellow Gloucester man W. G. Grace by bowling him and brother Fred at the MCG in March 1874; how he set off for England three weeks after the Second Test and became one of Grace's cricket retinue; how when he tried to reunite with the Australian team of 1878, Grace regained his services by . . . well . . . abduction. He had in the meantime at least top-scored for the Australians in their astonishing turkey shoot-out at Lord's: he made 10. The modern commuter cricket had nothing on 'Mid': to play six consecutive summers in Australia and England, he had to chalk up almost a year in travelling time.

What anchored Midwinter to Australia at last was love. In June 1883, he married a Bendigo girl, Lizzie McLaughlan, and became the publican at Carlton's Clyde Hotel, then an eponymous hotel in South Melbourne, and finally the Victoria Hotel in Bourke Street. Lizzie bore a son in 1886, Albert, and a daughter and son in 1888, Elsie and William Jnr. At the end of that year, however, the Midwinters were struck by the first of a series of consuming family tragedies: infant Elsie died of pneumonia; within a year, Lizzie and Albert also died, and William Jnr was hospitalized with a crippling hip problem.

The effect on Billy Midwinter can be imagined . . . or actually, maybe it can't All we really know is that while staying with a married sister back in his old neighbourhood of California Gully, Midwinter became violent, attempted self-immolation, threw candles at his hosts, and was found in possession of arms and ammunition – the police took him to Bendigo Hospital, from where he was decanted to Kew Asylum and designated 'dangerous'. Within months, reported Horan in *The Australasian*, he had degenerated into a 'helpless imbecile'.

The diagnosis of 'general paralysis of the insane' contained in his Kew Asylum records is unhelpfully vague. GPI was basically any neurological collapse the 'alienists' of the time could not explain: in William Julius Mickle's comprehensive 1880 textbook, its causes ranged from emotional strain to an excess of alcohol or sex. Interestingly, the admitting staff at Kew conscientiously absolved Midwinter of the latter ('Habits of life: Steady') and stressed the former ('Cause: domestic bereavement'). But later diagnosticians would establish a connection between GPI and untreated syphilis, and it's possible that Midwinter's infection was the unwitting cause of his family's annihilation.

Whatever the case, he knew but one final brief lapse into lucidity, reported by the *Singleton Argus*:

> H. F. Boyle went out to Kew (Vic.) Asylum one day last week to see his old Bendigo comrade Midwinter. The asylum authorities said that Midwinter would not recognize anybody, but, strange to say, he recognized Boyle, and also remembered W. G. Grace's name when it was mentioned, and said, 'Grace, good man.' Dave Scott was also present, and Mid knew him too. When they left he relapsed into his condition of mental oblivion. His lower limbs are completely paralysed, and it is thought that he cannot live for another twelve month.

In fact, Midwinter did not live another week. His funeral was well-attended, the actress Maggie Moore, wife of J. C. Williamson, sending a bat composed of immortelles (everlasting flowers), which was placed on the coffin. But there was no money for a headstone, and the grave remained unmarked for almost a hundred years, until the plot was identified by the Australian Cricket Society. Richie Benaud used to balk at the use of the word 'tragedy' in the context of cricket, but this story might have satisfied his criteria: within twenty years of the first Test five-for, the man who took it, his wife and his three children were all dead.

# W. G. Grace

## THE GRAND OLD MAN (2022)

For W. G. Grace, the challenge of Test cricket against Australia materialized in the nick of time. In 1880, the nineteenth century's greatest cricketer turned thirty-two. He was a father of three, had just become a doctor, and was committed for five years to a practice in a poor part of Bristol. For fifteen years, he had built a first-class cricket record beyond compare, averaging 50, producing more hundreds than almost all the rest of the world's batsmen put together. What else was there to aim for?

In fact, Grace sensed the waft of change. The great travelling elevens of his youth were fading; the County Championship was formalizing; but above all there was competition from beyond the seas, which he had seen first-hand on his cricket tour cum honeymoon in 1873–74. Here was a rival worthy of his mettle, with whom he tangled again, and came off second best, at Lord's, on that signal day in 1878 when Dave Gregory's unheralded Australians routed Marylebone by ten wickets.

When the Australian team of 1880 arrived under the shadow of the infamous Sydney Cricket Ground riot a year earlier, they struggled to fill a fixture list until Grace, in consultation with the industrious Surrey secretary Charles Alcock, successfully pushed for a full-dress match at The Oval. It was so late in the season that Grace was almost on holiday. In the last week of August, he accepted an invitation to Kingsclere from John Porter, a leading horse trainer, to go shooting. Grace prepared for his Test debut with a social match against Newbury in which he took eleven wickets, made a catch and a stumping.

'I came straight up to London for the Test match, and as I had not been playing in first-class cricket for some little time, I did not expect any conspicuous personal success,' he recalled. 'Nevertheless, I scored 152 out of the 420 made by England in the first innings.' And, characteristically of *Cricket Reminiscences & Personal Recollections* (1899), that's it: the only first-hand description of the first Test century by an Englishman.

This was not for want of trying from his amanuensis, the pertinacious Arthur Porritt, former editor of the *Church Times*, who undertook the blood-from-stone task of extracting Grace's memories. It's to Porritt's own lively memoir, *The Best I Remember* (1922), that we owe some of the most incisive glimpses of Grace, 'a singularly inarticulate man' with 'the simple faith of a child' who disliked talking about himself and mangled every story yet was oddly magnetic: 'He was a big grown-up boy, just what a man who only lived when he was in the open air might be expected to be. A wonderful kindliness ran through his nature, mingling strangely with the arbitrary temper of a man who had been accustomed to be dominant over other men.'

Thus, perhaps, Grace's relationship with Australians, who shared his favour for the open air, while jibing at times with his tactless quest for advantage. 'Thus, perhaps, was born the

Whingeing Pom,' says Simon Rae in *W. G. Grace: A Life* (1998) of that first fractious expedition down under. 'I do not think it redounds much to any man's credit to endeavor to win a match by resorting to what might not inaptly be called sharp practice,' complained the Australian Tom Horan of Grace's sly run out of Sammy Jones in the Ashes-making Oval Test of 1882. Yet Grace was no grudge holder in the vein of Lords Harris and Hawke. And for all his posthumous reputation for rapacity, the sense you obtain from the sheer density of Grace's career, powerfully evoked by the 2000 matches enumerated in Joe Webber's 1102-page *Chronicle of WG* (1998), is of a man who almost could hardly stop himself from playing cricket. No wonder he warmed to Australians: they meant he did not have to.

His Test figures provide a mean estimation of Grace: 1098 runs at 32.29 in twenty-two Tests spaced over nineteen years in this establishing phase of the format when teams were seldom altogether representative and administration was in constant flux. What's notable in that, nonetheless, is the stimulus of rivalry. Grace's 152 was immediately counterweighted by the Australian Billy Murdoch's 153 not out; having lost his English record score when Arthur Shrewsbury compiled 164 in the Test at Lord's in 1886, Grace wrested it back with 170 in the Test at The Oval. Grace wasn't about to share anything that day. No cricketer has rivalled the ratio of runs he scored while at the wicket in that match: a staggering 78 per cent. On the same pitch, Australia was bowled out for 68 and 149.

In that summer, Grace batted fifty-five times: a third of those innings were against Australia. By the end of his career, Webber tells us, he had packed in no fewer than 99 games against Antipodean XIs, with 4500 runs, 158 wickets and 111 catches – more than any other opponent. It was Australia, too, that persuaded Grace he was done: after the Trent Bridge Test of 1899, fifty-one-year-old Grace told his fellow selectors he was no longer worth his place. By then he was widely known as 'The Old Man'. His girth was ample, his beard flecked with grey, his feet sore after a day's play. In *Life Worth Living* (1939), C. B. Fry recounted Grace's explanation at the fateful meeting: 'It's the ground, Charlie. It's too far away.'

Nor did Australians forget. In *The Old Man* (1948), a biographical radio play on the BBC by John Arlott broadcast on Grace's centenary, fellow commentator Alan McGilvray played the role of Billy Murdoch. Donald Bradman's Australian 'Invincibles' sent a wreath to Grace's half-ruined grave at Elmers End: 'In memory of the great cricketer, from all Australia.' 'In W. G.,' notes Grace's latest biographer, Richard Tomlinson, in *Amazing Grace* (2018), 'they recognized a fellow spirit.' That might be regarded as putting a seal on the relationship: that, down the decades, Australians have played cricket more like Grace than his countrymen.

# Billy Murdoch

## WORLD CLASS (2019)*

Sometimes a book is published only for a late-breaking development to undermine a key assertion. Usually this is disappointing and frustrating. For the authors of a new biography of the Australian cricketer Billy Murdoch, however, the occurrence will be altogether welcome.

In *Cricketing Colossus*, to be launched today at the Melbourne Cricket Ground, Richard Cashman and Ric Sissons argue that Murdoch, maker of the first Test double-century and the first Australian first-class triple-century, should at once be inducted in the Australian Cricket Hall of Fame 'to rectify more than a century of neglect of this great player'.

They were not to know that even as they wrote this the decision had been made to do so – by, among others, me – ahead of its announcement at Monday's Australian Cricket Awards. Murdoch was indeed, as Cashman and Sissons argue,

---

* Review of *Cricket Colossus* by Ric Sissons and Richard Cashman (Walla Walla Press).

'the first Australian batsman to develop a world-class reputation'; maybe, also, the first captain.

Murdoch presented Australian batting credentials at the earliest opportunity, at The Oval during Australia's inaugural Test in England, where W. G. Grace made 152, and Murdoch replied with 153 not out. His leadership spurs were gained on the same ground two years later when he led Australia to a first Test victory abroad, in the match from which emerged the Ashes tradition.

One of the reasons for his overlooking since, I suspect, has been the lack of a thorough biography – a service that, in Murdoch's generation, Cashman has performed for Fred Spofforth and Sissons for Charlie Turner. And the reason for *this* is that Murdoch does not surrender readily to researchers: David Frith observes in his foreword, Murdoch's 'vacillating fortunes read like a novel'. He is a sporting Richard Mahony.*

Has any Australian cricketer had such an incomparably vivid patrimony? When American Gilbert Murdoch married Tasmanian Susanna Flegg in California in 1851, he was twenty-five and she was fifteen. Gilbert had been a corporal in a volunteer regiment from Maryland involved in the Mexican war and served as the second mayor of Monterey as part of a corrupt and violent Democrat clique; Susanna was the daughter of illiterate convicts, travelling with her mother and a consignment of goods on what was virtually a pirate ship.

No sooner had the newlyweds returned to Hobart than they embarked for the Victorian goldfields, where Billy would duly be born, and Gilbert become a flamboyant scapegrace, a

---

* For English readers, Henry Handel Richardson's trilogy *The Fortunes of Richard Mahony* (1930) is arguably the outstanding literary artefact of colonial Australia, the mercurial Dr Richard Townshend-Mahony perhaps our most fully realized fictional character.

merchant and auctioneer always on the edge of the law, eventually toppling in to jail in Bathurst and Beechworth.

Later profile writers drew a veil over Gilbert's infamies, but Cashman and Sissons believe that he abandoned his family circa 1856, when Billy was an infant, and Australia just over a decade later. Returning to Monterey, he claimed that his family had perished in a shipwreck after which he had escaped from savages; setting up as a greengrocer, he contracted a bigamous marriage to an epileptic women thirty years his junior.

Of the impact on Billy, who can say? But there assuredly emerged competing parts of his character: a streak of entrepreneurship and tendency to improvidence versus an arriviste's craving of respectability. This suited the Australian cricket teams he led between 1880 and 1884, which played with aggressively commercial intent while arrogating to themselves the status of amateurs. But it mainly showed up in his life, where he had an early brush with bankruptcy, then married money – or, to be more exact, eloped with it, hastily wedding a daughter of mining tycoon John Boyd Watson without approval.

In seeming atonement, Murdoch renounced cricket between the ages of thirty and thirty-five in favour of the life of a country solicitor, only resuming when old man Watson died – Murdoch promptly returned to Sydney, and was ceded the Australian captaincy for the 1890 Ashes tour. The team was a flop but the trip facilitated Murdoch's relocation to England, whose leisure class his family joined, returning to Australia only twice in his remaining two decades.

Mind you, this outwardly cheerful and festive existence proved harder to sustain than the family let on. Cashman and Sissons have obtained some fascinating begging letters to the Watson estate, in which Murdoch's wife touchingly if enigmatically defends his honour: 'Other than his one little fault he could not be a better husband to me.'

Though Murdoch would play many years for Sussex, it also queered his Test career. In addition to his residence, Murdoch's visiting South Africa with a team of English cricketers in 1891–92, including a match retrospectively accorded Test status, seems to have confounded his expectation of leading the next Australian team to tour England.

From Sydney, its manager Victor Cohen counselled Murdoch candidly that 'there is a decided antipathy to the inclusion of any Anglo-Australians out here'. Murdoch's retort was to call himself 'an Australian pure and simple'. But his having to make such an insistence implied the opposite. It could be argued that he fell victim to prejudices he played a part in instilling, the achievements of Australian cricketers building a proto-national consciousness.

A year before his death in 1911, *Melbourne Punch* commented cattily on Murdoch's diffuse allegiances: 'The old cricket captain is thoroughly anglicized now, and regards Australia with horror as a little place set by itself as far as possible from everywhere else. He has become cosmopolitan, and cannot bear the thought of being more than a day's journey from London, Berlin, Vienna, Paris, St Petersburg. That is the worst of a long and wealthy residence abroad, the best Australians becoming un-Australianized under such conditions.'

One hundred and nine years later, the fifty-second member of the Australian Cricket Hall of Fame is in a category with a membership of one: he is the first and only inductee to have also represented England.

# George Giffen

## ATLAS (2020)<sup>*</sup>

For eight decades, the George Giffen Stand was part of the patriotic topography of the Adelaide Oval, as distinctive and resonant as the Victor Richardson Gates. It was a fitting tribute. The cricketer for whom the stand was named was very nearly as permanent – a player who stopped only because it was impossible to play on one's own, who had bowlers been allowed to bowl from both ends or batsmen been free to face their own bowling would have given nobody else a sniff.

Giffen, however, has been slow to achieve other recognition. The Chappells, Clem Hill and Clarrie Grimmett are the only other full-fledged South Australians in the Australian Cricket Hall of Fame. But Bernard Whimpress's is the first biography, fully 122 years after Giffen published his own pioneering autobiography – the first of its kind, ghosted by Test cricket's great taxonomist Clarence Moody.

---

* Foreword to Bernard Whimpress's *George Giffen* (2020).

The surname Giffen, Bernard tells us, emerged from Flanders. It is a coincidence, but an apt one, that some have posited Flanders as the birthplace of cricket, the name being an adaptation of a Flemish phrase for 'to chase with a curved stick'. There is about Giffen, to be sure, something elemental and foundational. He took out the Australian patent on the all-round cricketer – classically defined as the player worthy of selection as either a batsman or a bowler. He was a cricketer, too, built to the specifications of timeless cricket, with a love of tall scores and unbroken spells, and an iron man's physique. To the latter, Giffen's contemporary Tom Horan paid sweaty tribute: 'I saw him once in football rig at a fancy dress ball on board ship, and even the ladies paused to watch the muscular play of his finely developed arm.'

Giffen was also, in his way, a modern figure. He never married. He never had children. He travelled only for cricket. He stayed with the Post Office because it was amenable to his playing. When his playing ended, his coaching and writing began. He then passed quickly from mortal to permanent, his name transferring to the aforementioned stand just six months after his death; the stand has since been succeeded by a statue. Nearly 150 years since the boy Giffen threw himself into bowling at W. G. Grace's Englishmen as they practised there, then, the Oval continues to make his name and reputation a feature. Read Bernard's book and you'll find out why.

# The Ashes of 1894–95
## 'I SAY, OLD MAN . . .' (1994)

'I say, "Old Man", who's got those Ashes?'

The inquiry, in a contemporary cartoon by George Ashton, was polite but pointed. The off-field welcome was hospitable, the on-field intent explicitly hostile. England's cricketers came to Australia holding an Ashes trophy some eleven years old, but it was in the 1894–95 series that their rivalry first showed its staying power.

In a new book on the series, *Stoddy's Mission* (1994), David Frith has called it 'the first Great Test Series'. It meets objective criteria. The rubber's unfolding was perfect: England won the first two Tests. Australia the next two, and England the decider. These games featured passages so dramatic and captivating that even Queen Victoria asked to be kept abreast of scores. The patriotic pride involved in the result, moreover, reached a new intensity.

The British Empire was at a peak, and the country to which its Andrew Stoddart led his thirteen Englishmen was one recovering from the trauma of a banking crash while also experiencing the early rapture of proto-nationalism. Ethel

Turner published her *Seven Little Australians* and Tom Roberts painted his 'Golden Fleece' in 1894. *The Bulletin* incorporated both 'fair dinkum' and 'cobber' into the local vernacular. Cricket presaged the incipient federalism. A gratuity left by Lord Sheffield, a patron of the previous English touring team, had been invested by the embryonic Australian Cricket Council in an intercolonial championship shield. Its first season, 1892–93, also saw Western Australia and Queensland join New South Wales, Victoria, South Australia and Tasmania as first-class cricket competitors. And Stoddart's team was the first invited by colonies in cooperation rather than competition.

Stoddart himself was an eminent Corinthian, who had stayed behind after the 1887–88 tour of Australia to captain England at rugby and even play a few Australian rules fixtures. His troupe of five amateurs and eight professionals was one of the best assembled, including the destructive Surrey fast bowling duo of Tom Richardson and Bill Lockwood, two prodigious Yorkshiremen in batsmen John Brown and left-arm spinner Bobby Peel, plus the uncapped Lancastarian opening batsman Archie MacLaren. They resembled well-to-do holiday makers as they relaxed for the camera in Adelaide's Botanical Gardens on arrival. But when his team was soundly defeated by South Australia in the first big match of the trip – with the inexhaustible thirty-five-year-old local hero George Giffen taking 11 wickets and top scoring in both innings – they knew they had their work cut out.

Perhaps it was ship-lag. It would be more than seventy years until an English team flew all the way to Australia. Stoddart's men had boarded *RMS Ophir*, flagship of the Orient Line, at Tilbury on 21 September and not arrived in Adelaide until 2 November, MacLaren meeting his future wife en route. Such wanderlust was gradually outlining a global cricket.

English teams had visited South Africa, India, North America by 1894; another would set off for the West Indies at the start of 1895. Since the pioneering visit of Australian aborigines, England itself had also received a great variety of touring teams, ranging from the Philadelphians to Indian Parsis.

The venue for the first Test for Stoddart's team was the Sydney Cricket Ground which, with a century of development ahead of it, was a far cry from today's arena. Plans had only just been laid for the Ladies Stand, and there was a lot of airspace for cricketers to play with: South Australian Joe Darling would hit a six there that carried 110 yards, through the location of the present M.A. Noble Stand, into the tennis courts outside. But, after years in which the venue had simply been the nebulous 'Association Cricket Ground', the flag 'SCG' was hoisted indicating its name change. Its pitch square had also been drastically improved by the introduction in August 1894 of Bulli soil.

No match in first-class cricket history had lasted as long as the First Test's six days, produced as many as its 1514 runs, or involved so many twists. Australia recovered from three for 21 on the first day to make a Test record 586 in just seven hours and ten minutes, with Syd Gregory compiling the first Test double-century in Australia and joining in a record Australian ninth-wicket partnership that still stands.

England followed on after trailing by 261 runs and MacLaren was one of the few brave enough to stake four pounds on his team, when the odds against their win lengthened to 50/1. But rain fell on the fifth evening as Australia contemplated victory with eight wickets in hand and just 64 runs to get, and Stoddart sobered up the notoriously bibulous Peel beneath a cold shower so that he could exploit the uncovered surface. Australia's 10-run defeat was mean reward for Giffen, who'd taken eight wickets from 118 overs and scored 202 runs, and not until 1981 at Headingley did a team win again after following on.

The First Test must have been agony for faraway English cricket followers. The cablegram service to London broke down at the end of the third day with the tourists on their knees, and those at home caught up with the match's last three days in a single despatch that some would have suspected was a work of fiction. Mind you, watching the game and catching the score was difficult even in Australia. Although almost 600,000 attended the first-class season – in a country with a population of about 3.5 million – the smaller grounds meant that many spectators were turned away. The offices of the major newspapers where scores were posted regularly were thronged by thousands daily.

The Second Test at the MCG seemed almost as fanciful as the First. England lost MacLaren to the game's first ball, were all out before lunch for 75, but still prevailed by 94 runs. The Third Test at Adelaide Oval was then marked by an all-round Test debut performance still unmatched: Australia's Albert Trott made 110 runs without being dismissed and took eight for 43 as his team romped home by 362 runs. It was an ill-advised heresy when Stoddart became the first Test captain to insert his opponents in the Fourth Test: he lost in a day and a half on a rain-affected surface exploited by Giffen and Charlie Turner, in the process even throwing financial markets into confusion. When trade on the Ballarat Stock Exchange was interrupted by London-born brokers chorusing 'Rule Brit-annia', Australian colleagues responded by raising a Southern Cross and singing 'The Men of Australia'. Communications between the Ballarat bourse and its Melbourne counterpart were limited one afternoon to a cable: 'Nothing doing; cricket mad; Stoddart out'.

More than 100,000 attended a game for the first time

as the Fifth Test was fought out at the MCG in an atmosphere tense from the moment of the toss. Australia's captain Giffen wrote of the preliminaries: 'He [Stoddart] was white as a sheet, and I have been told that the pallor of my own countenance matched his.' Australia banked a robust 414, but MacLaren's century ensured England's virtual parity. Richardson's tireless strivings on a blameless wicket gave England the edge and Brown saw his team home by seven wickets with what was then the fastest century in Ashes cricket in ninety-three minutes. Nobody in Test cricket has made it to 50 faster than his twenty-eight minutes.

Stoddart was a popular victor. *Melbourne Punch* versified: 'Then spoke the Queen of England/Whose hand is blessed by God/I must do something handsome/For my dear victorious Stod/Let him return without delay/And shall dub him pat/A baronet that he may be/Sir Andrew Stoddart (Bat).' But though its players had not recaptured the Ashes, the rubber did much to restore Australian self-confidence. *The Argus* opined: 'A wise government desiring to improve our credit abroad may do worse than send away thousands of photographs of the scene on the MCG on Saturday. There appears to be an idea somewhere else that there is depression here. To the spectator on Saturday the word had no meaning.' Three new loans were negotiated with London's financiers during 1895.

Australian cricket had crossed a Rubicon. Giffen had become the country's first great all-rounder – allegedly turning up in the children's prayers ('God bless Mummy, Daddy and George Giffen . . .') – and his seasonal first-class double of 903 runs and 93 wickets has never been surpassed. The past was honoured: Syd Gregory was son of SCG groundsman Ned, veteran of the inaugural Test. The future was in the offing: 1894 also featured the birth of Victor Richardson, founder of the greatest of South Australian sporting dynasties, and Robert

Menzies, longest-lasting and most cricket-fond of prime ministers. A tradition was emerging. Who had those Ashes? Nobody permanently.

# Harry Trott

## THE MADNESS OF KING HARRY (2004)

Cricketers great and humble meet one opponent equally. Sooner or later, all defer to time. Usually the end comes stealthily: muscles stiffen, reflexes slow, eyes dim. In some cases, though, it is abrupt, unceremonious, unkind; so sudden that it's as though the individual was never there to begin with.

One hundred and five years ago, in the summer of 1897–98, Harry Trott led Australia to its first win in a five-Test Ashes series. At thirty-one, he was in his athletic prime, and by common consent the world's wisest cricket captain. On his watch had emerged what historian Bill Mandle has called 'the unfilial yearning to thrash the mother country', even as the constitutional undergirding of an Australian commonwealth was being erected. But at the peak of his fame, Harry Trott disappeared, never to play let alone captain another Test. And though he reappeared as a man, it was as a marginal figure, and a source of stifled embarrassment. For – didn't you know? – poor Harry went mad.

Trott was born on 5 August 1866, third of eight children.

Father Adolphus, an accountant, was scorer for the South Melbourne Cricket Club, whose batting and bowling averages eighteen-year-old Harry topped in his inaugural season. He was marked out from the first by uncommon temperament, batting with easy grace, giving his leg-breaks an optimistic loop. As befitted one destined to spend his whole working life in the Post Office as a postman and mail-sorter, he met everyone alike. On one occasion he was introduced to the Prince of Wales, who after a long and convivial conversation conferred on him a royal cigar. Later he was asked what he had done with it: the fashion was for preserving anything of royal provenance as a keepsake. Trott, though, simply looked puzzled. 'I smoked it,' he said.

In his equanimity, Trott was a rarity. Australian teams of the time were notoriously combustible, riven by intercolonial jealousies. Trott's first skipper, Percy McDonnell, survived a 'muffled mutiny' against his leadership because of his over-reliance on New South Welshmen; his second, Jack Blackham, was weak, suggestible, and felt to be the cat's paw of other Victorians; his third, George Giffen, asserted South Australian primacy simply by bowling himself interminably. Discipline was lamentable, with Australia's 1893 tour of England especially unruly. 'It was impossible to keep some of them straight,' complained their manager. 'One of them was altogether useless because of his drinking propensities . . . Some were in the habit of holding receptions in their rooms and would not go to bed until all hours.'

Appointed to lead Australia's next trip to England in 1896, Harry Trott changed everything. He knew no favourites, was never quarrelsome, and above all showed a pioneering flair for tactics. At the time, rigid field settings and pre-determined bowling changes were standard; Trott set the trend of positioning fielders and employing bowlers with particular batsmen and match situations in mind, and rotating his attack to keep its members fresh. 'His bowlers felt that he understood the gruelling nature of their work,' said *The Referee*, 'and that they had his sympathy in the grimmest of battles.' To some, this sympathy seemed uncanny. Trott's star bowler Hugh Trumble had days, he confessed, when his usual sting and snap were missing; Trott could sense such occasions within a few balls, and would whip him off. Sydney batsman Frank Iredale, meanwhile, was gifted but highly strung, a teetotaller. 'Look here, Noss, what you need is a tonic,' Trott counselled. 'I'll mix you one.' Iredale made more centuries than any other batsman on tour, fortified by what Trott later admitted was brandy and soda.

In the end, the Australians were pipped 1–2 in the series, the defeats being narrow, their victory stirring. Opening the bowling on a whim at Manchester, Trott had W. G. Grace and Drewy Stoddart stumped in his first two overs: a decisive breakthrough. His leadership was then seen to even better advantage when England next visited Australia, and was overwhelmed 4–1. 'It didn't seem to matter to Mr Trott whom he put on,' lamented Stoddart, 'for each change ended in a wicket.' *Wisden* thought him 'incomparably the best captain the Australians have ever had'; the Anglo-Indian batting guru Ranjitsinhji concluded that he was 'without a superior today anywhere'. The Melbourne Test of January 1898 not only drew many of the delegates from the marathon Constitutional Convention smoothing the path to Federation, it wholly distracted the public. As John Hirst says in *Sentimental Nation* (2000): 'The Australian cricketers were better than the English. Who cared whether Australian judges were up to the mark?' Victory could also be deemed a vindication of the cause. *The Bulletin* exulted: 'This ruthless rout of English cricket will do – and has done – more to enhance the cause of

Australian nationality than could be achieved by miles of erudite essays and impassioned appeal.' Trott joined the Albert Park branch of the Australian Natives' Association, and his double-fronted weatherboard in Phillipson Street became a place of pilgrimage. Trott's employers, when some complained about the leave lavished on their most famous functionary, explained: 'Harry Trott is a national institution.'

The precipitous decline of that institution, veiled in euphemism for more than a century, began on 8 August 1898. Visiting mother Mary in Doncaster, Harry Trott collapsed; in the words of *The Argus*, he 'fell suddenly into a fit', losing consciousness. With wife Violet on the train home, he suffered another violent paroxysm; despite a doctor's presence, he was convulsed a third time at 10 p.m. For four weeks, Trott lapsed in and out of consciousness, unable to work, barely able to communicate. Public anxiety was acute. When *The Australasian* stated it was 'an absolute necessity that he should have a trip into the country where he will have the benefit of . . . a much-needed rest', supporters subscribed more than £400. Trott left Melbourne on 10 September with Test teammate Harry Graham and a nurse, bound for Woodend; the *Woodend Star* reported his intention of 'recovering from a recent severe attack of illness'. But he was unchanged by his fortnight at 'Bon Air', a private retreat, and many were shocked by his appearance at the MCG on 15 October bearing 'unmistakable traces of the terrible sufferings he had undergone during his severe illness'. He was tormented by insomnia, loss of memory and an enfeebling apathy. Hope he would recuperate in time to lead Australia to England to defend the Ashes gradually evaporated. On 3 May 1899, a green and gold flag fluttered over London's Inns of Court Hotel advertising the arrival of Australian cricketers under the captaincy of Joe Darling; that same day, a world away, Darling's predecessor entered Kew Asylum.

# HARRY TROTT

*

Opened in December 1871, Kew Asylum served as a mental hospital for 117 years. In that time, observes Dr Cheryl Day in her thesis *Magnificence, Misery and Madness*, 'any resident or long-term visitor to Melbourne understood what was meant by the phrase "you should be sent to Kew".' The building, however, was representative of a brief moment in psychiatric care when giant asylums seemed the way of the future. Kew echoed the theories of British alienist John Conolly, who had recommended first and foremost 'a healthy site, freely admitting light and air . . . on a gentle eminence in a fertile and agreeable country'. It was believed that Kew's position – set on 170 hectares, thirty metres above river level, eight kilometres from the city – would 'conduce to the happiness and comfort of patients and facilitate their recovery'. Built in the shape of an E enclosing two courtyards surrounded by roofed walkways, with a facade and steep mansard roof in the French Second Empire style, it was the most ambitious and expensive such project in Australian history.

Yet within five years, mental health meliorists had changed their minds. A government inquiry concluded: 'It has been well said that a magnificent asylum for the insane means, and must ever mean, the crowding of cases together which ought to be kept apart.' A royal commission eight years later investigating asylums at Kew, Yarra Bend, Ararat and Beechworth condemned them all: 'It is hard to say why the dwellings of lunatics should cost such extravagant sums as were lavished on the edifices in question.' The commission concluded, nonetheless, that the sunk cost justified keeping asylums open, and that the government might as well exploit their one advantage: economy. Policy trends reversed altogether: "In dealing with a large number of pauper lunatics . . . their actual wants and powers of appreciation should be regarded. Palatial residences, equipped with Chippendale furniture, would not make them happier, or minister to the wants of minds diseased. The majority of these people belong to the poorer classes and if they were supplied with the most elegant surroundings, they would be unable, even in their most lucid moments, to appreciate the refinements of better life.' Kew Asylum became Melbourne's Potemkin village of the insane. Boosters saw its external splendour as an index of wealth and sophistication: 'Our prisons and madhouses prove our civilization to be equal to that of any of the older cities of Europe.' Inside, the great madhouse was growing madder. Designed for 600, it seldom accommodated fewer than 1000, ranging from eccentrics and the elderly to drunks and criminals – including several convicted murderers. For these, there were never more than three medical officers.

The asylum mimicked some rituals of ordinary life. There was a cricket green, a tennis court and a billiard room, though mainly used by attendants. Patients were also expected to work; it wouldn't make them free, but might keep them calm. Kew's first superintendent had described 'employment' as 'the chief means of curing insanity of all kinds', and patients by the turn of the century followed a clockwork routine from 6.30 a.m. A basic farm operated, not to mention workshops and washing houses, while ornamental and kitchen gardens were maintained. But drudgery tended to deaden rather than discipline. In January 1898, *The Argus* stormed: 'A distinguished specialist attending patients at Kew stated only the other day that the state of things at that asylum was now so bad that a person just mad enough to be put under restraint ran the risk of becoming much worse instead of receiving medical treatment likely to restore his senses.' This risk Harry Trott's friends were prepared to run.

# HARRY TROTT

*

The contents of Kew's calf-bound casebooks reveal a world rich, strange and occluded. Two cases admitted the same week as Harry Trott convey that world's extremes. One, an ageing bootmaker suffering 'mania', believed that the Salvation Army had paid for his murder and that his tongue would be cut off; he 'took possession of the WC' and covered himself in excrement in order to ward attendants off. The other, a 'thin, pale and anaemic-looking' mining student, was afflicted with a 'melancholia' associated with his 'having practised self-abuse for some time'; the examining doctor noted his pessimistic conviction 'that people are fated to go through certain experiences which it is hopeless to strive against'.

Harry Trott might have taken this counsel to heart. Standing in one place, showing no interest in surrounding events, he seemed lost within himself. 'Refuses to converse not appearing to be able to follow what is said to him,' summarized a doctor. 'Answers questions in monosyllables. Does not rouse up when subjects are spoken of that formerly he was keenly interested in – has a vacant dull expression.' After four days, Trott was given an enema; his 'bowels freely moved, a number of hard masses coming away'. His colon had no effect on his consciousness. Sent optimistically to the cricket green, he took 'no interest', batting and bowling 'in a mechanical, indifferent fashion'.

The official diagnosis was 'dementia', the official cause 'alcoholic', though both reflect medical convention rather than empirical evidence. Kew's superintendent Dr William Beattie-Smith believed that alcohol was 'the most common cause of insanity', and that 'all the pity in the world will never conquer a weak will, selfish desires and moral perversion'. Nor was Smith's recommended cure – 'manual labour, cheerful

society, liberal and wholesome diet' – ever likely to be effica-
cious. Baffled staff took one chance. Kew Asylum traditionally
prohibited newspapers, convinced that isolation had 'a seda-
tive effect' and removed 'any delusions which they [patients]
may entertain'. After a few weeks, Trott was shown newspapers
sent to him, including the doings of Darling's team in England.
His 'heavy, dull expression' was unaltered. Trott's identity as
sportsman, indeed, was steadily subsumed by his identity
as inmate. Between 24 June and 14 December 1899, not a
single case note was taken. One whom eighteen months
earlier had been among Australia's most famous was now
among its most anonymous.

A remarkable vignette survives of Trott at this time. Paul
Farmer was a Collins Street physician who, for obscure reasons,
was abducted by friends on 13 September 1899 and briefly
incarcerated. In *Three Weeks in the Kew Lunatic Asylum*, a sixty-
four-page pamphlet about his ordeal privately published the
following year, Farmer profiled several fellow patients. 'Case
VII' was almost certainly Trott: 'Here is a well-known cricketer,
whom we once treated as a hero. But alas! Like everything
else, times have changed, and he is almost forgotten. He
stands about and is very reserved. Probably he has been badly
treated, or thinks he has been, by some person or persons, and
is one of the many disappointed men.' Trott's immiseration,
in fact, suggests what would now probably be identified as a
classic depressive psychosis and treated either pharmaco-
logically or with electro-convulsive therapy; Kew's medical
staff at the time, however, were merely doctors, who observed
the mind but treated only the body. Nothing, as Farmer noted,
prevented deeper loneliness: 'Surely such a man as this might
be tended by someone more closely related to him and given
his only chance of being restored to health. If he has gone
mad in the cause of cricket, then the cricketers should see that

he gets a few of life's comforts and look him up occasionally. For though that man may appear indifferent to such attentions, he is not so.' Farmer's conviction about Trott's isolation makes sense. The Melbourne Cricket Club's secretary Ben Wardill visited at the end of November, but left unrecognized; no others from the sporting community seem to have made the journey. Not, at least, until Trott trod tentatively back into the sporting community.

On 10 February 1900, a Kew Asylum XI hosted a club called North Melbourne Rovers. Not surprisingly, the quondam Test captain appeared, albeit with a man to run for him, on account of his leaden gait. To universal astonishment, Trott began swinging his bat in mighty arcs: his 98 in forty minutes contained twenty fours and a six. A doctor examining him shortly after cautioned against over-optimism: 'Considerable mental dullness still exists. Memory still impaired. Reads papers sometimes but does not remember the contents much.' But when Wardill took Test keeper Alf Johns to Kew a fortnight later, Trott piped perkily: 'Hello Alf! How are you?'

'Dr Smith says Harry played really well,' Wardill reported in a letter to Trott's South Melbourne colleague Bob McLeod. 'There was no soft stuff set up for him to hit, and he bowled and caught well. He was more talkative and brighter altogether.' Muscle memory reactivated other recollections; he played a string of forceful innings against other visitors, and in April secured six for 30 including a hat-trick against a team from the Commercial Travellers Association. Trott was moved to be presented in token of his feat with a hat. He was famously fond of them; a teammate once described him as 'the only man I have seen who, in the nude, had to have a hat on his head'. The doctor who visited the following week thought his 'improvement marked'. After 400 days, Trott's file was inscribed: 'Discharged. Recovered.' But not, perhaps, rehabilitated. The following year, he was declared bankrupt.

Though only thirty-three, Trott was never again a con-spicuous cricketing figure. A transfer to Bendigo Post Office limited him to half a dozen first-class games in seven years. There was little diminution in his abilities: returning to South Melbourne in 1910–11, he again led batting and bowling averages. But the circumstances of his Test career's end were henceforward unmentioned. Trott himself alluded to them only once, during a December 1913 skirmish with the Victorian Cricket Association's Mat Ellis in the letter pages of *The Argus*. 'Mr Ellis asks me why [John] Giller did not go to England when he was at his zenith as a cricketer,' wrote Trott. 'This was in 1899 and Mr Ellis, unless he is still suffering from bad memory, knows that months before that team was chosen I was laid up with a very serious illness and had no say in selection.' Ellis was probably mortified. When Trott died in November 1917, it was he who moved that the VCA raise money for a suitable tombstone. The settings of much of Trott's life have been erased by time – even the green on which he played his resurrecting innings has gone, occupied by a residential development near the long-dormant asylum. But Trott's memorial, a marble column on a granite base in Brighton Cemetery, survives.

The June 1919 dedication ceremony was a curious affair. The war was not long concluded, and the address by VCA president Donald McKinnon, also Director-General of Recruit-ment, was replete with martial allusions: 'Our greatest heroes were those 60,000 men who had died to keep the country free and the men who had fought with them. Harry Trott was a hero because he had excelled in a great sport.' In token of Harry Trott's inner battle, of course, no laurels were bestowed.

# Ranjitsinhji

## THE PRINCE OF CRICKET (2009)

No cricketer in history has been as romanticized and sentimentalized as Ranjitsinhji. It testifies to his uniqueness that this romance and sentimentality do not significantly enlarge on reality. W. G. Grace prophesied that there would not be a batsman like Ranji for a hundred years. This is inherently untestable, but it did set a remarkably high standard.

Ranji was not only the first well-known Indian cricketer, but 'the first Indian of any kind to become universally known and popular' – as John Lord puts it in *The Maharajahs* (1971). And this through a concatenation of circumstances that has inspired not only four biographies but two novels: John Masters's *The Ravi Lancers* (1972) and Ian Buruma's *Playing the Game* (1999).

There was, of course, always a mythic element to 'Prince Ranji'. He was, in reality, only fleetingly a real prince, adopted as heir to the Jam Saheb of Nawanagar as a precaution against that ruler's inability to father an heir of his own. Ranji's princely status was revoked when an heir appeared four years later, and not restored for the next quarter of a century. In fact, this caprice was integral to Ranji's first exposure to cricket. Apprehension about court intrigues in Jamnagar resulted in his enrolling 80km away at Rajkot's Rajkumar College, the 'Indian Eton', where he developed as a promising all-round athlete before leaving for England in March 1888 to further his education.

Simon Wilde, one of Ranji's biographers, suggests that this disinheritance explains Ranji's determination at Cambridge to 'make himself the prince of cricket'. The unique batting style that seemed to flow directly from Ranji's exotic origins belied his self-mastering dedication and the valuable tutelage of Surrey professionals who came to coach undergraduates. Ranji reputedly tackled them in relays. 'I must practise endurance,' he told F. S. Jackson. 'I find it difficult to go on after thirty minutes.' Legend has it that one of these professionals nailed Ranji's back boot to the crease to cure the young Indian's tendency to retreat from the ball. True or not, the facility that Ranji subsequently developed for deflecting balls to leg changed the course of batsmanship for ever, opening previously unexplored run-scoring quadrants of the field.

Cricket, hitherto, had been an off-side game, as Ranji's great friend C. B. Fry had been told as a Repton schoolboy: 'If one hit the ball in an unexpected direction on the on side, intentionally or otherwise, one apologized to the bowler . . . The opposing captain never, by any chance, put a fieldsman there; he expected you to drive on the off side like a gentleman.' Ranji's *Jubilee Book of Cricket* (1897) contained diagrams of fifteen recommended fields for bowlers of various types: only one, for lob bowlers, contains more than three leg-side fielders and most feature only one or two. Ironically, more than any other batsman, Ranji rendered such formations obsolete. Ranji's harnessing of the pace of the ball in the power of the stroke was also revelatory. As Gerald Brodribb contended in *Next Man In* (1952), it 'suggested a completely new way of getting runs'. With wrist, eye and timing, batting became a discipline of touch and subtlety as much as of strength and force.

Even a modern batsman would not make so bold as Ranji, if Fry's description of his contemporary's 'forward-glance-to-leg' is anything to go by. 'The peculiarity,' Fry wrote in *Batsmanship* (1912), 'was that he did more than advance his left foot at the ball . . . he advanced it well clear of the line of the ball to the right of it, and he somehow got his bat to the left of his left leg in line with the ball, and finished the stroke with a supple turn at the waist and an extraordinarily supple follow-through of wrist-work.'

How Ranji's colour hampered his advance is difficult to ascertain. There was prejudice at Trinity College against 'a nigger showing us how to play cricket', and Sir Home Gordon revealed in *Background of Cricket* (1939) that Ranji's signature habit of buttoning his sleeves to the wrist was 'acquired at Cambridge to mitigate his dusky appearance'. Gordon also recalls that Ranji's selection for the 1896 Ashes series was debated at Lord's despite his stupendous Old Trafford debut, when he made 62 and 154 not out: 'Old gentlemen waxing plethoric declared that if England could not win without resorting to the assistance of coloured individuals of Asiatic extraction, it had better devote its skill to marbles. Feelings grew so acrimonious as to sever lifelong friendships . . . one veteran told me that if it were possible he would have me expelled from MCC for having "the disgusting degeneracy to praise a dirty black".'

Yet it is remarkable, as Alan Ross commented in *Ranji* (1988), how quickly 'the Prince' became 'a character'. By the end of Ranji's debut series, the ramparts of Victorian England had yielded to him utterly. 'At the present time,' judged *The Strand*, 'it would be difficult to discover a more popular player throughout the length and breadth of the Empire.' And his fame would only grow: he published a string of books, was the subject of a biography by Percy Cross Standing, a painting by Henry Tuke, and a host of Anglicizing nicknames, from 'Ramsgate Jimmy' to 'Run-get Singhy'; he would later appear in James Joyce's *Finnegan's Wake* (1939) as 'Ringeysingey'.

The time was ripe for a crowd-pleaser of Ranji's kind, and he ascended still greater heights of fame in Australia on tour in 1897–98 after opening the series with a match-winning 175. 'Ranji, Ranji everywhere' read the headline in the *Evening News*:

> It is being said by those in Australia that the natives of the present time are mad to a man – madder than their own proverbial hares in March. They have a craze which 'is exciting interest even more than any of the innumerable American crazes [that] have excited the Yankees. The Australians, in short, have Prince Ranjit Sinhji, Ranji, Ranji everywhere! ' No touring cricket club, no travelling show of any description, has ever possessed such an attraction as Mr. Stoddart has gained for his club by the inclusion of the Indian Prince. There have been men in other days who have excited popular admiration to fever heat by their personalities – Dr Nansen, for instance, Dr Jameson, Dr Grace, Dan Leno, and scores of others of recent times. Yet none of these have made a bigger 'boom' than the little Indian cricketer, Ranji, Ranji everywhere! He is the one topic of conversation, the one topic of writing, the one topic of discussion at the present time in Australia. The natives come hundreds

of miles to see him, to shake his hand, to watch him play. They don't mind whether he scores or not – he is the hero of the hour.

With county cricket blossoming, Ranji also made the most of the expanding first-class programme: between 1898 and 1901, he and Fry, a combination unmatched in glamour, amassed 16,500 runs for Sussex. Standing noted that visitors were disappointed at Ranji's indifference to cricket's history: 'What's he to Fuller Pilch, or Fuller Pilch to him? Nothing. On the other hand, today's weather forecast is everything.' Perhaps Ranji intuited that history was of little account, save for the history he might make himself.

In an era usually identified with imperialism and white supremacism, why was Ranji's passage relatively frictionless? David Cannadine, in his *Ornamentalism: How The British Saw Their Empire* (2001), contends that rank, as much as race, was the key to imperial order: 'India's was a hierarchy that became the more alluring because it seemed to represent an ordering of society . . . that was increasingly under threat in Britain.' Ranji, famous for his ostentatious regalia and extravagant flourishes of wealth, colluded in those fantasies of an imagined east. On one occasion, dining at Hyde Park Hotel, Sir Home Gordon was struck by the shabbiness of Ranji's suit, then noted that at a military tournament later in the evening Ranji appeared 'resplendent in Oriental attire and ablaze with jewellery'.

Appreciations of Ranji's batting, too, often come from a perspective of inferiority, even gratitude. 'We had got into a groove,' wrote the England professional Tom Hayward in his primer *Cricket* (1907), 'out of which the daring of a revolutionary alone could move us. The Indian Prince has proven himself an innovator. He recognizes no teaching which is not progressive, and frankly he has tilted, by his play, at our stereotyped creations.' By this time Ranji had essentially renounced cricket, his political ambitions having borne fruit with the restoration of his inheritance after the death of the Jam Saheb in August 1906. But Neville Cardus's remark that 'when Ranji passed out of cricket a wonder and a glory departed from the game for ever' was both right and wrong. Cricket's inheritance from him endures.

# Archie MacLaren

## ODD MAN IN (2006)

In his final year at Harrow, Archie MacLaren had as his fag a particularly 'snotty little bugger', uppity but damn near useless, with no aptitude even for sport: the youth had actually once been pelted by boys with cricket balls, and felt an everlasting shame from having cowered behind trees.

Embarassing, really. For MacLaren, even as a teenager, was earmarked for great attainments. He would that year compile an effortless maiden first-class century for Lancashire; within four years he would set a record score in England to withstand all rivals for nigh on a century. That damnable, feeble fag. Never amount to anything, that Winston bloody Churchill.

MacLaren lived long enough to see the schoolboy upstart achieve fame throughout the world; one wonders if it ever occurred to him that his own closest brush with international renown beyond the cricket field was his walk-on part as a monocled veteran of the Crimean War in Alexander Korda's *The Four Feathers* (1939). Likewise, while Churchill's greatness endures, MacLaren is nowadays at best a period curio, like an antimacassar or an aspidistra.

There's little disputing MacLaren's skill and stature in his time. He inherited England's captaincy, at home from Grace and away from Stoddart, on the authority of his opening batsmanship, taking the lead in twenty-two of thirty-five Tests. He had unusual qualifications as an Ashes leader, being, like Andrew Strauss, married to an Australian. Australians liked him, too. 'One wonders if ever a finer batsman played for England than A. C. MacLaren,' said his rival in the 1909 Ashes, Monty Noble, in *The Game's The Thing* (1926). 'Certainly there never was a better sportsman.' Yet if ever a cricketer was the creation of a single writer, it is MacLaren, his luminosity owing in large degree to youthful acolyte Neville Cardus. Among the most famous passages in *Autobiography* (1947) is Cardus's paralleling his first glimpse of MacLaren with his first experience of the actor Henry Irving ('They wakened the incurable romantic in me which saves a grown man from foolishness'). Later he elevates the cricketer to the stature of creative genius ('MacLaren was not just a cricketer any more than Wagner was just a composer') and supreme English artist ('Among exponents of the recognized arts in England there is only Sir Thomas Beecham whom I have found fit to compare in character and gusto of life . . . with A. C. MacLaren, on or off the field').

Like Jad Leland in *Citizen Kane*, unable to wash from his memory the adolescent glimpse of a woman in white, young Cardus never forgot that initial sight of MacLaren, on 'the greenest grass in England', playing a drive 'far to the distant boundary, straight and powerfully'. The memory turned him back into a twelve-year-old in the sixpenny seats at Old Trafford. 'I cannot remember the bowler's name; he has passed with all other details of the match into the limbo, but I can still see the swing of MacLaren's bat, the great follow-through, finishing high and held there with the body poised as he himself contemplated the grandeur of the stroke and savoured it . . . This brief sight of MacLaren thrilled my blood, for it gave shape and reality to things I had till then only vaguely felt and dreamed about of romance.'

Other observers verify the spacious flourishes of MacLaren's batting. 'He lifted his bat round his neck like a golfer at the top of his swing,' recalled his contemporary C. B. Fry. 'He stood bolt upright and swept into every stroke, even a defensive backstroke, with dominating completeness.' But for Cardus, it was the thought of MacLaren as much as the deeds that did the trick. The climactic moment of their relationship, of course, was MacLaren's invitation to Cardus to Eastbourne in August 1921, where his makeshift English XI was taking on the might of Warwick Armstrong's unbeaten Australians. MacLaren made a first-ball duck. In the *Manchester Guardian*, Cardus nonetheless spent 150 words describing it: a passage, I might add, that is decidedly moving for its faith. The faith was repaid when MacLaren's team won two days later, not only handing Cardus the scoop of a lifetime, but personal affirmation.

By then, however, MacLaren was by most measures a failure. Clinging tenaciously to his amateur status, he had hazarded a host of careers: from banker to teacher, from Ranji's secretary, warding off his army of creditors, to limousine salesman, with 'a gaudy line in patter and a sunny indifference to his customers' real needs' (to quote a lovely essay on MacLaren by Jeremy Mailes). Eternally beyond his means, he had been invalided out of the army and run a failed magazine; he'd go on to start an unsuccessful stud farm and an inhospitable hotel; he would fail in attempts to manufacture Spanish willow cricket bats and inflatable pads.

Nor were these misfortunes; on the contrary, they were the failures of a frankly unpleasant personality. Cardus admired him from the perfect distance. Teammates and business partners alike found MacLaren brusque, boorish, overbearing. Even admirers who grew close enough came away disabused. 'It is disillusioning to one of my youthful loyalties,' wrote the Etonian *littérateur* George Lyttleton to his former pupil Rupert Hart-Davis, 'to realize that the Majestic MacLaren was an extremely stupid, prejudiced and pig-headed man.' In *Batter's Castle* (1958), Ian Peebles recalls perhaps his most notorious habit: 'I have heard old timers say he was liable to enter the dressing room clutching his head and saying, "Look what they've given me this time." Or "gracious me! Don't tell me you're playing!" Which cannot have been very good for morale.'

No, indeed. But for Cardus, in fact, MacLaren might have faded altogether: *Autobiography*, today probably the most popular of Cardus's work, still tends his monument, if in a slightly unusual way. Cardus's MacLaren is the archetypal object of youthful devotion to whose faults and failings we are impervious. There was only one MacLaren, but everyone has *a* MacLaren.

# Victor Trumper

## PRINTING THE LEGEND (2016)*

O ne of my first cricket books was a slim black Sun paperback called *Great Australian Cricket Pictures* (1975). When I retrieve it from the shelf now, it falls open at page 87, testifying to my boyhood fascination with the image thereon.

'Trumpered' read the bad-pun heading for the short caption, which described Victor Trumper as 'one of our truly great cricketers', told me that he was 'the first to score a century before lunch in a Test match', which proved to be true, and 'once hit the first ball of a match for six', which was not. So, in the context of assertion, fact and myth, was I introduced to the first cricketer of the past that ever registered with me and to what remains perhaps its oldest truly treasured image.

I had also, though I would be unaware of it for many more

---

* Essay on the publication of *Stroke of Genius: Victor Trumper and the Shot That Changed Cricket* (2016).

years, been introduced to the work of the pioneering Edwardian photographer George Beldam, in whose book *Great Batsmen: Their Methods at a Glance* (1905) the picture first appeared. Instead, as it usually is, the photograph of Trumper in *Great Australian Cricket Pictures* appeared uncredited, undated, unaccounted for, as though it had taken itself – or even as though it wasn't a photograph at all, but a keyhole vantage on the past. When not long after I commenced reading about Trumper, it can only have been with the image of him jumping out to drive in mind.

That was then, of course, although now may be less different than we think. Nobody's found a great many more photographs of Trumper, or at least thought to make the others that do exist more readily available to the online browser. Today's ten-year-old would encounter Trumper pretty much the same way as I did, simultaneously with his most famous pictorial representation: google 'Victor Trumper', and one is led to the image. For the more mature fan, meanwhile, the image attests the residual Trumper reputation, even if a good deal of the residual Trumper reputation is based on the image.

When in 2015 I first contemplated writing a book about Trumper, convention drew me towards a biography. Yet I also experienced misgivings. It was 113 years since his zenith when, on the 1902 tour of England, he made 2570 runs at 48.49 with eleven hundreds, including one before lunch on the first day of the Old Trafford Test: though perhaps no batsman had ever batted so brilliantly in a Test match, no eyewitness surived.

Of Trumper, three previous biographers had struggled to make much. The primary material was thin, the residual mythology thick. To write about any figure of the past is essentially to make a claim for them, to make a mission of substantiating their significance. In sport, the allure is of great deeds, stirring victories, public approbation. Yet legend is an uneasy companion of biography, if not an outright enemy. And to track the Trumper story through the standard sources is a little like entering a hall of mirrors. Everyone is quoting everyone else. Stories and their origins have long since parted ways. Did he really farm the bowling of Walter Mead to protect senior colleagues in his 135 not out in the Lord's Test of 1899? Did he really skewer Len Braund's leg-spin during his 185 not out in the Sydney Test of 1903? One channels, instead, impressions. My excellently icono-clastic friend Jarrod Kimber wrote about Trumper in *Test Cricket: The Unauthorized Biography* (2015) in terms of which Neville Cardus would not have disapproved – and let's just say that these two writers would not normally be thought of as kinsmen.

So I struck a kind of bargain with antiquity. Why not look legend in the eye rather than try to peer around it? Why not evaluate knowingly what a conventional biography would be unavoidably transacting in anyway? 'Fable is more historical than fact,' Chesterton reminds us, 'because fact tells us about one man and fable tells us about a million men.'

That didn't mean ignoring fact. What became *Stroke of Genius* still needed extensive biographical underpinnings – partly to illustrate legend's deviations from them, partly because Trumper has been gradually winnowed away to a name and an image. But I was anxious to avoid what so many works about cricket history seem to become – chronologies of scores, transcriptions of match reports, recitations of anecdote. That's not only because these are seldom truly enlightening, but because so much now lies within reach of the interested reader. Want to find out Trumper's scores in 1903–04? Use Cricket Archive. Want to read what people said about these scores? Try Trove or the British Newspaper Archive. In some ways, those of us enticed by cricket's past have yet to adapt to the modern accessibility of informational riches. In any case, what differentiated Trumper was not his scores so much as their interpretation, the heights of lyricism ascended in describing him and the remarkable unanimity of opinion, so that their evocation by a single image did not in the end seem so unnatural – indeed, it would steadily become 'proof' of claims for his aesthetic superiority.

Heading down this track, I grew interested in how cricket was 'seen' before the First World War. Cricket, of course, is a challenging game to watch live, for reasons of distance and speed, without some kind of technological enhancement. Way back when, illustrative forms – painting, engraving, early photography – tended to reflect that. They hovered at the boundary edge, and perforce took in the whole scene. Classics of illustration like Mason's 'A Cricket Match' and Ponsonby Staples's 'An Imaginary Cricket Match' foregrounded the crowd and recessed the cricket. The Victorian Age's outstanding cricket photographic work, Alcock's *Famous Cricketers and Cricket Grounds* (1892), posed players for wistful portraits, provided venues as tranquil panoramas. Intimacy with action was undreamed of – until George Beldam.

Quite why Beldam is not better known amazes me. Perhaps it is because he is *sui generis* – he belongs to a leisure society swallowed up by the First World War. He was an amateur cricketer, for Middlesex and London County, who doubled as an amateur photographer: indeed it was one of the passing intrigues of researching my book to learn that photography underwent debates similar to those in cricket about amateurism and professionalism. A century on, we're apt to deem amateurism a kind of effete dabbling. In photography as in cricket, Beldam was a furiously industrious perfectionist. Between 1904 and 1908, he took thousands of photographs for eight works of sports photography, five of them sub-stantial: not just cricket, but tennis, golf and even ju-jitsu. Nor is this just a matter of versatility. He had the confi-dence of his caste and skill. It's not a coincidence that Beldam persuaded cricketers to do what they did for no other photographer: he was one of them, and, as an amateur, atop cricket's social heap.

Beldam had the further cachet of a creative partnership with the era's *arbiter elegentiae*, C. B. Fry. Not only was Fry the finest flower of English amateur sport – batsman, footballer, rugby player, athlete, scholar – but a prolific journalist and editor of an eponymous magazine of outdoor recreation. Fry had both the Victorian fascination with technique and the Edwardian infatuation with style – which he defined with a Ruskinian formulation about the maximum effect for the least apparent effort. Long entranced by the unique elan and deftness of his Sussex and England teammate Ranjitsinhji, Fry was captivated by a photograph that Beldam took of Ranji at Hove in September 1904.

These were not action photographs as we would now understand them. To bridge that abiding gap between bound-ary edge and action, Beldam circulated among his subjects during practice sessions and at intervals; sometimes he invited them to his home where he enjoyed the gentlemanly indulgence of an outdoor and an indoor pitch. Photography being such a novelty, and the idea of a glimmer of action so alluring, that few if any seemed to say no to him.

The photograph of Ranji was one of a portfolio collected after a Middlesex v Sussex county match, in which Beldam hit the winning run, put on his blazer, fetched his camera, erected his tripod, and pressed Ranji into going through his repertoire to Fry's bowling – not even Philip Brown has pulled that off. One of the images clearly anticipates the photograph Beldam would take of Trumper – Ranji is prancing out to drive, eyes flashing, front foot in mid-air. Fry, who had previously expressed reservations about photography, felt them give way: the image took up a full page of the next issue of *C. B. Fry's Magazine of Action and Outdoor Life* alongside an appreciative exposition.

Beldam's collaborations with Fry, *Great Batsmen* (1905) and *Great Bowlers and Fielders* (1906), signify such a breakthrough in the representation of cricket that they might almost have been of another sport, given their departure from the norms of the portrait and the panorama, and their accent on the capture of the figure in motion. They reverse, in fact, cricket's existing descriptive grammar. It was the first time cricketers had been shown in close quarters in the physical performance of their deeds; it was the first time image had taken true precedence over text, Fry's captions serving only to tease out what Beldam's photographs introduced. In detail and comprehensiveness these companion volumes may never even have been equalled – certainly, but for them, we would have no idea what cricket looked like before the First World War. You can spend countless hours poring over them. You can spend countless hours poring over one photograph alone – and I should know, because I did.

In *Great Batsmen's* section on Trumper there are no fewer than thirty-three photographs – more than for any other subject. They were accumulated across two sessions during the Ashes summer of 1905, at Lord's and at The Oval, separated by roughly two weeks. Pare those sessions apart, and they are fascinatingly distinct. The former are a wide range of shots taken from more or less the same front of the wicket off-side position, with Beldam acting as bowler while taking the photographs by means of a pneumatic push connected to the camera by a long cord – we know this because it was included in a diary entry by the painter Henry Scott Tuke who was present on the occasion. The latter are, in the main, attempts to capture one stroke, a straight drive, from a variety of positions in an arc from mid-on to about fourth slip – we can surmise this from a photograph of Beldam at work at The Oval photographing Clem Hill published the same week in a London illustrated paper.

Nothing like a contact sheet survives, but Beldam's objective is apparent. He craves the sense of motion conveyed by the airborne front foot, which he had succeeded in capturing while photographing Ranji the year before. He craves it so badly that for a few plates he does something very unusual in his oeuvre: he adopts a landscape framing, wider-than-high, rather than a portrait shape. What becomes 'Plate XXVII: Jumping out for a straight drive', taken from side-on, is a photograph as audacious as the shot it immortalized. Trumper is launching from outside his ground: the crease line is falling away at bottom left. Trumper is surging into light: the gap in the skyline caused by Clayton Street stretching away from The Oval. Trumper is alone in his estate: there are no stumps, no fielders, no square leg umpire. Trumper's bat is poised at the moment of perfect stillness before commencing its downswing, which is foretold by the horizontals and verticals of the background, and the empty space at top right into which we can imagine the ball vanishing. You come to the photograph for Trumper, but stay as much out of admiration for Beldam.

What's almost as fascinating, especially in our present day and age, is that the photograph was not immediately identified as a classic, as distinct from simply of superior quality. Like the aforementioned image of Ranji and another of F. S. Jackson, it was offered as a limited-edition photogravure. Yet none of them sold out. And while *Great Batsmen* and *Great Bowlers and Fielders* were critically acclaimed, they were too expensive to sell widely. Reprographic and communications technologies were inadequate for the broad diffusion of Beldam's images – a hundred years ago the only things that 'went viral' were . . . well, viruses.

At the time, this actually didn't matter: Trumper had no immediate need of pictorial elaboration. And in the annals of iconic photography, delayed appreciation is not unusual. On the recent death of Muhammad Ali, virtually every news outlet adorned their obituary with Neil Leifer's 1964 image of all-conquering Ali towering over the prone form of Sonny Liston. Yet fifty-two years earlier, the photograph had been buried deep in the recesses of *Sports Illustrated*, garnered little attention, won no award. It had been rediscovered only when people had forgotten that the fight itself was a squib, and that what looks like Ali's bray of triumph was actually a demand that Liston, widely suspected of taking a dive, get up.

To say as I have heard it said that Trumper's greatness is 'based on a photograph', therefore, is a gross oversimplification. At the time and in the earthly decade he had remaining, Trumper was not just hugely admired, but deeply loved: contemporaneous responses to him have an emotional incandescence that I suspect is almost unique. He also remained an enigma – something excluded from almost every account of his life, for example, is that he was an obdurate resister of administrative encroachments on what had been to that stage a player-led game. He would not sign his contract for the 1909 England tour, because to do so would have been to accept the dominion of the new Board of Control; he stood aside from the 1912 England tour at that Board's insistence on appointing their own manager, over the wishes of the players. Perhaps it is this that accounts for his adaptable reputation, that by his reticence he kept it free of complication, and also that he died in 1915, along with a great many more beautiful, comforting, transitory things.

For the Anglosphere after the First World War, memory was an exquisite self-torture. So much loss, so much waste and decay. Looking back on Trumper was at least only bittersweet. At first he was recalled chiefly in print. His extoller-in-chief, in an ecumenical gesture, was the rising star of English cricket writing, Neville Cardus, who wrote in the *Manchester Guardian* as 'Cricketer'. Cardus, of course, sought pitches of eloquence never before attempted in cricket writing; central to his critique, too, was the irrefutable inferiority of the cricket of his adulthood, with its serried professional ranks, to the cricket of his youth, with its swaggering amateur leadership. Of the latter, Trumper became the personification, unsullied and unageing. And it was in an elegy for Trumper in July 1926 that Cardus first trialled an evocative expression: 'Trumper's winged batsmanship was seen in *the golden age of cricket* [my italics]; he was, at his finest, master of some of the greatest bowlers the game has ever known.'

It was a conception Cardus would expand, burnish, celebrate and mourn the rest of his lengthy career. By the 1940s the 'golden age' had been entrenched by upper cases for G and A; by the 1960s it had been historicized by book-length treatments. Trumper did not hold the Golden Age up by itself. But by being Australian, being beautiful and being dead, he gave it a roundness and completedness that made it sound like more than an assuagement of fading class certainties.

Then, in October 1927, fully twenty-two years after it was taken, Beldam's photograph of Trumper was published for the first time in Australia, in the *Sydney Mail*, a popular weekly published on art paper. Whose decision it was we do not know, but it almost certainly involved the paper's brilliant English-born pictorial editor, Herbert Fishwick. There were no jpegs and tifs: the *Mail* relied on a copy of the gravure taken down from the wall of the New South Wales Cricket Association, still reproduced a little hazily. But the caption writer's excitement was unfeigned.

'Victor!'

To look at this picture (kindly lent by the N.S.W. Cricket Association) is to see Victor Trumper as we used to see him from the pavilions. See him and marvel! It does not show his face clearly, but as an action picture it is wonderful. No hesitancy here. He is stepping out to meet the ball. Strength, grace, and balance, combine to reveal joyous and youthful sense of mastery. What was the secret of this joyous freedom? Simply the beautiful character of Victor. All young players should know all that can be told of him, whose other name was Modesty.

The odd thing is that had I elected to write a conventional biography of Trumper, I'd have left him in 1915, when his definition and significance were still far from clear. As it is, Trumper took on a new posthumous effulgence from the late 1920s, thanks to an image which slipped seamlessly into a mass media with an expanding pictorial quotient. The year after the *Sydney Mail* published the Trumper photograph, it published Fishwick's stirring action portrait of Walter Hammond cover-driving – a perfect counterpart, in a way, the Englishman in Australia to balance the Australian in England as they helped establish an aesthetic continuum. But a greater influence still, I suspect, was just hoving into view.

We tend to think now of Donald Bradman as becoming the monopolist of cricket fame from the 1930s, arising as he did in the age of radio, the wire photo, and a ceaselessly expanding newspaper and publishing industry. Yet Trumper was kept flickeringly alive by all those with reservations about the on-rush of modernity, materialism, industrialization and professionalism that Bradman embodied. Originating his dichotomy of Trumper as 'the bird in flight' and Bradman as 'the aeroplane', Cardus could now flourish the most modern of empirical proofs. 'Look at the photographs of him [Trumper], doubting young Thomases of the skeptical present, and see how far he would venture beyond the crease's rim at the sight of a well-tossed ball,' Cardus wrote in *Cricket* (1930). 'His bat is held up behind him punitively, he is leaping to the ball, his every muscle responding to the demands of the will to power and victory.' Administrators discomfited by Bradman's popular heft also looked back fondly: in 1930, the NSWCA placed a line drawing inspired by Beldam's Trumper on the cover of its yearbook, where it remained twenty-five years.

As deeply as Bradman interred his precursor's records, then, he preserved a role for Trumper as a kind of romantic counterpoint to his overpowering rationalism. And while Trumper receded perhaps from the very front rank of fame, his spirit remained available for criticism of modern mores, from joyless professionalism to flamboyant entrepreneurship. Trumper's centenary happened to fall on the eve of Kerry Packer's World Series Cricket. The first public duty of Australia's 'establishment' captain Bob Simpson was to place a wreath on Trumper's grave – somewhat of an irony given that Trumper had so frequently been at loggerheads with the establishment of his own generation.

In the generation or so since that centenary, the image has evolved further, and almost shaken off its subject: it is 'Trumper', the equivalent of an artist known by a single work, or even a public man by a solitary, resonant if only partially grasped idea or phrase, like, in Australia, A. A. 'The Cultural

Cringe' Phillips or Donald 'The Lucky Country' Horne. The concluding chapter of *Stroke of Genius*, which could easily have been several times as long, is concerned with the appropriation of the photograph as a free-floating art object. It turned out, for example, that the owner of the most superb representation, Louis Laumen's one and a quarter times life-size bronze of the image, has no interest in cricket: he is a collector who had some spare cash.

The basis of iconoclasm as it was originally understood, if we recall, was the objection that icons had heretical powers to destroy the divine presence – that they, rather than what they represent, become the object of veneration. Perhaps in a secular and sporting sense, this is the fate that has befallen Victor Trumper, effaced by his own image, reduced at times simply to a leap, so that every *Cricinfo* reader knows what is meant when it is said that 'Victor Trumper would have been proud' of AB De Villiers [http://www.thecricketmonthly.com/story/910981/the-audacity-of-ab] or a youth batting near Premadasa Stadium is making a 'salute to Victor Trumper' [http://www.espncricinfo.com/blogs/content/story/1011061.html].

Yet to complain of this would be pernickety. It is the image that has kept for Trumper an irreducible corner of this visual age, that brings him effortlessly up-to-date every time we see it. For all that Bradman is Australian cricket's historical lodestar, no photographer ever succeeded in obtaining his aesthetic signature as Beldam did Trumper. Without Beldam's photograph, Trumper would be no more than a distant name with a fading echo, a statistical remnant buried deep beneath a century's further achievement. And without Beldam's photograph, I doubt his name would ever have detained me at an impressionable age, and lodged in my mind to the degree that I wished to write a book about him.

# Tip Foster

## 287 AND ALL THAT (2015)

R. E. Foster's 111-year-old record for a score by a visiting batsman in Australia, which with an epic 290 New Zealand's Ross Taylor broke yesterday [15 November 2015] at the WACA Ground, has for long been a great cricket trivia question. For most of the last century, people have been looking at it in tabulations of high scores and asking . . . who?

That's understandable. For most of his career, Reginald Erskine Foster had no time for sport, despite being the only man to captain England at cricket and football, and representing Oxford at racquets and golf as well. He came from perhaps the most omnicompetent sporting family of all: all seven brothers represented Worcestershire at cricket while their three sisters represented Worcestershire at golf. But 'Tip', third and most gifted of the brethren, was a stockbroker for whom cricket tours were not an option after his first, to Australia in 1903–04.

Foster's mighty 287 came at the very first opportunity, and under acute pressure. Australia had made 285, but the uncovered pitch was damp from overnight rain when England began its reply. Johnny Tyldesley and a lunch watchman Ted Arnold bought time, so that conditions were improving in the afternoon when Foster came to the wicket at three for 73, but there was still a match to win. The innings was in two stages: after a rather laboured 71 in three hours at the close of the second day, Foster added 216 in four and a half hours on the third, including 80 in his last hour with last man Wilf Rhodes for company.

We sometimes imagine the ancients to be less figure-minded than we, but the account by his captain Pelham Warner in *How We Recovered the Ashes* (1904) suggests the presence of some eager stattos. There were cheers at the first record to fall, Charles Bannerman's 65, highest score on Test debut; there were cheers at the next, Ranjitsinhji's 175, the record score for England against Australia. Then:

> Shortly afterwards he passed Gregory's 201 against
> England at Sydney in 1894 – curiously enough Gregory
> was bowling at the time – and then a few minutes later
> amid cheering which W. L. Murdoch might have heard
> in faraway England, he beat that great batsman's 211 at
> Kennington Oval in 1884. That innings had been the
> benchmark for nearly twenty years, on what seemed an
> inaccessible pinnacle, and here Foster comes along and
> in his first Test match beats it.

With a nice sense of posterity, Warner thought to photograph the scoreboard afterwards, ahead of its adornment by Trumper's masterful 185 not out. The following year in England, Foster also went through his paces for the estimable George Beldam, showing off a rather stiff front leg, but a dramatic leap and a decidedly modern pull shot. Another of the photographs also made it, via a chalk rendering by Albert

Chevallier Tayler, onto an incomparably rare Australian cigarette card.

There was not much more, of cricket or life: diabetes claimed Foster, aged thirty-six. Twenty fourteen marked the centenary of his death, which was commemorated at Great Malvern Cemetery and New Road. It's been Foster's score that's shown the staying power. It stood for twenty-seven years as the highest Ashes score (broken by Bradman), for another eight as the highest Ashes score by an Englishman (broken by Hutton); it endures as the highest score at Sydney (where it survived menacing by Brian Lara in 1993) and the highest score on debut (where nobody has come closer than Jacques Rudolph). That last, I suspect, has a few years ahead of it yet. Although if they continue producing Test wickets like this one, who knows?

# BODYLINE AND OTHER LINES

*I've borrowed this intertitle, of course, from the subtitle to Jack Fingleton's Cricket Crisis (1949), still as good a book as has been written from the middle of an Ashes. Bodyline is at the middle of our imagined Ashes heritage, too, that instant when the great measure of Bradman met the arch countermeasure of Larwood, and the incipient violence of the age found sporting expression. But their clash, perhaps, had been coming anyway, from reversed origins. The first subject here, England's Sir Jack Hobbs, was a new benchmark in batting mastery; the second, Australia's Warwick Armstrong, was the first to harness pace bowling ruthlessly, in the persons of two other subjects, Jack Gregory and Ted McDonald. A keen cricket intelligence, Douglas Jardine, was watching. A ten-year-old boy, Ken Farnes, would grow into the nearest thing to Larwood's heir.*

# Sir Jack Hobbs

## THE MASTER (2001)

After his monopedal hundred in the Oval Test in 2001, Steve Waugh was asked by Channel 4 to explain his overpowering desire to participate in the game. 'I'm a professional cricketer,' he replied, 'and I love playing for Australia.' It was a typical Waughism, succinct and direct. Yet at one time the remark would have sounded paradoxical, even dangerous. There was cricket for pleasure and cricket for profit: amateur and professional, oil and water. Then along came Jack Hobbs – 'a professional who bats exactly like an amateur', said Sir Pelham Warner, as though describing one of the marvels of the age.

Hobbs was the only Englishman garlanded as one of *Wisden*'s Five Cricketers of the Century.* His status as the greatest first-class run scorer (61,237) and century-maker (197) clearly counted for something; his serene and sportsmanlike demeanour for something more. Yet seventy respondents to

---

* The other four were Bradman, Warne, Garry Sobers and Viv Richards.

the survey did not figure him in their calculations, and the editor Matthew Engel's *Almanack* tribute seemed somewhat tepid: Hobbs was called 'pragmatic', 'businesslike' and 'the supreme craftsman', though 'not an artist'.

But was Hobbs really like that? Study the images in the primer *The Perfect Batsman* (1926) and one obtains a different impression. The book's '98 Cinema-Photographs of JB Hobbs at the wicket' were taken for author Archie MacLaren in 1914, when Hobbs felt himself at his peak. And they are anything but staid, or even conventional, and not a bit 'pragmatic': the bat speed and brio are breathtaking. In *Jack Hobbs* (1981), John Arlott remarks on his subject's tight bottom-hand grip – 'contrary to the advice of most coaches' – and it is evident in the sequences that illustrate 'Driving to the Right of Cover Point' and 'A True Cover Drive Along the Ground'. It is batting at its most spontaneous and original; 'The Master' and 'The Master Blaster' were not quite so dissimilar as might be imagined. Hampshire's Alex Kennedy once recalled bowling the first ball of a match to Hobbs at The Oval. It was a late outswinger on off stump; Hobbs dispatched it through square leg for four. The anecdote's only un-Vivish aspect is that Hobbs smilingly apologized: 'I shouldn't have done that, should I? I was a bit lucky.'

To appreciate Hobbs's full significance, we must con-template the class rigidities of his time. The discrimination that placed amateur and professional in separate dressing rooms and hotels, and had them enter the field by different gates and travel in different railway carriages, now seems as remote from our experience of cricket as sectarianism or McCarthyism. Yet it was very real and even seemed the natural order, not least to Hobbs, who enumerated his Surrey colleagues with careful acknowledgement of necessary honorifics: 'There was Tom Shepherd, Andy Ducat, Mr Jardine,

Mr Jeacocke, Mr Fender, Bob Gregory, as well as Andy [Sandham].'

Quietly but categorically, Hobbs upset that precedence. Before him professionals had been largely chained to the bowling crease. Only a handful of 'players' had represented England as batsmen: Arthur Shrewsbury, Bobby Abel, Johnny Tyldesley, Tom Hayward. And these were business cricketers. When Hayward received merely a fiver in talent money for scoring 315 not out at The Oval, he remarked: 'Well, it's no use me getting 300 again.' Heavily influenced by Hayward, Hobbs was clear-eyed about his vocation: 'Unless you get to the top where the plums are, it is a bare living, and when your cricket days are over, you have to find a new career.' Yet he bucked the stereotype of the workman pro. Commercial realities never restrained his adventure or compromised the pleasure he took in his craft. 'Of course I was earning my living,' he said. 'But it was batting I enjoyed.'

Hobbs was not an agitator for the rights of the professional; rather, the excellence of his example provided a personification of the cause. His Surrey captain Percy Fender was one of the first to lead his team through a single gate, earning him a reproach from Lord Harris: 'We do not want that sort of thing at Lord's, Fender.' It was because of Hobbs that Fender felt free to advocate the unthinkable notion of professional captaincy: 'My experience of professional cricketers does not teach me that cricket would necessarily go to the dogs if a professional happened to be in charge.' And it was Hobbs that Cecil Parkin invoked as the best leader he had played under in his famous January 1925 article in the *Weekly Dispatch* disputing Arthur Gilligan's captaincy credentials, provoking Lord Hawke's even more famous retort: 'Pray God that no professional will ever captain England.'

The ire Hawke incurred after that address was the greatest

testimony to Hobbs's renown. Even the former Australian Governor-General, Lord Forster, weighed in, stating that he would 'never hesitate to play under the captaincy of a man like Jack Hobbs'. So it came to pass that on 26 July 1926, Hobbs was asked to lead England when Arthur Carr fell ill during an Ashes Test at Old Trafford: the first professional appointment since Shrewsbury.

Hobbs was reticent. He disliked the responsibility of leadership and said publicly that 'most professionals' preferred an amateur skipper. But he took the job, drew the Test and foresaw others following in his footsteps. 'We are such sticklers for tradition in insisting on an amateur captain, regardless of the question of whether he can pull his weight as a player,' he wrote in *My Life Story* (1935). 'The time is coming when we will have to change our views ... when there will be no amateurs of sufficient ability to put into an England side.'

Cricket, as so often, found ways to defer change. And as a standard bearer for the exploited, Hobbs would not appeal to a Marxist: he overthrew nothing, stormed no citadel. Yet, in a way, he so dignified his profession that the archaisms of class distinction in cricket had ceased to matter long before the annulment of the gentleman–player divide. Alec Bedser commented that using the players' gate at The Oval was no hardship, because if it had been good enough for Hobbs it was good enough for him. That Hobbs became the first professional games player to be knighted in 1953 is one of cricket history's better coincidences: England was in the course of winning the Ashes under its first professional captain of the twentieth century, Len Hutton.

If all this seems like history – and no remark in the contemporary sporting vernacular is more dismissive than 'that's ancient history' – Hobbs's career had two other trappings of modernity that loosely link him with Waugh. Hobbs was the first professional to take his wife on an Ashes tour. He did it characteristically, initially declining to make the 1924–25 trip, then agreeing to join the team as an 'extra member' when Lord Harris granted Ada Hobbs permission to accompany her husband. Waugh took up a similar cudgel, championing a new Australian regime that welcomed players' partners on tour. Likewise did Waugh follow in Hobbs's literary path, capitalizing on his fame through the publication of books. Nine books bear Hobbs's name. Nine* bear Waugh's.

---

* Now thirteen.

# Warwick Armstrong

## MR BIG (2006)

At his final playing dimensions of nearly 140 kg and 193 cm, Warwick Armstrong was Australia's heftiest Test cricketer. It suited him. Everything about Armstrong was outsized, from his first-class record of 16,158 runs at 47 and 832 wickets at less than 20, to his impatience with authority and capacity for resistance.

Moderns fans know him mostly by his voluminous shirt, like the spinnaker on a yacht, now draped on a tailor's dummy in the Australian Cricket Hall of Fame. But he has left many other traces: the highest Australian partnership for the sixth wicket (with Monty Noble), the second highest for the seventh wicket (with Joe Darling), the third highest for the ninth wicket (with Ted Windsor), a century and five wickets in an innings on four occasions, a hundred runs and ten wickets in a match twice. Among the eleven Australians with 10,000 first-class runs and 500 first-class wickets, Armstrong has the highest batting average and second-lowest bowling average.*

For his huge and heavy boots, also in the Hall, authorities

always thought Armstrong too big. A man of few, mainly terse words, he could be found at the bottom of disputes with the Victorian Cricket Association, and subsequently the Board of Control, on an almost annual basis for twenty years. Partly this was because Armstrong was a representative of Melbourne Cricket Club, whose influence the VCA and Board were intent on extirpating; mainly it was because Armstrong was a cricketer who played only on terms satisfactory to him, and who knew his value to the last shilling. As teammate Arthur Mailey commented, Armstrong 'didn't have much time for arbitration unless he himself could act as the arbitrator'.

Most of Armstrong's career was before the First World War, when he was a roundhead among cavaliers, a batsman of prodigious strength restrained by great patience, and a leg-spin bowler who made up what he lacked in spin with immense accuracy and endurance. No Australian will better his 1902 runs at 50 and 122 wickets at 18.2 on a tour of England just over a century ago. He made 133 at Adelaide Oval in February 1908, took six for 35 at Lord's in June 1909, both match-winning efforts.

After the war, he was more belligerent, taking only 205 minutes to score 158, the first post-war Test hundred, against England at the SCG: 'Even the great Victor Trumper in his heyday had shown us nothing better,' said the umpire Bob Crockett. But he was never other than an entirely uncompromising opponent. He made a timed out appeal against an opening pair in a grade match. He attempted a 'Mankad' run-out in a first-class match more than thirty years before Mankad.

---

* The ten others make an excellent trivia question, being skewed towards those who played regular county cricket in England: George Giffen, Monty Noble and Richie Benaud are joined by Sammy Woods, Albert Trott, Frank Tarrant, George Tribe, Vic Jackson, Colin McCool and Bill Alley.

Most famously, having earlier pointed out that his rival captain had declared illegally, he became the first man to bowl consecutive overs in a Test. Asked if this had been deliberate, he simply 'smiled and looked away'.

In Armstrong's dealings with administrators, there was no ambiguity: everything, especially the coat trailing, was deliberate. In 1902–03, he flouted the VCA by refusing to play under the state's captain, Jack Worrall, on account of Worrall's published remarks about a teammate's bowling action. In 1903–04 and 1904–05, he enraged the VCA by playing as a professional because they had refused to pay his expenses as an amateur. In 1905–06, he was censured by the VCA for captaining Melbourne in New Zealand rather than playing in the Sheffield Shield. In 1906–07, he censured the VCA for selecting him in a match for which he had notified them he was unavailable because of work commitments. In 1907–08, the VCA very nearly banned him permanently after another dispute over expenses, and he was ousted by fellow players as Victorian captain. When the Board of Control then mooted taking over the finances of Australian tours to England, Armstrong was at the forefront of player objections. 'What are they going to do with the money?' he asked at a meeting of the players of Victoria and New South Wales in December 1908. 'The players are taking all the hard knocks and making all the money. We should have a little idea where the money is going.' He joined Victor Trumper in refusing to sign his contract for the 1909 Ashes tour as a protest against the Board voting themselves a cut, and only a job offer from the Melbourne Cricket Club kept him from accepting a lucrative coaching contract in New Zealand early the following year.

Victorian administrators would have been glad to see his broad back. In 1910–11, he wrangled with the VCA about his players' entitlement to complimentary tickets, then declined to represent an Australian XI because the fee was too small. In 1911–12, teammate Jim Kyle revealed that the VCA was intent on engineering Armstrong's removal as Victoria's captain. In 1912–13, Kyle having been excommunicated and others sidelined, Armstrong *was* replaced as Victoria's captain by a stooge at a gerrymandered player vote. In 1913–14, reappointed as a stand-in captain following that stooge's failure, he resigned at lunchtime on the first day when the VCA declined to make the appointment permanent. After all that, in 1914–15, he led Victoria to victory in the Sheffield Shield, maybe simply to annoy his detractors.

Between times, Armstrong was at the heart of Australian cricket's seminal dispute, being one of the six refuseniks opposed to the Board's organization of the team to England in 1912. When the Board stripped Australian players of their last remaining right, to choose their own manager, Armstrong affirmed his allegiance to the players' choice: his Victorian teammate and friend Frank Laver. With Trumper, Clem Hill, Hanson Carter, Albert Cotter and Vernon Ransford, he forfeited selection. This disobedience was forgiven but not forgotten. When Armstrong became Australia's captain in November 1920 after the Great War, the Board appointed him for only one Test, and only on the odd vote. Had they imagined this would unsettle him, they were mistaken. In the next year, Armstrong scored 2282 runs at 56, bowled 5420 deliveries for 117 wickets at 15.5, and turned that one Test appointment into ten, for eight wins and two draws.

The VCA made one last bid to dispossess him, sacking him from the Victorian team in February 1921, ostensibly as a punishment for withdrawing with an injury from a Sheffield Shield game without informing the team manager, more generally for behaving like a state within a state in Australian cricket. But after 10,000 gathered outside the MCG to protest,

Armstrong was recalled and Victoria's selectors narrowly averted a vote of no-confidence. The climax of his career was a wildly successful Ashes tour, harnessing Australia's first great pace bowling partnership: Jack Gregory and Ted McDonald.

For a generation, Armstrong was a personification of Australia: big, tough, taciturn, insouciant, yielding nothing. After watching Armstrong in England in 1921, dramatist Louis Esson wrote to the novelist Vance Palmer that its cricketers better represented Australia than its artists and politicians put together: 'England are really scared of Armstrong and the fast bowlers . . . They are not pleasant players. A good English journalist described them as "hard-bitten", "grim", and "pitiless". We shouldn't be a soft, mushy, maudlin race. In politics we're a shingle short, a nation of grinning village idiots. The cricketers fill me with great enthusiasm. They can lose, for there is luck in cricket, but they'll never crack up like the English.' More than a century after Armstrong played his maiden Test, Australians would like to imagine that this still holds.

# Herbie Collins and Ted McDonald

## LIVES ENTWINED (2015)<sup>*</sup>

C ricket and the punt – two great Australian recreations, frequently coexistent in individuals. Think Keith Miller at Royal Ascot, with his encyclopaedic recall of Melbourne Cups ('1947 – the year of Hiraji'). Think Doug Walters with a transistor earplug in his ear, Mark Waugh with a tip on his tongue, Ricky Ponting with a dog on his mind. Not always is the overlap of interests so wholesome, as evinced by two new biographies, linked also by their historical period and the meter of their titles: Max Bonnell's *Lucky: The Life of H. L. 'Bert' Collins* and Nick Richardson's *The Silk Express: The Story of E. A. 'Ted' McDonald*.

Lucky was among many nicknames worn by Herbie Collins: he was also Horseshoe, Nutty, The Squirrel and Mauldy. Bonnell has chosen it as a title for his excellent monograph, because of the irony of Collins's reputation for

---

\* Review of Max Bonnell's *Lucky: The Life of H. L. 'Bert' Collins* and Nick Richardson's *The Silk Express: The Story of E. A. 'Ted' McDonald*.

good fortune. Certainly Collins was reprieved on a few key occasions during his career as a Test opener, but fortune followed him little further. Livelihood as a bookmaker, stipendiary steward and commission agent was insufficient to support him, an invalid sister, an elderly mother and a gambling habit. Five years after he ceased to captain Australia, he was seeking financial assistance from the NSW Cricket Association, and he found late-life marriage to a beautiful and expensive young woman impossible to sustain. Mind you, at least he stayed the right side of the law, unlike an older brother who deserted his own wife, and later did time for separating lonely women from their savings in the style of Ernest Gorse.

'As a batsman I took no risks,' Collins wrote of himself. 'I built up a reputation as a solid, reliable opener, always orthodox. They say there's two sides to everybody's character. Perhaps my cricket and private lives were two sides to mine. On the racecourse I took risks . . . I don't intend to offer advice to anyone. But let me say racing didn't make me wealthy.'

Nor did cricket, although that was, perhaps, to be expected. All the same, Collins was treated cruelly by the game, which he did so much to put back on its feet after the First World War as captain of the Australian Imperial Forces XI. When the Australian selection panel, of whom he was a member, excluded his Waverley teammate Alan Kippax from the 1926 Ashes team, the club not only shrank from offering Collins the customary send-off but sacked him as skipper. He lost his jobs as state captain and selector while he was away, too. Collins never retired from Australian cricket, notes Bonnell: Australian cricket, almost uniquely, retired him.

McDonald, the premier fast bowler of the 1920s, earned much more from the game – indeed, he made sure to, virtually sacrificing his Test career in order to become probably the highest-paid professional cricketer in the world with the Lancashire League club Nelson in 1922. As Richardson notes, the £500 he earned per season, first for Nelson, then for Lancashire, were equivalent to $1 million today.

Yet financial insecurity was his constant companion also, from the instant he had to leave his native Tasmania for Victoria to stay a step ahead of a scandal about his defalcations from an insurance company to meet gambling debts. And even once he was settled in England, expenditure had a way of rising to meet, and exceed, income: Richardson reveals that McDonald was constantly importuning advances from his employers to meet the demands of bookmaking creditors. His stunning death by a roadside in 1931 aged forty-six left a wife in straitened circumstances, and children only vaguely aware of their father, believing in family lore that McDonald had been with the ANZACs at Gallipoli – in fact, the enigmatic McDonald never enlisted, and went on playing sport, featuring in the 1916 Victorian Football League Grand Final for Fitzroy.

Both Bonnell and Richardson seek to redress their subjects' relative obscurity. Bonnell points out that Collins's 1926 Australians lost only one match – the best record of an Australian touring team in England until the Invincibles. Alas, that defeat in the Oval Test turned the Ashes over, and Collins has suffered the odium ever since of a posthumous allegation by Stork Hendry, credulously repeated, that he fixed the decisive game. After a methodical demolition of the case, Bonnell dismisses the proposition crisply: 'It will never be possible to acquit Bert Collins of the charge made against him by Hendry. But the case against him is based on innuendo rather than evidence and, taken all in all, the circumstantial evidence is unpersuasive.'

To make a case for *his* subject, Richardson need only point to McDonald's record as one of eleven Australians with more than 1000 first-class wickets, and at a superior strike rate to Shane Warne and Clarrie Grimmett. He presents McDonald as presaging a revolution in cricket by opening the bowling with Jack Gregory at Adelaide in January 1921 – it was the first time in Australia's history that two fast bowlers had opened the bowling, ahead of a year in which the pair carried all before them.

Richardson also argues for his subject as an inadvertent and indirect progenitor of Bodyline. The doping of wickets in England after the summer of 1921 compelled bowlers to seek redress in other ways, Harold Larwood among them, and McDonald would have been first to applaud a bowler who treated the batsman not just as an opponent but an enemy. When Larwood's teammate Bill Bowes felt a little sheepish about hitting India's Wazir Ali at Lord's in 1932, he called the counsel of the relentless Aussie to mind: 'I remembered Ted McDonald's advice . . . and that was the last time I hurried to offer sympathy to a victim. From then onwards I put on an act. I never said sorry to a batsman who I'd hit and never went to inquire how he was.'

The allure of the wager to cricketers? To a degree, of course, they are like endeavours: the cricketer stakes their ability against the skill of an opponent amid surrounds of randomness. Collins told a story from his life as a pony race steward, of taking up with a trainer the inconsistency of one of his stable. 'Now look here, Mr Collins,' replied the trainer. 'Not long ago I saw you get a beautiful hundred in the first innings of a Test match. The next innings you got a blob; that's like my horse. We can't be consistent all the time.' A lively paradox, that last line: Collins couldn't think of a reply. In recent times, Shane Warne has described poker as providing a substitute for his cricket rush: 'This is the same buzz I used to get from playing cricket.' Profiling Warne the poker player a couple of years ago, Andrew Miller wrote: 'It is not hard to see why Warne is hooked. In poker, as in spin bowling, the mind-games can be gladiatorial.'

A key difference is that the only measure of success in gambling is winnings. Cricket also offers fame as a spur. What if Nelson had not pursued and recruited McDonald in 1921, which Charlie Macartney called 'one of the greatest tragedies of Australian cricket'? What if Collins had had McDonald to throw the ball to in England in 1926? They might now be the subject of bigger and more laudatory biographies. As it is, their stories are of sporting success and human frailty – well worth your perusal, too.

# Jack Gregory
## CRICKET DYNAMITE (2004)

The camera loved Jack Gregory. Photographers of his day had still to conquer the distance between boundary and pitch, but Gregory's expansive, vibrant cricket reached out to meet them, advancing, radiating from the middle.

There's a famous image of him in his delivery while practising at Lord's: the front leg hanging in mid-air, the right arm at the bottom of its swing, the left arm aloft. The body's slight backward tilt lends him a palpable energy. Another picture features him batting at Sydney a few years later. With the completion of a drive, the hands have ended up over the right shoulder. The force of the stroke has turned Gregory's trunk to face down the wicket, although the ball is disappearing through mid-off, and the front foot hovers just off the ground. Here again is energy, a glad, spontaneous vitality. To enhance the breezy naturalness, Gregory is bare-armed, bare-headed and gloveless; indeed, we have it on Ray Robinson's authority that he even scorned a protector.

Not so long ago, I chanced on another photograph, on the

front of a copy of Sydney's *Referee*. It was Gregory taking a slip catch, and a blinder, too: he was parallel to the ground, the ball snug in an outstretched right hand, while wicketkeeper Hanson Carter cast a startled glance over his right shoulder. More than seventy years have elapsed since Jack Gregory played cricket, but age hasn't wearied him; photographs show Gregory as he was, the most magnetic and expressive player of his day. Donald Bradman revered the 'vital and vehement' Gregory: 'His bowling in the early days was positively violent in its intensity. His whole attitude towards the game was so dynamic, his slip fielding so sensational, his brilliant batting so pleasing . . . that thousands would flock to see Gregory play anywhere at any time.' Another who 'venerated' Gregory was Harold Larwood: 'Gregory's bowling was the essence of savagery, his great kangaroo leap at the last instant presenting an awesome sight to any batsman.' It is surely something to have both Bradman and Larwood in the same corner on any subject.

Gregory's career might easily never have happened. He had the perfect genealogy. Father Charles had played for New South Wales. Uncles Dave and Ned represented Australia, the former as captain in the inaugural Test match at Melbourne in March 1877, the latter becoming the Sydney Cricket Ground's groundsman; another uncle, Albert, was renowned for owning Australia's most comprehensive cricket library. Ten months before Jack's birth, cousin Syd relieved England of the first Test double-century on Australian soil.

Yet Jack the Lad evinced no particular aptitude for cricket. He captained Shore's first XI in 1911 and 1912, but as a batsman, and impressed at least as much as a hurdler and first XV rugby player. On leaving school, he went jackerooing in Queensland; a source, he wrote later, of deep disappointment to his family. By twenty, he cut a striking figure: six feet three inches tall, bronzed, blue-eyed and rugged. In portrait photographs, he has an air of quivering alertness bordering on impatience, as though in a hurry to be elsewhere. But it was not to be playing cricket.

Cricket's prospects of claiming Gregory dwindled further when he enlisted as an artillery gunner in January 1916. He served in the 7th, 10th, 11th and 23rd Field Artillery Brigades and 3rd and 4th Division Artillery Brigades, undertaking two tours of France. He played regimental cricket, and there first toyed with fast bowling: the legendary Charlie Macartney first met Gregory in an inter-unit game on a matting pitch at Larkhill, Salisbury Plain, and remembered him for ending the match by hitting a batsman in the eye with a lifter. Gregory's off-duty recreational energies were otherwise devoted to winning the hurdles over 120 yards, the sprint over 100, and his unit's tennis championship.

With peace, however, came the notion, mooted by the MCC grandee Pelham Warner, of a touring cricket team selected from AIF ranks; so much of the services' recruiting effort had been aimed at sportsmen that it was heavily endowed with cricketers, and a number of unofficial internationals had already been staged between England and an ersatz Dominions XI. Players were invited to join training sessions preparatory to selection at The Oval; Lt J. M. Gregory was one. It's unclear why. Before enlisting, he'd played exactly one game in Sydney first-grade. According to historian Ron Cardwell, the summons was on the recommendation of another officer in Gregory's unit, former NSW Shield batsman Frank Buckle. Gregory himself heard that his invitation came direct from Warner, who'd spied him in a social match between the Artillery Officers' School and Red Cross, intuiting latent ability from the family name. In the event, the twenty-four-year-old was the last of the touring sixteen picked, and then largely on the basis of physique; if he couldn't play much, it looked like Gregory could learn.

In hindsight, the AIF team was a powerful one. Lance-Corporal Herbie Collins, who became its captain, went on to lead Australia. Corporal Bert Oldfield, Captain Clarence Pellew and Gunner Johnny Taylor would serve under him as Test men. Then there was Gregory himself, all his cricket ahead. Yet at the time, their quality was unknown, their resilience unascertainable. Some had endured very hard wars indeed: Oldfield had spent five months in a military hospital with shell-shock; Captain Bill Trenerry had been wounded twice and Lt Charles Kellaway no fewer than four times. Gregory advanced by accident. Early on, he reported having cut his hand by stepping on it at fine leg. He was ribbed mercilessly; he was nicknamed 'Pavlova', an ironic reference to the dancer; Collins commented that he had all the elegance of a tank rolling into action and ruefully directed him to convalesce at slip.

To universal surprise, 'the long'un' proved a close catcher of uncanny reflex and reach; scorer Bill Ferguson likened his arms to an octopus's tentacles, 'only they seemed twice as many and twice as long'. Impressed, Collins tossed him the ball when the leader of the team's attack, Captain Cyril Docker, broke down. It was like removing a genie from a bottle. In the tour's third match, against Cambridge University at Fenners, Gregory claimed six for 68, and in bowling two batsmen didn't simply disarrange the stumps but knocked them flying like ninepins. On a benign surface at Lord's a few days later, he struck the chest of Middlesex's Mordaunt Doll so hard that the ball lifted the batsman off his feet, before trickling cruelly onto the stumps. Doll departed. Gregory had arrived.

*

Gregory would bag 178 wickets at less than 17 on that trip, and collect 1352 runs at 31. But a recitation of his successes wouldn't convey the force of his initial impact. Here was a mediocre grade cricketer, three years at war, suddenly transformed into a self-taught fast bowler, hitter and catcher. And he was dramatic. Oldfield described his run as 'ungainly', for his stride was immense, and his boots so voluminous that teammates could fit their own shod feet inside them. The 'kangaroo hop' delivery stride was completed with a follow-through that had him bounding down the pitch. The effect of Gregory's hyperkinetic exertion was fearful. Writing 55 years later in *Wisden*, Sir Neville Cardus insisted that Gregory 'ran some twenty yards to release the ball'. In fact, Gregory's approach was only fifteen yards, twelve paces; it must simply have 'seemed' longer.

As the ball descended from almost eight feet, it could do almost anything. When he pitched up, Oldfield thought, Gregory swung the new ball as much as any bowler he ever took. When he pitched short, Collins remembered, the ball seemed to whoosh like a mortar. For he was un-relievedly, inexhaustibly quick, once sending a bail flying forty metres.

Gregory's batting, initially primitive, always uninhibited, also developed on that AIF tour. He scored his maiden first-class hundred against Northants, and was eventually trusted to open the innings. Then there was the fielding, infallible at slip, electric anywhere. Against Natal at Durban on the first three days of November 1919, Gregory harvested nine for 32 and threw the last man out for good measure.

When the AIF team landed in Melbourne two months later, Gregory was the object of insatiable curiosity. Games were arranged to test the mettle of Collins's now-celebrated cohorts. At his first Australian gallop, Gregory claimed seven for 22 against Victoria, bowling flat out on a rain-affected Melbourne surface. A fortnight later against New South Wales, opening both batting *and* bowling, the great SCG scoreboard that his uncle Ned had built registered Jack's scoring 122 and 102, taking eight wickets and three catches. In eighty years since, no one has even approximated such a feat, let alone paralleled it.

Johnny Douglas's English team, which toured the Antipodes the following season, must have sensed what it was in for. And, in 1920–21, Australian cricket had a pitiless edge: new captain Warwick Armstrong was a leader who took the tact out of tactics. The hosts won all five contests and, if Gregory did not completely dominate the rubber, that was only because Armstrong had such a constellation of talent at his disposal: the left/right opening alliance of Collins and Bardsley, the hawk-eyed Macartney and the googly guru Arthur Mailey among them.

As it was, Gregory would almost certainly have been man-of-the-series, had such awards been in vogue. No Australian has approached his seven for 69 and chanceless hundred in 137 minutes in the Second Test at Melbourne over New Year. For good measure, he also accepted no fewer than fifteen chances. Sir Jack Hobbs said Gregory stood closer than any slip catcher of the time, and was unmistakably ravenous for the ball; sometimes, when Mailey loosed his wrong'un, Gregory would take a couple of giant strides from his normal post and materialize, like an apparition, at leg slip.

Gregory formed two vital strategic alliances during this series. The first was with his captain. Armstrong was a figure more respected than admired by contemporaries; sooner or later, he seems to have antagonized most opponents and more than a few comrades. Yet Gregory revered the vast Victorian, referring to him in two very rare articles some years later for *Sporting Globe* as 'my ideal cricketer' and 'the greatest of my time'.

Gregory also aligned with another Victorian: Ted McDonald had begun cricket as a batsman, before discovering a natural gift for bowling fast; the great Englishman Frank Woolley thought him speedier even than Larwood. Their combination was contrasting. Where Gregory's approach shook the earth, McDonald's flowed like a river. While the former enjoyed the wind at his back and swung the ball mostly away, the latter didn't mind breasting a breeze and possessed a sinister off-cutter. To Cardus, Gregory was 'atomic-powered', McDonald 'Satanic'. On one key question, however, Gregory and McDonald were as one. As McDonald's future Lancashire teammate Cec Parkin put it: 'He always maintains – that there never was a captain to equal Warwick Armstrong.'

McDonald actually achieved little in the three Tests of that 1920–21 Ashes series, and had reason for gratitude to Armstrong at its conclusion; the captain insisted on his selection to partner Gregory for the forthcoming tour of England. It was a ground-breaking recommendation. Hitherto, the concept of entrusting the new ball to pace at both ends had been almost unknown; the great Australian pacemen of yore had been solo venturers (Fred Spofforth, Ernie Jones, Tibby Cotter), usually sharing the new ball with a medium-pace bowler or even a spinner. With Gregory and McDonald, speed was now in the ascendant; now, in fact, and ever more.

Neither Gregory nor McDonald fit the contemporary fast bowler's mould of histrionic aggression and attention seeking. Gregory was anything but a limelighter. As Armstrong's Australians crossed the continent to board the England-bound *Osterley* in Fremantle in March 1921, their train had to stop in country South Australia for a civic reception at Quorn.

During manager Syd Smith's address to the crowd, a cry went up for Gregory and a posse of locals boarded the train in search of him. The first player they encountered was Gregory himself but, in those days when news was vested in word rather than image, he went unrecognized. Thinking quickly, Gregory confided that the man they sought had slipped off the other side of the train, sending his admirers off in comic pursuit.

Bradman noticed that Gregory, though 'generous-hearted', could never be drawn to discussing his on-field accomplishments; Larwood likewise found him the gentlest of men away from the fray: 'Off the field you could not meet a more friendly and amiable chap.' Leery of the press after once being misquoted, the only interview he granted was a most reluctant one in the year before his death, an aspiring cricket writer called David Frith driving 200 miles on the off-chance of catching him in his shack at Narooma on NSW's south coast, and coaxing him into a few quiet reminiscences. There were no visible trophies or mementoes. 'Here,' recalled Frith, 'was a cricketing Garbo.'

McDonald, likewise, was a self-contained character with little smalltalk, among strangers as inscrutable as a cigar-store Indian; Ronald Mason thought that he 'harboured in a not very approachable personality a genuine vein of genius'. His energy seemed almost supernatural. Even bowling at his fiercest, Oldfield recalled, he did not seem to perspire. On one occasion, he arrived late for a day's play, drained a glass of water, took a couple of drags on a cigarette, and bowled unchanged till lunch.

Yet that summer of 1921, Gregory and McDonald sapped English spirit where the bombs of the Kaiser's Zeppelins had failed. In the first innings of the First Test at Trent Bridge, Gregory had Donald Knight caught behind then bowled

Ernest Tyldesley and Patsy Hendren in one hectic, breathless over. In the second innings, he bowled Tyldesley again, this time off his head. No Man's Land had been recreated over twenty-two yards of turf.

For the Second Test at Lord's England picked a batsman called A. J. Evans: a good player, and a courageous man. As a pilot he'd won the Military Cross and bar. As a POW, he'd organized escape attempts of such reckless derring-do that he'd been persuaded to pen a book, *The Escaping Club*, describing how his mother had sent him maps and compasses concealed inside cakes and jars of anchovy paste. Yet on the day of his Test debut, a teammate remembered: 'He was so nervous that he could hardly hold his bat, and his knees were literally knocking together . . . His nerve had gone and the first straight ball was enough for him.'

Australia won those Tests, and the next at Leeds, to retain the Ashes, and against the counties waged a reign of terror. Even Wally Hammond, then a rising star with Gloucestershire on the brink of a brilliant thirty-year career, had not the stomach for the fight: 'Jack Gregory had cultivated a fearsome stare and gave me the treatment. With knees trembling and hands shaking, I was relieved when he bowled me first ball.'

It was Armstrong's turn for gratitude. No Australian touring party has won more first-class games. Gregory and McDonald claimed 116 and 138 wickets in England respectively, each at the pin's fee of 16.6. In twenty-seven matches, Gregory also accumulated 1135 runs at 36.6 and hauled in thirty-seven catches; no Australian all-rounder has performed such a 'double' since. En route home via South Africa, he then annexed the honour of the fastest Test century, belting 34 from his first twelve deliveries, and cruising to three figures in ten minutes over the hour. Those who regard packed inter-national schedules as a feature only of the jet age should inspect Jack Gregory's figures in the first three years of his cricket career: eighty first-class matches on three continents for more than 4000 runs at almost 40, and 400 wickets at 17.

Perhaps it was too much. On his return, Gregory foreshadowed retirement, and a return to rural life; his right knee was by now constantly painful and inflamed. In the event, he found a job with a Sydney sheet metal manufacturer, Kavanagh & English, and submitted to a surgeon removing a cartilage from the afflicted joint: an operation at the time from which recovery was never total. Indeed, despite being an absentee from the next two domestic seasons, Gregory was seldom the same. On occasion, he offered glimpses of his former threat, once breaking the shoulder of Arthur Richardson's bat in a Shield match at Adelaide Oval as he had him taken at slip. More often, he was merely a good bowler rather than a great one.

By coincidence, his admirers Larwood and Bradman were both present when Gregory's knee finally buckled during the Brisbane Test of December 1928: Larwood batting in his first Australian international, Bradman making his Test debut. As Gregory dived headlong for a return catch, his knee bore the brunt of the fall. Larwood recalled the Australian's tears 'not from the pain of the injury, but from the realization that he could no longer play the game he loved'. Bradman recorded Gregory's words when he was carried to the dressing room: 'Boys, I'm through, I have played my last game.'

A photograph exists of the moment Gregory was maimed; as I said, cameras were seldom idle in his presence. Two features compel attention. Larwood's bat has shattered at the shoulder; a final attestation of Gregory's force. And Gregory's prone figure lies more than half-way down the pitch; a last intimation of his athleticism. Jack Gregory was right; he never played again. But, at a glance, he continues to come alive.

# Don Bradman

## THE LEGEND LIVES ON (2010)

S ome day in our lifetimes, the last person to have seen Sir Donald Bradman bat in a Test match will pass away. It may not be marked, like the deaths of the last survivors of the *Titanic* or of the first day of the Somme; in cricket's terms it will be as significant.

Of no cricketer has it been truer to say that their every innings was an event, in both the anticipation and recollection, too. Only Sachin Tendulkar since has been accompanied to the crease by such uniformity of expectations, and even then these seldom ramify far beyond India. In fact, while assertions of Bradman's uniqueness usually concentrate on the phenomenon of his record as a statistical outlier, it's the combination of his level of performance with the fascination of his society that makes him not only a one-of-a-kind batsman, but a one-of-a-kind cricket hero.

Cricket in the 1930s and 1940s enjoyed a cultural primacy in the Anglosphere since rather diminished, and a status in Australia enhanced by the country's general modesty in other senses. 'Who will write a biography of Sir Donald Bradman,' noted C. L. R. James, 'must be able to write a history of Australia in the same period.'

Here was a nation of unparalleled emptiness, of more than one square kilometre per person. At the outset of Bradman's career, Australia's population was about the same as that of Jordan today; when his cricket ended, Australians were still less numerous than modern Austrians. Bradman filled that hollow, made it echo, made it resound, throughout an Empire still worth the title, and a world that grasped mastery even if it struggled to wrap its mind around cricket – the subject, on receipt of his knighthood of an editorial in the *New York Times*. 'There is no other kind of game but cricket in the British lexicon,' the paper concluded. 'Bradman was the unchallenged shining light for almost twenty years.'

The tightness of the fit between Bradman's feats and his public's fancies was exquisite. His was the contemporary Australian journey. Still fewer than half Bradman's fellow Australians lived in cities; Bradman himself was off the land, as it were. But he also embodied the country's transition to an urban, white-collar future, and its belief in social mobility: he was the country boy who became an estate agent, retail assistant, stockbroker and finally company director; he was the poor boy who came to walk among kings and prime ministers, and to enjoy an (unostentatious) wealth and (merited) honour; he was the ordinary man, small, compact, anatomically commonplace, prowess deriving not from fast-twitch fibres like a sprinter or flipper-like feet like a swimmer but from something *about* him, something *in* him, generally concealed, but when he came to the crease on show for the world to see.

As a representative of Australia's prevailing white Anglo-Saxon monoculture, and its protestant majority, Bradman grew into democratic privileges not really earned, and a dominant culture mainly imported. In the speech he gave at the Empire Theatre in February 1930 before departing on his first Ashes tour, Bradman faithfully espoused the values not of the bush frontiersman or the Anzac warrior but those of the English public schoolboy and muscular Christian:

> First my parents taught me to be a cricketer off the field as well as on. It was not 'did you win' but 'did you play the game' that made the man . . . I have no doubt that it [cricket] moulds in an individual the right type of character better than any other sport. If that can be substantiated, no other recommendation is required, because character must surely be one of the greatest assets any nation through its citizens can possess.

The acute sense of national identification with cricket's new hero, meanwhile, sprang from a deep hankering for home-grown accomplishment. His feats, in their widely visible, verifiable and quantifiable nature, spoke not just of progress but of possibilities. In his lively 1951 memoir, *Don Bradman*, the poet and novelist Philip Lindsay, son of the artist Norman, provides one of the best descriptions of the particular pang of watching him:

> Reading poetry and watching cricket were the sum of my world, and the two are not as far apart as many aesthetes might believe; and when into this world came talk of a young phenomenon from Bowral, a lad of near my own age, I began to look towards him with nervous hope as though he were myself.
>
> Most of us need an ideal. Nor is it necessary for that ideal to symbolize one's particular ambition. An actor can prove to be the spur, rousing one's spirit to a

realization of the greatness in mankind and the latent
powers within oneself, but more often it is a work of art,
the reading of a poem, the hearing of music, the sight of
a great painting . . . and to me Don Bradman became
that symbol of achievement, of mastery over fate, all the
more powerful because it was impossible for me, a
cricketing rabbit, to compare myself with him.

Indeed, while the everyman aspect of Bradman's achievements
has been widely attested, his feats in the 1930s engaged the
emergent Australia intelligentsia, too. The critic Vance Palmer
describes a visit to Henry Handel Richardson in which the
great novelist could scarcely speak of anything but Bradman;
the historian Manning Clark reports the frustration of a
foreign economist with local professors obsessed by cricket
scores. Bradman offered Australians not just a corroboration
of their sporting prowess but, to use Thomas Keneally's phrase,
a 'great way out of cultural ignominy'.

The other salient precondition of the rise of Bradman is
the coincidence of his career with the adaptation of newspapers
to the role of investigation, interpretation and lionization,
and the diffusion of radio, cinema and wire photographs as
forms of mass communication. Radio in particular, with its
exhilarating immediacy and its free availability, was the ideal
messenger for the steady unfolding of feats of scale like
Bradman's scores. The merest fraction of those who revered
Bradman ever saw him bat in person, yet in the 1930s and
1940s they were able to partake of his records and thereby feel
a share in them.

Australian cricketers before him had regarded writing
about the game, and themselves in it, as almost taboo:
Bradman published his first autobiography age twenty-one.
Australian cricketers had been filmed only from far away for

newsreel purposes: Bradman appeared in his own instructional movie, *That's Cricket*. His captain Bill Woodfull introduces him in the film in terms of another entertainment technology, as having 'more records than a gramaphone company'. Bringing modernity to cricket, he brought it also to the game's promotion and dissemination.

In this way, Bradman became perhaps the first cricket hero to genuinely transcend his game. Watching the thrall he exerted on his English hosts in 1948, John Arlott noted astutely: 'More people are interested in Bradman, and not in cricket, than are interested in Bradman *and* cricket.' Arlott summed Bradman's up as a general rather than a cricket-specific remarkableness:

> He is the supremely capable man. Satisfied with the
> terms of his employment, he would make the perfect
> executive. He prefers, however, to make his efforts on his
> own behalf . . . He was given, and has maintained, a
> good average body and a good average brain; he has
> directed them with rare perfect single-mindedness which
> makes for the attaining of objectives.

Arlott expressed a certain pity of Bradman in his burden of expectation on that tour:

> An old-hand county batsman . . . can have a swish and
> get out and catch the early train home, or can say, 'Don't
> send me in, skipper – give one of the lads a chance and
> put me down at number ten, my feet are sore.' But when
> Bradman rests for one match on an arduous tour of
> England, the local spectators are hurt and they adduce
> fifty 'good' reasons why Bradman ought to have played.
> If he moves himself down in the batting order he 'insults

our players'. If he throws his wicket away, he has robbed
ten thousand people of the conversational gambit,
'When I saw Bradman make his hundred at _____.'

But those spectators were onto something: to have been part
of the legend at close quarters was something considerable as
perhaps for no other cricketer, in the sense that no other
cricketer had so resonated with audiences of their time. To see
Bradman bat in a Test match was as ennobling as to have
watched Babe Ruth at Yankee Stadium and Ali at Madison
Square Garden, and perhaps Caruso at La Scala and the Beatles
at the Cavern as well. In a choice tribute to the Australian,
Michael Parkinson recalls his father, a miner from Barnsley in
south Yorkshire, walking thirty miles to see Bradman bat,
then wondering why this was thought at all strange.

Upon his return he faced a family who clearly believed
he had a slate loose. Who, in their right mind, would
waste that much precious shoe-leather to see a cricket
match? My father went to his grave unrepentant.
Retelling the story – as he did many times – he'd say,
'But I saw HIM bat and they didn't.'

# Bradman's 254
## CRACKING NOISES (2001)

Sir Donald Bradman's career involves many totemic numbers. In a cricket publication it is almost superfluous to mention the contexts in which 99.94, 6996, 334 or 974 arise. But no number resonates quite like 254, because no innings ended up holding for its maker quite the same significance.

The first of Bradman's great Ashes innings, at Lord's in June 1930, was like his very own Operation Shock and Awe, with English cricket's dismay as its objective. It commenced at 3.30 p.m. on the second day of the Second Test with what remained Bradman's fastest Test 50, in forty-five minutes. What Neville Cardus called 'the most murderous onslaught I have ever known in a Test match' finished at 2.50 p.m. on the third day after five hours and twenty minutes, 376 deliveries and a century in boundaries.

The particular significance of the 254 derives, however, from Bradman's own estimation of it. While doubt attaches to other choices posthumously ascribed to him, Bradman left no ambiguity about where he ranked this feat, volunteering in

*Farewell to Cricket* (1950) that it was technically the best innings of his career. 'Practically without exception every ball went where it was intended,' he opined – and 'practically' is, with Bradman, not an inconsiderable word.

This is not merely a premium endorsement either, but an insight into Bradman himself. In his restless quest for perfection, this exploit was the pinnacle of efficiency to which he himself always aspired: speed without noticeble haste, risk without obvious recklessness. If Bradman's feats now seem scarcely human, the self-scrutiny that singled this innings out implies that they cannot have been altogether unconscious.

By the same token, it is interesting that Bradman made his distinctions on a technical basis. In echoing him since, critics have been inclined to let the innings' specifications and dynamics efface its circumstances. At the time, Percy Chapman's Englishmen had Bill Woodfull's Australians very much under the cosh. The hosts held the Ashes, led 1–0 in the series and had compiled 425 in their first innings on the game's most venerable ground. The trail to a Test double-century, moreover, had been blazed by only five Australians in more than fifty years of international competition.

The stage was ideally set by Woodfull and his opening partner Bill Ponsford, whose 162 for the first wicket survived every challenge save a teatime visit from King George V. Indeed, it was Woodfull whom Bradman credited with his approach: he was 'playing so finely . . . that I could afford to go for the bowling'.

Despite being 'naturally anxious to do well' in view of the occasion and the audience, he surged forward to meet his first ball from England's 'Farmer' White, punched it to mid-off and sauntered a single. The stroke was as clean and clear as a proclamation. 'It was,' wrote England's former captain Pelham Warner, 'as if he had already made a century.'

White, a famously parsimonious left-arm spinner, could not curb him. Nor could Maurice Tate, still probably the world's best medium-paced bowler. The young Gubby Allen and Walter Robins were harshly manhandled. Yet what was striking at once about Bradman's batting was less its power than its poise. He had held for six months the record for the biggest first-class innings: his 452 not out for NSW against Queensland. But this was more than humdrum accumulation of runs. It was calm, carefree, precocious; as if nobody had explained to Bradman why the occasion should daunt him and whose were the reputations he was trampling. 'Young Bradman,' said Cardus, in one of his crispest phrases, 'knocked solemnity to smithereens.'

That Cardus was present as the correspondent of the *Manchester Guardian* is history's good fortune; in cricket terms it's as if A. J. P. Taylor had been around to report the signing of Magna Carta. 'The bat sent out cracking noises; they were noises quite contemptuous,' wrote the dean of English sports journalism. 'When he batted eleven men were not enough. Lord's was too big to cover; holes were to be seen in the English field everywhere. Chapman tried his best to fill them up, but in vain.'

After tea, everyone appeared to become a spectator. To cut off Bradman's scoring seemed like trying to cap a Yellowstone geyser or a Spindletop gusher. He barely paused for the applause that greeted his 105-minute century – his third hundred in consecutive Tests – and ploughed on to the more remarkable landmark of a century in a session. Despite Woodfull's 78-run and 170-minute head start, Bradman had caught up with his captain by the time their 160-minute partnership of 231 was ended. England's impressive total was in sight by stumps, and being judged according to an entirely different scale: suddenly no score, no statistic, no history was safe.

Given the curious queasiness that has emerged in recent years about Bradman's records, it's worth noting that the man himself knew no such taboo. When he resumed on Monday at 155, he cast intrepid and covetous eyes on the benchmark Test score of 287 by England's 'Tip' Foster. He even thought there might be something appropriate about his consigning it to oblivion: he would seize for Sydney the record set at its cricket ground twenty-seven years earlier.

With this in mind, Bradman introduced a note of care to his play before lunch, even allowing Tate to bowl him a maiden, and partner Alan Kippax to take greater initiative. Still he overhauled a double-century in 245 minutes at 12.50 p.m. – becoming, at 21 years 307 days, considerably the youngest to achieve the feat. His lunchtime 231 was already the highest score by an Australian, the highest against England, and highest at Lord's – and still wasn't over.

Foster's citadel, in the end, did not fall. The elastic Chapman stuck his right hand aloft at extra cover to arrest a screaming drive – 'a magnificent piece of work', wrote Bradman admiringly – with the batsman 34 shy of his goal. His 254 had been made from 423 added while he'd been at the crease, and his third-wicket partnership of 192 with Kippax was another Lord's record.

Perhaps the only aspect of Bradman's innings as remarkable as the number of records is their brief durations – the cause, of course, was Bradman himself. His 254 was the Australian Test best for precisely one match; his 334 at Headingley two weeks later put everyone in the shade, including himself. Bradman's 974 runs in the five-Test series, including another 232 at The Oval in August, would remain a record seemingly beyond challenge.

It was the beginning of a sporting monopoly so unsparing it should almost have been dissolved by anti-trust regulators.

## ON THE ASHES

To break a record is one thing; to break one's own is quite another. To make big scores is one thing; to compile them so memorably that they become associated with you for ever is a mark of genuine greatness.

# Walter Hammond

## LOST HORIZONS (2022)

In 1988, *The Cricketer* magazine published a plaintive letter signed Valerie Guareschi. Guareschi was one of the daughters of Walter Hammond by his second wife Sybil, whom it emerged was the reason for the enquiry. 'Unfortunately, after the death of my father, my mother either gave away or burnt most of his things,' she explained. 'My son is very keen on cricket and of course the one thing that I really wish for is to see him become a good player. It seems such a shame not to have anything of value left of such a wonderful man.'

It's unknown whether anyone responded to Guareschi's solicitation of 'anything regarding my father – trinkets, photographs etc.', but anyone familiar with the Hammond legacy would have been pardoned a rueful nod. Most great cricketers summon a host of warm memories, of feats, of gestures, of sentiments. For all his Olympian achievements – 7249 runs in 85 Tests at 58, 83 wickets at 37 – Hammond left a residue of sadness, partly because they seemed to leave him unmoved, unfulfilled, unavailed. David Foot reached the end

115

of a fine biography, *The Reasons Why* (1996), by admitting that the subject rather eluded him: 'He wished he had more friends: and then, in evenings of tormented reverie, he accepted that maybe he had not deserved more . . . In terms of personality, he remained without any easily defined shape or purpose.'

Foot's controversial explanation for that personal elusiveness was the effects of mercury, administered to counteract venereal disease contracted on Hammond's first tour, to the West Indies in 1925–26. But that reaching for an exogenous explanation says something about our own psychic needs – we who love cricket cannot imagine anything more uplifting than success and accomplishment at it. That he was sublimely gifted at and utterly dedicated to something that ultimately failed to satisfy him must have been a source of deeper unhappiness.

Perhaps we should accentuate the positive as Hammond failed to. There may never have been a greater cover driver; there has barely been a more successful English batter in Australia. At the age of thirty, Hammond was monarch of all he surveyed, with thirteen hundreds in thirty-eight Tests, an average of 67, and a renown for patrician elegance that abided. Even a decade afterwards, R. C. Robertson-Glasgow was calling him 'quite simply, the greatest cricketer who began in the last twenty years, and that, too, by a long distance' for the 'effect on a match of his presence alone'.

Hammond could take the ball and deliver a match-winning spell of medium pace; he could stoop at slip and pluck a crowd-dazzling catch; not until Viv Richards did a player so inspire simply by walking. Said R. C. Robertson-Glasgow: 'It is something to have seen Hammond walk out to the Australians from the pavilion at Lord's: a ship in full sail.' Said J. M. Kilburn: 'Hammond's walk was the most handsome in all cricket, smooth in the evenness of stride, precise in balance. It was a flow of movement linking stillness to stillness.'

But, gradually, other sensations settled over him, and above all one personality. In 1928–29, Hammond had heaped up a run pile it seemed would never be bettered: 905 runs at 117.12 in five Tests in Australia, with a highest score of 251. But in 1930, Bradman had built an adjacent peak taller still: 974 runs at 139.14 in five Tests in England, with a highest score of 334. Hammond reclaimed the record Test score by making 336 not out against New Zealand in 1933. The following year, Hammond was cut down as few truly great cricketers have been, averaging a listless 20 across a home Ashes. He blamed it on 'bad health' and worry: 'My throat gave me a lot of trouble, and as is always the way when a man depends on his health for his income, I became very worried and depressed.' Yet he made 2000 runs in twenty-one innings for Gloucestershire, and his benefit year yielded a bumper £2500 even as eavesdropping teammates heard him grumbling of 'bloody Bradman'. It smarted, as Alan Gibson observed in *The Cricket Captains of England* (1981): 'For the rest of his career, Hammond was destined to be only the second best batsman in the world . . . and he was not, as far as cricket went, a man content to be second-best.'

This came out most clearly in November 1937 when Hammond foreshadowed turning amateur by taking a cushy job with a motor company and in doing so making himself eligible to captain England. Whether this relieved Hammond of worry is unknowable; it certainly appealed to his streak of west country snobbery. He polished his accent; he smartened his dress; he broadened his contacts, and the leadership duly came his way, facilitated by the Lord's potentate Sir Pelham Warner.

During his convalescence from that mysterious Caribbean infection, Warner had promised him: 'You'll make plenty of hundreds for England, so keep your heart up, my boy.' So it seemed when Hammond made a magisterial 240 against Bradman's Australians under Warner's gaze at Lord's in 1938. Then, at The Oval, the young Len Hutton overtopped Hammond's Test record score with his own mountainous achievement, 364. A new rival, and in his own camp. And though neither knew it, the future belonged to the younger man, succeeding to the same office fifteen years later without the necessity of revoking his professional status.

Hutton was himself a great admirer. 'The most perfect batsman I ever saw,' he said of Hammond. 'More enjoyable to watch than Sir Don.' Yet he looked on his skipper with pathos when they toured Australia after the Second World War. Hammond took his new class distinction to heart, travelling alone everywhere. One day, Hutton was granted the rare privilege of being passenger in the captain's car on a 700-mile road journey. 'We need petrol,' was the only remark Hammond passed. 'Keep your eye out for a station.'

An ever harder man to know, it was agreed. The shrewd Bob Wyatt was sympathetic: 'A shy, complex man.' The young Denis Compton was anxious: 'I was never at ease with him.' That 1946–47 Ashes saw Hammond and Bradman opposed again, the former deploying his fine new seam bowler Alec Bedser against the Australian champion in Brisbane: 'Bedser, sweating with eagerness to take Don's wicket for a 0, sent up a wicked one – and Don snicked it involuntarily, like a schoolboy, through the slips. If my arm had been a little longer . . . but the red streak was out of reach.' So was everything else: forty-three by now, Hammond had come on his tour too many. The umpiring reprieve granted Bradman soon after, following a convincing appeal for a slip catch, simply made it official. Soon enough, it would be Hutton and Compton who personified English batsmanship, with Hammond a dwindling, darkening, doleful memory, fading away almost to nothing.

# Douglas Jardine

## THE IRON DUKE (2016)

The harlequin cap. The rigid bearing. The mirthless aquiline features. Modern spin doctors would tell Douglas Jardine he had an image problem – and perhaps, in historical terms, he does. Assessments of him usually accent the personal characteristics that emerged during the Bodyline series of 1932–33 – his determination phasing into stubbornness, his imperviousness up to and past the point of antagonism. His skills as captain have been overlooked.

The long chapter about captaincy in his *Cricket* (1936), for example, is wonderfully shrewd. Written from the point of view of a fielding captain manipulating a five-man attack trying to prevent an opposition scoring 340 at a run-a-minute in a fourth innings, Jardine presents 'The Skipper' with a series of problems. The ground has a slope. A stiff breeze is blowing. Bowlers have preferences as to ends, and to particular batsmen. There are issues of temperament. The fast bowler is a bit of a fusspot. The slow bowler is collared. A batsman gets set and needs to be isolated. A new ball falls due. There is luck. There is rain. There are debates about fields, which are illustrated diagrammatically. It might not be *The Art of Captaincy*, but the relish is evident and the thinking disarmingly supple: 'A good side works like a good machine, but this is not to say that it works mechanically. No side will run according to plan, but this does not say that its captain should not have a plan, and a very definite plan. The plan must, however, be capable of instant modification to an almost infinite degree.'

No plan was more definite than leg-theory, which Jardine first discussed over dinner in the Piccadilly Grill Room in August 1932 with Harold Larwood, Bill Voce and their county captain Arthur Carr. But at the time, Bradman, Test average then 112.29, was modifying all before him. The likelihood was an Ashes series as high-scoring as the two preceding it. There's no reason to doubt Jardine when, in his *In Quest of the Ashes* (1933), he states that he was not in advance 'inclined to rate the possibilities of leg-theory very highly', because he harboured 'a very healthy respect for their [Australians'] play off the leg stump.' Never imagining that leg theory 'would stand such a test as would prove its effectiveness throughout the whole tour', he thought merely that it 'might occasionally prove a profitable variation when two batsmen were well set'. He persevered, then, not only because he was ruthless, Spartan, not for turning; he also persevered because he intuited, sometimes against the run of play, that it was working.

*In Quest* provides further evidence for a view of Bodyline as more dynamic and evolving than usually imagined. Jardine describes his observations of timeless cricket in Australia in 1928–29 – how attritional the tone, how skiddy the wickets, and how necessary they made it to attack the stumps rather than persevere in an off-stump line at which the batsman could in theory refrain from strokes all day. He also notes how Australian wickets in the intervening years changed, being flattened and top dressed to such a degree that medium-pacers could extract next to no sideways movement, but on which 'parabolic' bounce suited the fast and the slow – and for all its retrospective definition as the series of pace, the summer of 1932–33 featured 1000 (8-ball) overs of spin. The host country, then, played an unwitting part in rendering Bodyline more effective.

'He's a queer'un,' confided the Yorkshireman Maurice Leyland of Jardine, and he was the martinet's martinet: he scowled at players playing golf, forbade them whisky, fell out with his emollient manager Pelham Warner, and, of course, treated colonials with contempt. But consider the man-management challenges facing a captain eighty-five years ago. There was no coach, no support staff, no media minders. English cricket was also a good deal more diverse than today: Jardine had to mix coal miners with old Etonians, ex-servicemen with Indian aristocrats. But if his amateurs sometimes chafed, his professionals offered more than dumb obedience. 'Everyone respected and admired him and many of us liked him,' said Larwood. 'One of the greatest men I have ever met,' thought Herbert Sutcliffe. 'He planned for us, cared for us and fought for us on that tour,' said Bill Bowes. Hedley Verity named his son for Jardine, and when weak-kneed Warner convened a team meeting about Jardine's captaincy after the unruly Adelaide Test, the Yorkshire leg-spinner Tommy Mitchell is said to have growled: 'It's got nowt to do with thee.' If Jardine had no WAGs to corral on tour, he was also solicitous of those far away: he had team members send cases of Australian produce to wives and mothers for Christmas, with a card 'To The Old Folks At Home' designed by Australia's Arthur Mailey. And if captaincy is about leaving a mark, well, who will be debating Michael Vaughan's merits in 2090, or Andrew Strauss's in 2095?

Bradman? Of course it was about Bradman, for whom Jardine worked up a pathological distaste, and who also inflicted on him his only Test defeat (otherwise his record was of nine wins and five draws). In twenty years no captain so got under Bradman's skin and skull, so that by the Fifth Test the Australian was spooked: the bluff of parking the injured Larwood in Bradman's eyeline ('I want you to stand there and just stare at him') was mental disintegration *avant le lettre*. Yet in its way Bodyline was the greatest tribute ever paid Bradman, the saga becoming integral to his legend. And Bradman was paid no more sincere compliment by an opponent than Jardine's concession, twenty years later to John Arlott, in the spirit of his ruminations on the complexities of captaincy in *Cricket*: 'You know, we nearly didn't do it. The little man was bloody good.'

# Harold Larwood

## THE ANTI-BRADMAN (2004)*

In the years after he settled in Sydney, Harold Larwood's humble Kingsford home became a place of pilgrimage for English cricketers, especially those mandated by nature to bowl fast. They usually came away twice marvelled, at the patch of English patriotism to be found just five kilometres from the Sydney Cricket Ground, and at the seemingly frail figure who cultivated it. Had this diminutive, bespectacled pensioner *really* been the terror of all Australia?

Nor was this merely a matter of age. When picked for England, Larwood stood just five feet seven inches tall and weighed less than eleven stone, and seemed as likely to be a source of controversy as Michael Ramsey, born the same day and destined to become Archbishop of Canterbury. One of Larwood's most vivid anecdotes from the Bodyline tour of 1932–33 was overhearing a little girl quizzing her mother:

---

* Written on the centenary of the birth of Harold Larwood, 14 November 2004.

'Why mummy, he doesn't *look* like a murderer . . .' Yet as few in cricket cannot know, Larwood achieved a notoriety as Australia's Least Wanted usually confined to criminals; he competed for headlines with the likes of the Lindbergh kidnapper Bruno Hauptmann and the mobster Al Capone.

Reviewing his legend a century after his birth, one obtains a slightly different feeling, from a sense of cricket's abiding search for a statistical and aesthetic equilibrium between bat and ball. In his autobiography *The Larwood Story* (1965), ghosted by Kevin Perkins, the Englishman pleads guilty to a degree of batsmanslaughter, but presents himself as acting in legitimate self-defence: 'They said I was a killer with the ball without taking into account that Bradman with the bat was the greatest killer of all.' Indeed, had Larwood not existed, it might have been necessary to invent him.

Larwood was born on 14 November 1904 in Nuncargate, a midlands village that served a colliery at Annesley in the Leen Valley five kilometres away. Although his origins have commonly been depicted as underprivileged, the mine was actually an enduring and not ungenerous employer, lasting until January 2000. Larwood's parents owned their own home, and his teetotal Methodist father Robert captained the colliery's cricket team, which at various stages contained Test cricketers-to-be Bill Voce, Dodge Whysall, Joe Hardstaff and Sam Staples; at fourteen, Harold both went down the mine as a pit-pony boy, and took to cricket with a will. The game, he would explain, soon became his 'reason for living'.

In June 1922, Larwood saw his first game of county cricket, heading to Trent Bridge for the day so that he might bask in his idol Jack Hobbs's glory. Instead, Hobbs was dismissed first ball by local boy Fred Barratt, who not only haled from Nuncargate but had worked the same coal seams; at once, the seventeen-year-old saw a future teeming with possibilities. A year later, Larwood left the pit behind when he trialled successfully for Nottinghamshire.

Tiny, earnest, polite, etiolated from his years underground, running in an improbable distance, he was nonetheless recognized at once as a pace-bowling prospect, at a time when they did not abound. On one occasion, Larwood greeted the Leicestershire tailender Hayden Smith with a searing lifter, followed by a short one that looped from the edge and was taken on the bounce in the gully. Seeing Smith retreat, fielders assured him that the ball had not carried. 'Oh yes it bloody well did,' replied Smith, continuing on his way.

Curiously, the first time they met, his future captain Douglas Jardine was well-positioned to take Larwood's measure. It was at Folkestone in August 1926 where they were representing an England XI against the Australians; Jardine, standing in for Tiger Smith, was keeping. Larwood took seven for 95, including the wicket of top-scorer Warren Bardsley with a delivery that knocked the bat from his hands; the bat then hit the stumps as the ball lodged in Jardine's gloves. Though the umpire denied Jardine a catch by ruling the dismissal hit-wicket, the encounter impressed the Surrey amateur forcibly.

For a time, this was as close as the pair became. Larwood would tour Australia with Jardine a little over two years later, but both were men who observed the proprieties where players and gentlemen were concerned. On the evening in August 1932 of their famous dinner in the Piccadilly Grill Rooms with Larwood's fast bowling pitmate Bill Voce and their Nottinghamshire skipper Arthur Carr, the conversation was at first stilted and strained, before finding the common obsession of Bradman.

Though they 'didn't contribute much' as Jardine revealed his theory that Australians in general and Bradman in particular were vulnerable to pace bowling concentrated at leg stump, Larwood and Voce were immediately impressed with the thinking. Under Carr's captaincy, they had been experimenting with such methods all season, claiming almost 250 cheap wickets between them. Bradman's telephone-number scores, meanwhile, were the talk of cricket, and Larwood was one of many bowlers who'd found his line permanently crossed. Among Bradman's *Wisden*-busting 974 runs in the 1930 Ashes series, 137 had been from Larwood, pilfered from only 147 deliveries.

Larwood and Voce are sometimes depicted as clockwork toys wound up by the English establishment, bowling the leg-stump line Jardine demanded of them like obedient professional automata. This probably derives from Larwood's first published remarks on Bodyline in the *Daily Express* in July 1933, to the effect that 'in bowling as I did I was merely carrying out the prearranged plan'. The impression is erroneous. Larwood better explained the dynamic of the relationship, and his loyalty to Jardine, to Perkins: 'I wouldn't say I was told to bowl leg-theory. I was asked to do it and I complied. In any case, I was convinced that I wouldn't get many wickets any other way.' The motive was, in large part, redress: 'I had a score to settle with him [Bradman]. He had got on top of me. As a professional, any scheme that would keep him in check appealed to me a great deal.' Larwood was no deferential dupe. David Frith reports in *Bodyline Autopsy* (2002) that his favourite tune was Frank Sinatra's 'My Way': whenever he heard it, he would 'always smile and nod knowingly'.

The other reason why it is wrong to underestimate Larwood's agency is that leg-theory was an attack designed with his gifts in mind as much as Bradman's. Larwood seldom obtained swing: the handmade balls of the period had a small seam, and in Australia their poor-quality lacquer wore away within overs. His chief asset, after speed, was accuracy, and his most dangerous delivery a backbreak; he seldom had batsmen caught in the slips cordon even bowling an orthodox line. George Hele's close-up appreciation in *Bodyline Umpire* (1974) is worth citing:

> Harold Larwood was not only the fastest bowler I have watched. He also had the most beautiful action. While he was running in behind me I never heard him. He glided towards the wickets until the last three yards. Australian fast bowlers dragged their right or left toes as they gathered themselves into the delivery stride; Larwood dragged his entire right foot and at right angles to his course. He placed a tremendous strain upon that foot and his ankle. I have not seen a bowler gain greater impetus from his left and guiding arm. From here came his exceptional speed and exceptional accuracy. There was nothing loose, untidy or wasted about Larwood's action. It was a copybook, classic and utterly direct.

Too direct for Australians prone to walking in front of their stumps but leery of the hook – and too hot to hold. 'He's too fast for me,' confessed Alan Kippax after his first brush with Larwood – sentiments that would be echoed by many others before tour's end. Bradman's scheme of withdrawing to leg and flailing toward the depopulated bespoke desperation rather than daring. When he hit what was his first first-class six at Adelaide, Bradman explained it succinctly: 'Oh, I wanted to hit one bowler [the spinner Hedley Verity] before the other [Larwood] hit me.'

It was Bradman who continued his career, of course, rather than Larwood, whose retirement was rudely hastened in order to soften Bodyline's bruises on Anglo-Australian relations, and whose future so unexpectedly lay down under. But Larwood had helped reduce Bradman's Test average from its high-water mark of 112.9 to 99.7, which is where it pretty much stayed, apart from a brief post-war reflation. And in revealing Bradman's mortality and fallibility, Larwood not only gave heart to other bowlers, but provided the nemesis necessary to the hubris of his story. The narrative of Sir Donald Bradman's career is still among cricket's most inspiring. Yet it would not be quite so compelling without featuring, at some stage, a kind of anti-Bradman – the role Larwood fulfilled. Had there been no Larwood to cut his output down to size, to choose but one example, Bradman would never have needed four runs to secure his hundred average at The Oval in August 1948, and would never have failed to achieve it in such astonishing circumstances. Larwood, then, by introducing to the Bradman legend a tincture of the evitable, might be considered the embodiment of cricketing uncertainty.

# Bob Wyatt

## THE SURVIVOR (1995)[*]

B ob Wyatt opened the innings as England's captain at Jamaica's Sabina Park in 1935 and in the first over from Manny Martindale received a wicked bouncer that not only knocked him unconscious but broke his jaw in four places. Brought round in the dressing room, Wyatt signalled for pen and paper, and in a firm hand rewrote his team's batting order with the instruction 'we must not lose'. He then wrote a note to Martindale, saying that the bowler should not worry. The injury had been a batting error.

Such was the stamp of a cricketer respected for his ability and tactical acumen but admired above all for physical courage. The sequel to his injury is remarkable in itself: Wyatt came home with his team by sea, being fed on Horlicks, Ovaltine, Guinness and stewed spinach. Once his jaw was rebuilt with a bone graft from his hip, he began his rehabilitation with centuries at Lord's and Edgbaston and followed

---

[*] Written on the death of Bob Wyatt, 20 April 1995, aged ninety-three.

them with his highest test score: 149 against South Africa in the First Test at Trent Bridge.

Deputy to Douglas Jardine on England's famous 1932–33 Ashes tour, Wyatt registers in the annals of Australian cricket as nominally the first man to set, for fast bowlers Harold Larwood and Bill Voce, what became known as a 'Bodyline' field on an Australian cricket surface. The occasion was a tour match between the touring MCC and an Australian XI at the MCG a fortnight before the First Test at the SCG. As the tourists deployed Larwood against Don Bradman in Jardine's absence, Wyatt constructed a primitive leg-theory field by shifting his chevron of four slips into catching positions behind square leg. Bradman's discomfiture was noted: he fell to Larwood for only 36 and 13.

When Jardine heard empirical evidence that a form of the leg-theory trap he'd considered previously had worked, he set his own predatory field against Bradman when MCC played NSW at the SCG a week later and took them into history's most inflammable cricket contest. Yet highlighting such an ignominious honour disserves the Warwickshire right-hander. Though he remained steadfastly behind Jardine, Wyatt grew to revile Bodyline as deeply as the Australians: 'Jardine was not in any way contravening the laws of the game, but I was against leg theory being so ruthlessly applied. It bred ill feeling . . . It had been a fundamental mistake on his part to go to Australia at all. If you hate an opponent, you should not play against them.'

Wyatt even grew quite fond of Australian barrackers, one of whom protested mightily at his stoical double of 51 and 61 not out in the Final Test at Sydney. 'For God's sake get out, Wyatt!' Came a cry from the Hill. 'We've seen all your strokes bar one. That's sunstroke.' Recalled Wyatt: 'It put the crowd in good humour. I took it as a compliment.'

Educated at Coventry's King Henry the Eighth School and cousin of the MP Woodrow Wyatt, Bob Wyatt scored 1839 runs for England in forty Tests and almost 40,000 first-class runs in a thirty-four-year career with eighty-five hundreds. He began his county career in 1923 as an all-rounder and first toured with the MCC in India in 1926 and South Africa in 1927. In 1929, he made 2630 first-class runs at 54 including a punitive 113 at Old Trafford against South Africa.

Wyatt inherited England's captaincy and a distinctly hostile press in August 1930, when the popular figure of Percy Chapman was displaced for the Final Test at The Oval. In the lead-up to the match Wyatt was the innocent butt of the disdain many commentators felt for England's selectors, and he recalled in his autobiography *Three Straight Sticks* (1951) the crowd's spontaneous popular support for him when coming into bat against Clarrie Grimmett in the last over before tea on the first day.

'I gritted my teeth, told myself not to be nervous, that I'd got to stay in whatever happened,' wrote Wyatt. 'As I started coming out of the entrance past the members in the pavilion, they all stood up and began to cheer. Taking their cue from the members in the pavilion, the whole of the vast crowd seemed to follow suit. The walk toward the wicket seemed an age. The roars buffeted my head and made my eyes swim. It was the cricket lovers' reply to the attacks which had been going on against me for the past week.'

Wyatt's 64 helped Herbert Sutcliffe add 170 for the fifth wicket, though it was insufficient to prevent an Australian victory. Wyatt again came off second-best to Bill Woodfull four years later, though he earned respect from the Australians for his flintiness. He battled two resolute hours at Lord's with a thumb that had been shattered in a county match by Ken Farnes protected only by a crude tin splint, which occasionally flew off when he swung with too great a vigour. One injury too many came on Wyatt's second Australian tour in 1936–37 when, in an up-country game before the First Test, his ulna was broken in two places. Despite registering his first class best of 232 against Derbyshire at Edgbaston a few months later, he could not again attract the selectors' attention.

Playing for Worcestershire after the Second World War, Wyatt participated by proxy in an English reclamation of the Ashes. In the last of his five years on the MCC selection panel, he helped pick a team led by Len Hutton at The Oval in 1953 that clinched a series against Australia for the first time since Jardine himself. In the introduction to Gerald Pawle's *R. E. S. Wyatt: Fighting Cricketer* (1985), Hutton wrote of him: 'No cricketer I've known had a greater love of cricket or was more knowledgeable about this complex game than Bob Wyatt. He was and remained a student of cricket throughout the whole of a remarkable life.'

Remarkable life it was: Wyatt died as the oldest English Test cricketer, old enough to have watched Warwickshire's first County Championship in 1911 aged ten, still in full possession of his faculties when interviewed last season as his former county was propelled to a triple crown by Brian Lara. A jaw still sensitive to changes in conditions testified to the fact that, long before Curtly Ambrose, the West Indies was no cricket arena for the faint hearted.

# Ken Farnes

## THE NATURAL (2006)

With our narrowing sense of what constitutes a properly athletic physique, cricketers of the past can seem increasingly remote. How did a figure so diminutive as Harold Larwood terrorize Australia, or a man as mountainous as Warwick Armstrong intimidate England? As for W. G. Grace, today he'd be nicknamed 'Dis'.

Ken Farnes represents a type far more recognizable, standing 195 cm, displacing 93 kg and bowling what would now be called a 'heavy ball', usually fast and often short. When he became one of only six Englishmen to secure ten wickets on his Test debut, he opened the bowling with the amiable forty-year-old pro George Geary; in his next Test he was partnered by the bespectacled and ungainly Bill Bowes. Yet nobody today would fail to pick Farnes as a fast bowler in a cricket identikit parade.

R. C. Robertson-Glasgow thought him a bowler 'who can suggest even by his run-up that the batsman would do well to stay firm', and batsmen stayed hit when he hit them. Jim Swanton offered his biographer David Thurlow a vivid aural vignette of Farnes in the 1932 Varsity match: 'I can still hear the ball thudding around Peter van der Bijl's ribs and Peter giving great groans. You could hear him in the Tavern.' And Player Bill Edrich left a memento of Farnes's eight for 43 for the Gentlemen at Lord's six years later which has a distinctly modern ring: 'I tried to play back, a defensive back stroke while turning my head and lifting my hands. The next thing I knew was that someone was saying smoothly, "have some water, there's no hurry."'

Long before cricketers began subscribing to the body cult, too, Farnes was an addict of physical culture. He undertook a Mr Universe course, and was often pestered in dressing rooms to show off his stomach muscles; his party piece was to contract first one half, then the other. In every team photo where you find him, he exudes a very contemporary strength and youth. He could have changed in the next cubicle to Michael Bevan without coyness.

In most other senses, Farnes was a distinctly unusual cricketer, even in his time. Pace in 1930s England was a professional vocation: Larwood, Tate, Voce, Bowes, Clark, Nichols, Copson. Farnes, a housemaster at Worksop College, was the most serene of amateurs, and the last of a line to pursue such hard labour. As a twelve-year-old, he watched Arthur Gilligan knocking a stump from the ground in a Test at Lord's, thought it 'a wonderful, unforgettable, inspiring sight', and never lost the love of doing it himself: 'The sight of a stump seen hurtling out of the ground has always struck me as one of the finest in cricket. It sends a shock through the spectators and from the middle you can hear a gasp all round.' To not then have bowled fast, with his physique and physicality, would have seemed like a denial of destiny. In anointing him a Cricketer of the Year in 1939, *Wisden* called him 'essentially a natural cricketer', and this was perhaps about more than talent; he revelled in what Frank Tyson would describe so memorably as 'the glad animal action', and the 'thrill in physical power' of fast bowling. Some passages in Farnes's 1940 autobiography *Tours and Tests* even have a kind of muted mysticism to them, like a recollection of fielding in the deep one day at Leyton against Kent: 'It was there too that a day's fielding in the late summer heat brought about in me an amazing evening's contentment. I cannot explain the reason – just positive physical well-being really. I had not done well myself, for Kent had thumped our bowling, but it was just the end of the season and I still remember the glow of pure contentment that I felt that evening.'

Teammates thought Farnes a little too susceptible to such reveries. He was a mystery to Len Hutton, who thought the absence of histrionics from his bowling suggested limited ambition despite his being 'the most ferocious fast bowling I ever had to deal with'. In fact, Farnes's ambitions were broader and vaster than Hutton's professional imaginings. The salient exhibit in Thurlow's biography is Farnes's diary of MCC's 1938–39 tour of South Africa, which gives surprising glimpses of his sensitive, restless, questing mind. Before the trip, Farnes set himself five objectives, none of them having anything to do with cricket; he would try instead, for instance, to 'remain conscious of my inner, natural, more realized self instead of being overcome by successive and accumulative environments experienced on tour'. He wrote of having seen some children in the East End, 'monstrous in their lack of realization', whose appearance 'seemed a horrible reflection on the state of civilization or education'. Yet he also confessed to feeling 'detached' and 'some what disgruntled with myself', and pledged himself a 'subjugation of self' that he felt might induce 'the required metaphysical state'.

Farnes had long had a literary bent: he was an aficianado

of the orientalist poet James Elroy Flecker and the Irish novelist George Moore. The diary reveals a fascination with the work of J. W. Dunne, an engineer turned philosopher who had developed an abstruse theory of sleep's effect on time after becoming obsessed with his dreams. Dunne was an eccentric and obscurantist; even his friend H. G. Wells thought his theories 'an entertaining paradox expanded into a humourless obsession'. But Farnes was 'absorbed and thrilled' by Dunne's *The New Immortality* (1939), and imagined himself 'glimpsing a new world' – which suggests that he was looking for one. Farnes was later introduced to the metaphysical lyrics of Rabindranath Tagore, which also resonated with him: 'The song that I came to sing remains unsung to this day . . . The time has not come true, the words have not been rightly set; only there is the agony of wishing in my heart.'

As well as an expression of patriotism, then, Farnes's enlistment in the Royal Air Force at the outbreak of war smacks of a continuation of a search for fulfilment, for a transcendent cause or duty. In *Gitanjali*, Tagore asks: 'On the day when death will knock at thy door what wilt thou offer him?' Farnes, perhaps, wished it to be more than wickets. The day turned out to be 20 October 1941, when thirty-year-old Farnes died as his plane crashed during a night-flying exercise. There were no more amateur fast bowlers of note; within two decades of war's end, there were no more amateurs. The love of speed remained, and the game now teems with towering athletes bowling fast. Yet to fast bowling's traditions, Farnes both belongs and does not – a big man in all senses.

# Bill Brown

## BLINKY BILL (2008)[*]

When Steve Waugh inaugurated the custom of a former Australian Test cricketer presenting baggy green caps to new selections, his choice settled without hesitation on eighty-seven-year-old Bill Brown. Brown was puzzled. Yes, he had batted with Don Bradman; captained Australia, too. But shouldn't they get someone important? He was just a battler, really.

On the contrary, insisted Waugh: 'Bill is a baggy green icon who represents all that is good about playing for your country. He is humble, self-effacing and respectful, proud to have been afforded the honour of being an Australian Test cricketer, and a man who always looks for the positive in people.' Waugh looked on delightedly as Brown settled a cap on Adam Gilchrist, feeling the old man's 'emotion and pride'.

Curiously, an Australian who played cricket less like the bristling, bustling Waugh can hardly be imagined: Brown,

---

[*] Written on the death of Bill Brown, aged ninety-five, on 16 March 2008.

born in Queensland but brought up in New South Wales, was a slight figure with a light touch at the crease, a serene man who made friends easily and lastingly. The last Australian pre-war Test player, he was amused by his late celebrity. Yet Brown was a better player than he let on, with an average of 51 to show for his 13,840 runs in 189 first-class games, and of 47 for his 1592 runs in twenty-two Tests. 'Immaculate, calm and old-headed,' thought Neville Cardus: 'His cricket is perpetually keeping an appointment leisurely with moments to spare. Does the bat have an engagement this over with a half-volley? Very well, then, put it down in the book. We'll be there for it. Plenty of time.'

Brown made a century in his first Test at Lord's in 1934, and a double-century there four years later. The latter, an unbeaten 206 in 375 minutes out of 422, came when Australia were under the cosh, chasing England's 494, and secured a draw that underwrote a successful Ashes defence. He was on the field from the start of the match until 5 p.m. on the fourth day.

Brown was then just twenty-five and at his peak. He made 1057 runs in eleven innings of the subsequent home summer – more even than Bradman. But thanks to the war, during which he served as a pilot officer in the Royal Australian Air Force, he would be thirty-three when next he toured, leading Australia to New Zealand, and win only five more caps at irregular intervals over the next two and a half years before his retirement. Brown would make less of his achievements than his misadventures, such as when he played a ball gently on to his stumps at Adelaide Oval in December 1938 without dislodging a bail. He turned his 27 at the time into an unbeaten 174, apologizing guiltily all the way.

In the summer of 1947–48, Brown was twice run out at the bowler's end in Sydney by the Indian Vinoo Mankad, bequeathing to cricket the term 'Mankaded'. Brown formed part of Bradman's much-feted Invincibles in England in 1948, scoring eight centuries, although he had only a modest impact on his two Tests. He enjoyed a story of the team's opening game at Worcester where sawdust was applied to damp run-ups. "'Ere, go easy with yon sawdust,' a spectator called. 'You're wasting a full month's ration of sausage meat.'

When Bradman left New South Wales for South Australia in 1935, Brown took over the job he held down for the men's outfitters FJ Palmer. Relocating to Queensland, he sold Chevrolets for the Brisbane firm of Egars, before running a sports store in the shadow of the giant emporium McDonnell and East. Brown celebrated his sixty-seventh wedding anniversary with Barbara last December. She survives him, as do three sons. 'They were well spaced,' Brown said. 'Like my centuries.'

# CRICKET'S COLD WAR

*The Ashes did not go out in the quarter century after the Second World War, but they smouldered rather than flared. Two captains stood tall: taciturn Len Hutton and ebullient Richie Benaud. But such flashes as there were came from fast bowling in the 1950s, Lindwall and Miller inspiring Tyson and Trueman leading back to Davidson and Meckiff. Between times, spin had its day: Laker's 46 wickets at less than 10 in the Ashes of 1956 set a benchmark nobody has approached. Then, in the 1960s, draws began piling up: in five series from 1962–63, seventeen out of twenty-six Tests ended inconclusively, and not losing seemed to be accorded more prestige than winning it. Rather like the Cold War itself.*

# Len Hutton and Denis Compton

## OPPOSITES ATTRACT (2022)

Before music fans were required to choose between the Beatles and the Stones, English cricket had an equivalent: whom out of Len Hutton and Denis Compton, the outstanding batsmen of their generation, to admire more? Northerner or southerner? Roundhead or cavalier? Faded, low-tugged cap or gleaming Brylcreemed head? Did you prefer a Gradgridge like Hutton, or a Slazenger like Compton? Cricket rejoices in such ready contrasts, such unresolvable oppositions: they are, in their way, self-set personality tests of those constructing them. Whom you choose is an act of personal definition. But in the 1940s and 1950s, their differences were more meaningful than we can perhaps imagine.

Hutton was England's great bulwark – the outcome of professional batsmanship's evolution from Shrewsbury and Hayward through Hobbs and Sutcliffe, further tempered by the post-war surge in pace bowling. Before the war, Hutton had been a record breaker; after it, pale and seemingly frail, he was more a record defender. In him the shots lay latent. Occasionally he revealed a majestic cover drive, a flash of the steel in his scabbard; he eschewed the hook after a war-time injury left him with one arm shorter than the other; generally he husbanded his energies as he husbanded English innings, as though wartime rationing had been extended to strokes also.

That strokes were, in fact, free to any good home was evident in half an hour of Compton. Two years Hutton's junior, he was strong, sturdy, sun-bronzed, a holiday week-end of a batsman, in tune with the gradual emergence of an English leisure consciousness and consumer mentality: his endorsements, brokered by the pioneering sports agent Bagenal Harvey, earned him more than his cricket. He had the full range of ravishing shots, with his signature the sweep. It was entirely self-taught, Compton claimed, and only twice in his career did it get him out – once in 1938, once in 1957.

Hutton was a shy man, mordant when not inscrutable. Alan Ross saw him as 'playing [a] heroic part in a drama of tragic dimensions, one in which he alone had to keep superior forces at bay', his 'curious magnetism' interrupted periodically by 'Queeg-like moments of dispirited confusion'. Revd David Sheppard told a story of his first opening partnership with Hutton. Not until they had been batting together for half an hour did Hutton approach, and then to ask no more than: 'Are you all right?' The line became so familiar that teammates on the 1954–55 Ashes tour inscribed it on the silver salver with which they presented him after their victory. Quotations of Hutton are characteristically brief and usually a little cryptic. He reminds you of Metternich's famous quip when Talleyrand died: 'I wonder what he meant by that.'

Compton was all easy charm and gleaming surfaces, a man for whom batting looked a pleasant pastime rather than an ordeal or vigil, who put onlookers in a similarly good mood: John Arlott described his 'easy, happy figure at the wicket', Neville Cardus spoke of his 'propulsion of happy, sane, healthy life'. With his Middlesex teammate Bill Edrich, Compton formed a partnership that ran the clock around; they approached batting in daylight and socializing after dark with a similarly casual air. The Australian John McMahon told a story of the pair running between wickets one day at the Oval. 'What are we doing?' asked one as they passed for the first run. 'Do you mean tonight?' replied the other as they returned for the second.

Notwithstanding the ramparts' resistance to a professional captain of England, Hutton was probably born to lead; Compton never looked all that fussed. Everything about them, in fact, seems accentuated by their differences. Hutton's mother burned his football boots lest he deviate from his rightful batting path; Compton continued dashing down the wing for Arsenal well into his cricket career. Hutton's earnest personal testament was entitled *Cricket Is My Life* (1949). With Edrich, Compton published the light-hearted *Cricket and All That* (1978): eight wives between them, there had been quite a lot of all that. Compton recalled coming in during the 1953 Lord's Test with Lindwall and Miller bowling swiftly, and Hutton's beckoning him. 'What is it, Len?' he asked, curious because his captain so seldom had anything to say. 'I've been thinking,' Hutton replied. 'There must be easier ways to earn a living.' On retiring, in fact, Hutton became representative of an engineering firm; Compton never needed to stop being Compton. But guiding England along their twin tracks, they kept their game alive. And for all the rivalry of the Beatles and the Stones, of course, music was richer with both.

# Ray Lindwall

## COMMISSIONED BY GOD (1996)*

F ast bowlers have eclipsed Ray Lindwall's feats of wicket taking and will continue doing so, but few will ever recapture the sense of alarm and danger he lent Test cricket in the decade after the war. When Lindwall arrived in Test cricket in March 1946, there were precious few bowlers with the speed to hasten strokes and none who combined this with the stamina and artfulness that continued his threat in discouraging conditions.

Lindwall seized on helpful surfaces with alacrity, as when he rumbled England for 52 with six for 20 at The Oval in August 1948. But he was just as capable of spells such as one of seven for 43 on a slow, turning wicket at Madras's Corporation Stadium in October 1956 when other quick bowlers might have reconsidered their vocation. No out-and-out fast bowler had lasted long enough to harvest 100 Test wickets until Lindwall did so in his twenty-sixth Test, and he

---

* Written on the death of Ray Lindwall, aged seventy-five, on 23 June 1996.

146

remains in Australian pace's top ten wicket-takers.

Lindwall was educated at the Marist Brothers High School in Sydney's Darlinghurst, and raised in Hurstville's Hudson St, a near neighbour to Bill O'Reilly, then Australia's most inexhaustibly combative bowler. Lindwall and his mates always redoubled their street cricketing efforts as O'Reilly, a schoolmaster, turned the corner on his way home. Though O'Reilly always feigned uninterest, he covertly gleaned a strong impression of Lindwall as a youngster 'commissioned by God to be a good athlete'. When Lindwall came under his aegis at St George CC in 1938, he insisted that the tyro seek speed. 'For the seconds and thirds, I've been bowling swingers against the wind,' Lindwall piped. O'Reilly rebuked him: 'I'm having none of that, my lad. You're to bowl fast and with the wind.'

Lindwall was capped by NSW a few weeks after his twentieth birthday but only a few weeks before Pearl Harbor, and duly spent the next four years in the Signals Corp in New Guinea and the Solomon Islands. He played for Australia first against New Zealand while on leave awaiting demobilization, when the after effects of tropical diseases and a dose of chickenpox curbed his exertions. But in March 1947 the twenty-five-year-old Lindwall stamped his authority on England with a bag of seven for 63 at the Sydney Cricket Ground. He went on to spearhead Don Bradman's 1948 Australians in England with 27 wickets in five Tests.

Lindwall was, and remained, an athlete's athlete, one whose ballistics inspired numberless backyard imitators. Ray Robinson summed him up thus: 'The mind's eye sees a sandy-haired player of Swedish Irish extraction almost 5 foot 11 inches tall. His step is short, making the least possible call on muscle and sinew until all-out effort is needed. Anxiously, the striker watches him move from two walking steps into the thirteen running strides which form a model of accelerating approach. On the twelfth stride a high leading left arm sets the line for a side-on delivery, with his back arched. Body momentum tows his arm over and a flick of the wrist propels the ball on its destructive way.'

It was on that 1948 trip that Lindwall was first regularly awarded joint custody of the new ball with Keith Miller. 'Jackson' Lindwall and 'Nugget' Miller, as they were known to one another, have been entwined ever after – Lindwall, smooth and relentless, Miller, brimming with nervous energy. In a halcyon era for Test cricket, Lindwall and Miller were the axis on which the Australian teams of Lindsay Hassett and Ian Johnson revolved. So successful were they that Lindwall scarcely tasted defeat for the first half of his career. Australia won twenty-six of his first thirty-six Tests and suffered only three defeats.

Numerous critics have described Lindwall taking the new ball to bowl to the Yorkshireman Len Hutton as the pinnacle of Test theatre. Perhaps their most famous encounter was at Headingley in July 1953, when Hutton won the toss as England's captain and batted before his home crowd. The lusty Northern salaams with which Hutton was greeted ceased when Lindwall yorked him second ball, the stumps reeling drunkenly. Lindwall's celebrations, even on capturing a scalp such as this, were more relieved thankfulness than exultant crowings. In triumph and disaster on the cricket field, he treated the two impostors just the same. J. M. Kilburn saw Lindwall as a pacific personality carrying 'an air of detachment between assaults'.

> He held, or assumed, a philosophy of contemplation
> born, no doubt, of slip catches gone astray or the
> inability of batsmen to touch his outswinger or the

imperfect sympathy to be found in umpires. His gestures of disappointment or satisfaction were few and became fewer with the ripeness of the years. The more he played in England, the more he accepted the English disinclination to discriminate, yet he could not have been mistaken for anything but an Australian. The stamp of independence, of equality between Jack and master, was firmly upon him. He looked as though he knew how to look after himself.

Lindwall moved to Queensland in 1954 to take a job with Cobb and Co and was dispensed with by Australia's selectors after the 1956 tour of England. He fought back. For three months before the 1958–59 season, he pedalled a stationary bicycle on his front lawn for half an hour each day and rehearsed his action with a self-designed pulley to correct a lowering of the left arm.

Lindwall's recall to the colours at the age of thirty-seven in the Adelaide Test of February 1959 against England was an emotional homecoming, not least for his new-ball partner and lifelong admirer, Alan Davidson. Davidson told Lindwall's biographer, John Ringwood: 'I found probably the hardest thing I ever did, when Ray came into the side in Adelaide in 1959, was to be bowling with the wind and downhill and seeing Ray coming uphill and into the wind. When you have a hero, you only see him as a hero. And I always had it in my mind that he was the greatest and it was silly for me to be over him.' In the next Test at Sydney, Lindwall claimed his 216th test wicket, breaking Clarrie Grimmett's Australian Test record.

Lindwall's Test batting – forthright and technically sound – is often neglected in discussion of Australian all-rounders. In addition to 794 first-class wickets at an average of 21, he made more than 5000 runs at almost 22, with five centuries. He also captained Australia in a Test – a drawn match against India at Brabourne Stadium, Bombay, in October 1956, where he stirred a fine performance from an under-resourced team – and Richie Benaud described him as 'one of the great tacticians of bowling and indeed of Australian cricket over the years'.

One of the best estimations of Lindwall's influence is in the manner in which other countries, having witnessed his match-winning properties, sought out speedmen during and after his career. Brushes with Lindwall and Miller provoked England to unmuzzle Fred Trueman, Frank Tyson and Brian Statham, South Africa to harness Peter Heine and Neil Adcock and the West Indies to combine Wes Hall and Charlie Griffith – not to mention, in due course, Sir Curtly Elconn Lynwall Ambrose. None, however, has rivalled Lindwall in combining speed with subtlety, flinty competitiveness with common decency.

# Keith Miller

## THE AUSTRALIAN IN EXCELSIS
## (2004)*

The office of Australia's longest-serving prime minister Sir Robert Menzies was famously decorated by two framed images. One was a painting by Tom Roberts, capturing the austere, sun-blasted beauty of a bush landscape; the other was a photograph of Keith Miller leaning back to put the finishing touch on a square cut at the Sydney Cricket Ground in 1950.

Any symbolism was unconscious. Yet here, perhaps, seemed the first and last word on Menzies's country: the primal antiquity of the land, and the expansive youthfulness of its people. For no one since the Second World War had so fitted the bill of Australian in excelsis as Miller. An Australian might hope to have been born a Bradman, but there was only really room for one Don in the firmament. Miller not only did everything a cricketer would want to do, but the way they would want to do it, wrapped in a personality radiating

---

* Written on the death of Keith Miller, 11 October 2004, aged eighty-four.

carefree ease one moment and virile hostility the next. He batted with classical technique and utter abandon, playing each ball, as R. C. Robertson-Glasgow put it, 'just that much below its supposed merits that scratches a bowler's pride'. He could touch speeds of bowling reserved for few, so that rivals were loath to rouse him. 'The worst mistake a batsman could make,' recalled Sir Leonard Hutton, 'was to hit him for four.'

Lounging deceptively at slip, Miller stood out even when unoccupied. He was a game of cricket in himself; he could even, when the circumstances dictated it, ooze an unstudied boredom. Though Australians distrust exhibitionism, they esteem the natural, the open, the spontaneous. Miller was more than simply an entertainer: he had that uncanny knack of commanding attention without seeming to seek it. And just as Bradman is often seen as sporting solace for the Great Depression, Miller is associated immediately with the Second World War, the warrior who beat his sword into a bat rather than a ploughshare.

A sense of destiny infests his name: Keith Ross Miller was christened as a tribute to the aviators Keith and Ross Smith, who in the week of his birth landed in Melbourne after a pioneering trip from England. There is little doubt that, in reversing their journey at the outbreak of war, Royal Australian Air Force pilot officer Miller underwent what was his defining life experience. In *Cricket Crossfire* (1958), Miller gives his war years ten pages that read at first light-heartedly. Then you notice, dropped in laconically, phrases such as 'who later in the war was killed', 'he crashed and was killed', and 'six or seven of my pals had been killed'. He tells of walking away from a crash-landing with the advice: 'Nearly stumps drawn that time, gents.' If his cricket had an air of insouciance in the face of danger, there is little wondering why.

His first big cricket ensued in the so-called Victory Tests of the English summer of 1945, which he capped off with an innings of 185 for Dominions, led by Learie Constantine, against England, led by Walter Hammond. In this extraordinary three-day match of 1241 runs, Miller's first 61, scored in the last seventy-five minutes of the second day, included one six on to the top tier of the pavilion. He followed it, on the third morning, with what Sir Pelham Warner reckoned the greatest exhibition of hitting he saw in sixty years as a player and administrator. In ninety minutes of mostly orthodox but startlingly powerful batting, Miller added 124, with six further sixes: one carried to Block Q on the right of the pavilion; another landed on the roof of the broadcasting box, falling into a shrapnel hole in the roof, from which it had to be dislodged with a stick.

The story goes that Miller's hitting was so violent that elderly MCC members abandoned their favourite positions and adjourned to the bar, where it was safer, though this may be fond Australian imagining. In any event, Lord's became a venue that Miller cherished as much as it cherished him: he made a fine Test hundred there in 1953, and scooped up ten wickets three years later.

Still, no appreciation of Miller should be overburdened with facts. It just wasn't him. Just about every Australian can tell you Bradman's batting average; only a real aficionado can be exact about Miller's statistics. He simply stood out. In an era when cricketers did not routinely resemble athletes, he assuredly did. In an age when cricketers were not famed for being photogenic, the camera sought him out. Cricket, too, was only to be played during the day; Miller did not care to think about it too deeply in hindsight. A journalist once accosted him, wanting to know how he had just taken seven for 12 in a Sheffield Shield match against South Australia. 'There's three reasons,' Miller replied. 'First, I bowled bloody well. Second, I, errr . . . second . . .' There was a pause. 'You can forget about the other two reasons.'

And make no mistake: Miller had 'it'. Presence, charisma, an aura – call it what you will. It was said that men wanted to be like him, women simply to be with him. He was thankful in later life that the media had in his own time been a relatively tactful institution. Over lunch in Sydney one day, a mutual friend opined that Miller would have been worth millions to the modern game and been paid accordingly. When I asked Keith if he would have wanted it that way, simply to play cricket, he looked askance. 'You know,' he said, 'Bill O'Reilly said to me just before he died: "Keith, we were lucky to play cricket when we did." He didn't have to say anything else. I knew exactly what he meant.'

I have one particular recollection of that meeting, for I did something I seldom do, and asked Miller for his autograph – to sign a copy, as it happens, of that same photograph that had hung in Menzies's office. The mutual friend laughed, not without reason, that a park-cricket plodder such as I should feel an affinity with such an image. Only after returning home did I peep at Keith's dedication. It reads: 'Good shot this. Try it some time.' It may explain something about Miller's personality that just contemplating this makes me think I ought to.

# Bill Johnston

## DEAR BILL (2007)<sup>*</sup>

B ill Johnston, who has died aged eighty-five, played cricket with a smile on his face, like someone who couldn't quite get over his unlikeliness as a Test player. He even let go his bouncer with an air of amiability, as if simply to amuse the crowd. 'The most popular man in cricket,' declared his contemporary Keith Miller, who himself had claims to the garland: 'Bill is one of the very few sports stars I know about whom nothing but good is spoken and written. He is a great bloke in every way.'

The looks were as deceptive as Johnston's left-arm bowling, which varied from waspish pace to teasing spin. Not that the personality was not as sunny as it seemed, but Johnston was as crafty and competitive as his 160 Test wickets at 24, and the 2.07 runs per over that he gave up, suggest.

Johnston not only came off the land but looked like it: tall, rangy, with big ears, and hands strengthened by milking the

---

* Written on the death of Bill Johnston, 25 May 2007, aged eighty-five.

herd on the family farm at Ondit, near Beeac in country Victoria. He and his older brother Allan, an all-rounder, did not converge on Melbourne until just before the war, which promptly spirited them both away as members of the Royal Australian Air Force. Allan, trained in the Empire Air Scheme in Rhodesia, was killed when his bomber crashed in Ireland; Bill became a radar technician, lucky enough to serve most of his time in the Australian north, and to be demobbed quickly on the cessation of hostilities.

Johnston then specialised in left-arm slows with the occasional surprise fast ball. His Richmond skipper Jack Ledward wanted him to stay that way; national selector Jack Ryder saw more promise in his quicker deliveries. Johnston always recalled sitting in the empty members' stand at Adelaide Oval after a Sheffield Shield match in October 1946, when Donald Bradman confided Ryder was onto something: fast bowlers were in short supply, and likelier to advance more quickly.

Johnston evolved a hybrid method, wheeling in from eleven yards, pumping his elbows through a seven-pace run, and whistling his arm over. Ray Robinson described him as dipping his head and hitching his shoulders 'like a swagman humping his blue on the track to Croajingalong'. His front foot would land parallel to the crease and his back foot perpendicular, so he had little follow through, always had to strap his ankles, and suffered from the first with shin soreness. But he was also wickedly difficult to read. His bouncer seemed to follow and corner the batsman; his cutters jagged; his slower ball hung teasingly. When he reverted to spin as a variation, it was always with accuracy. 'Johnston was faster than he looked,' Bradman recalled. 'When bowling spinners he was quicker than the normal type and had a difficult curving flight.'

Johnston was picked to tour England in 1948 with his

Richmond teammate and lifelong pal Doug Ring. They roomed together, and debated who might make the final cut. When Johnston did not play in the tour's opening match at Worcester, where Australia usually played its Test XI, he gave himself no chance. But there was rain in the air on the first morning at Trent Bridge, and Bradman told him that Ring had been made twelfth man: 'Bill, you're in the side. We think the conditions are in your favour.' Johnston proved them right by taking five for 36 from twenty-five overs, and 102 wickets at 16.8 on the trip including ten for 40 against Yorkshire in a game the Australians always regarded as their 'sixth Test'. He also radiated bonhomie, as Andy Flanagan commented in his travelogue *On Tour with Bradman*: 'Had a vote been taken as to the most popular man in the Australian side on the 1948 tour of England, I believe Bill Johnston would have won. He exudes friendliness and good fellowship, and worked like a horse, uncomplainingly.'

Johnston and Ring combined most famously in Melbourne in January 1952, when left 38 to win as the last-wicket pair in a Test against the West Indies. Cheered on by Richmond fans ('C'mon Tigers!'), they bridged the gap with judicious slogs and some nerveless defence. Johnston was not an agile figure: in fact, when they ran a helter-skelter three, he managed to run one short. 'Don't worry, Ringy!' he called to his partner. 'I think it was me!' But he took his batting seriously: Bradman had insisted on it. He worked the ball through square leg to win the game, running straight into history. Murray Shea, mayor of Richmond, granted the pair freedom of the city. Their names are permanently entwined in the Ring-Johnston Scoreboard that today overlooks Melbourne's picturesque Punt Road Oval.

His more famous batting accomplishment was averaging 102 on the 1953 Ashes tour: 102 runs for once out, caught and bowled at Southampton by Victor Cannings on 6 June. It was the *Herald*'s vigilant Percy Millard who alerted Johnston's captain Lindsay Hassett to the possibility of such a freak statistic when Johnston had accumulated about 70 runs. Hassett would send his bowler to the wicket with an explanatory note asking that the opposing captain try to refrain from dismissing him. Among others who urged Johnston on was Cannings himself, who wrote to him: 'Resist all offers of promotion. I want to be the only man who got you out.'

At his peak, Johnston would have been among the best three bowlers in the world, more consistent than the more celebrated Lindwall and Miller, as penetrative as the Englishman Alec Bedser and deceptive as Sonny Ramadhin. His first hundred Test wickets cost fewer than 19 runs each. The blow from which his bowling never quite recovered was a knee injury sustained in the opening match of the 1953 Ashes tour, at East Moseley, when overlong spikes stuck in the turf too long. He redesigned his action so that his front foot pointed down the wicket, which eased the pressure on his tortured cartilages, but cost him some of his disguise and late movement. When the knee went from under him at Bourda in April 1955, there was no more cricket for Bill Johnston.

Ray Robinson thought Johnston had 'the sunniest nature of any cricketer I ever met' – and he kept it. I remember walking into his bowls club on the Gold Coast to meet him, and everyone in the bar beaming at the mere mention of his name. He had a vivid memory for his cricket, but an infectious lack of seriousness about it. You would ask him, for example, about running out South Africa's Jack Nel at Johannesburg in February 1950. 'Yeah, I was fielding at short leg,' he'd nod. 'I chased it and threw the stumps down at the bowler's end.' Pause. Gusty laugh. 'How unlucky was he!'

Johnston was a treasure house of recollections of his time

as well. He married Judith, an air hostess, at Melbourne's St Paul's Anglican Cathedral, remembering how the Catholics, including Hassett, had to stand outside. And he cherished a January 1956 letter from his cricket-fancying prime minister Robert Menzies: 'My dear Bill, I am sorry to hear of your retirement. All those who recognize skill, courage and gaiety as the ingredients of good cricket will mourn your decision.' That kind of lover of the game will also mourn his passing.

# Neil Harvey

## THE LAST INVINCIBLE (2021)

Cricket is always quietly marking birthdays, more and less notable. Last weekend, rather nicely entwined, it was Ian Chappell and Bishan Bedi, charismatic captains both, turning seventy-eight and seventy-five respectively.

Sometimes, these anniversaries can be slightly confounding. On Monday, it's Rishabh Pant. Can he still only be twenty-four? On Thursday, it's Graham Yallop. Can he really be entering his seventieth year? On the day after falls the milestone of another Victorian left-handed Libran who captained Australia, Neil Harvey.

At ninety-three, Harvey is not our oldest Test cricketer: evergreen Ken Archer had a nine-month head start. But Harvey enjoys the eminence of being the sole survivor of Sir Donald Bradman's 1948 Australians – 'the last Invincible', to use the title of a new biography by Ashley Mallett, which sounds like it belongs on a fantasy novel or the latest *Star Wars*.

It's fifty-eight years since Harvey published his own autobiography, *My World of Cricket* (1963) – a short book, rather perfunctory even by the standards of a more reticent era. He has left this second innings late. But *The Last Invincible* is a welcome addition to cricket's library, and for the author a personal one. Harvey, you see, was Mallett's childhood hero. As a boy he watched Harvey bat at the Sydney Cricket Ground. He did so in the company of a beloved grandfather whose memory stretched, delectably, back to Victor Trumper – reflect a moment on the span of those recollections, effectively from nineteenth century to twenty-first.

Later, as Australian selector, Harvey would choose Mallett, a fine finger spinner and predatory gully fielder, in thirty-eight Tests. Plus he would advance the claims to the captaincy of Mallett's old mucka Chappell. Mallett reveals that Harvey cajoled his fellow Invincible Sam Loxton into replacing Bill Lawry with Chappell in January 1971 over the objections of their former captain Bradman – an uncharacteristic apostasy on the part of Loxton, who typically would not give the time of day without consulting the Don first.

Heroism is an unconscious theme of *The Last Invincible*. In quoting a long list of luminaries who shared Harvey as an idol, the book invites us to consider Harvey's appeal, and how cricketers lodge in imagination. In this, Harvey enjoyed certain unselfconscious advantages. Harvey made his Test debut aged nineteen and three months, at a time when cricket's ranks were still composed largely of individuals who had started before the Second World War. He was the youngest Invincible, seven years Loxton's junior. A generation then proceeded to grow up with him, measuring their own maturing against his.

There was a vernacular appeal to Harvey's story, as one of six working-class brothers who piled up more than 50,000 first-class and first-grade runs between them; he did not even own a bat when he was capped by Australia and made his first Test hundred with a Crockett borrowed from his state's kit bag.

Cricket in the 1950s welcomed a range of physiques, some rather aldermanic. Harvey was trim, athletic and active. He was sharp in the field, agile at the crease and speedy between the wickets, at a time when this mattered, when bats facilitated twos and threes rather than mainly ones or fours. Harvey was also instantly recognizable from scorning a cap let alone a helmet. In a photo of him walking off after a century at Hastings, Harvey's hair is immaculate, his parting still precise. His creams are spotless.

We are also inclined to forget, in an era in which they abound, how rare a left-hander was in Harvey's era. In seventy years' Test cricket before him, only half a dozen Australia lefties had made hundreds; the only higher scoring lefties to emerge all postdate Harvey. If you were a left-handed youth in the 1950s, like a South African boy called Graeme Pollock, you identified with Harvey immediately; if you were right-handed in the 1960s, like a lad in Adelaide called Greg Chappell, you batted the other way round when you imitated Harvey in backyard games with your brothers.

If, meanwhile, you never saw him, and into this category I fall, you have listened carefully to Harvey's contemporaries describe him. When many years ago I set out to write *The Summer Game*, a history of cricket in the generation before mine, I was struck by the unique tone of respect accorded Harvey. Bradman was unrepeatable, Keith Miller inimitable, but Harvey belonged to that very particular subset of cricketers who exert an unspoken authority in a dressing room, then by avoiding the limelight never cheapen it.

Harvey sidestepped the media after retirement, instead selling Tuppeware. His longest post-playing cricket commitment was a role as selector, where his $50 per diem was so paltry that he avoided taking cabs. In the age of long Covid, let's call this long heroism. 'Robert Neil Harvey,' concludes the author. 'He was my hero then; he is my hero still.'

So here is Harvey, birthday ushering in another season, like the smell of newly mown grass, and the pock of leather on willow. Later this month, another left-hander marks a birthday. David Warner will be thirty-five on 27 October. Marooned in a hotel room in the UAE, sidelined by his struggling Indian Premier League franchise, he'd be pardoned feeling rather older than his years.

# A draw at Lord's

## WATSON AND BAILEY HANG ON
## (1996)

Seldom in a series can two captains have afforded such a contrast as in 1953. Lindsay Hassett remained a leader well loved for his pawky good humour. On one occasion after a rain break in a county match, pressmen watched Hassett probing the pitch dubiously with his thumb. 'Any chance of play?' a reporter wondered. 'I dunno,' Hassett replied sardonically, 'I only do that to look intelligent in front of the crowd.'

England's Len Hutton would never have allowed himself such a quip. Like his Yorkshire mentor Herbert Sutcliffe, Hutton was the master builder of English batsmanship. Geff Noblet remembers bowling against the MCC for South Australia in 1950, and coyly launching a leg-cutter that he had spent years rehearsing in the nets. Hutton, at the non-striker's end, remarked: 'You didn't bowl that four years ago, Geff.' When Noblet bowled to him, Hutton pushed the leg-cutter back, grinning broadly.

From the local perspective, the most important aspect of Hutton's ascension was that he was a professional: the first to

lead his country in an era in which English cricket still distinguished between gentlemen (amateurs) and players
(professionals), still allotted them different changing rooms
and entry gates. The Australians knew that Hutton's leadership
would make England that much more formidable. He was
well versed in Australian methods, citing as his captaincy
primer *The Game's the Thing* (1929), the autobiography of the
former Australian Monty Noble: 'They [Australians] have
the utmost ability for producing that little extra, or instilling
into opposition an inferiority complex that can have, and has
had, a crushing effect. Australians have no inhibitions.'

The 150 journalists covering the series, accordingly, foresaw a tight contest. Hassett could still call on Lindwall, Miller
and Bill Johnston, but on the evidence of its drawn rubber
with South Africa was hinting at cyclical decline; a group of
young players round Hutton, like Trevor Bailey, Tom Graveney
and Peter May, implied an England on the cusp of a new age.
Even Sir Donald Bradman – who arrived in London on 5 June
with his wife to become the $10,000 guest columnist of the
*Daily Mail* – wrote in his first despatch: 'On paper England
must be conceded at least a 50–50 chance this time against
Australia. This is something no unbiased prophet has been
able to forecast for twenty years.'

By the Monday evening of the Second Test at Lord's,
Australia seemed about to confound their doubters. Thanks to
authoritative hundreds from Hassett and Miller, England
faced an almost unassailable 343 in the fourth innings. And
England's chase began badly, Lindwall reducing them to 3 for
12. In Jack Fingleton's words, the great fast bowler 'plunged a
double-edged dagger deep into English cricket'.

In the day's last over, however, Lindwall missed the chance
to twist that dagger. Left-handed Yorkshireman Willy Watson
turned Doug Ring low but straight to Lindwall at backward

short leg. 'Straight in, straight out', the bowler recalls. 'He should've got it. Of course, we didn't realize the significance at the time.' The significance was that Watson – a cool customer and football international who'd been part of England's 1950 World Cup squad – stubbornly refused to budge on Tuesday. Greeted pessimistically by a crowd of only 5000 at 11.30 a.m., he and Compton saw off the new ball, and settled solidly against the leg-spin of Ring and Benaud.

There were alarms. Bowling from the Pavilion end, Ring spun one into Watson that squeezed between bat and pad and rolled purposefully towards off stump. A soccer player's kick deflected it. And Compton, after seventy minutes, was lbw to a ball from Johnston that stayed low. But next came the obdurate Essex all-rounder Trevor Bailey, whose native stubbornness had been stiffened by perusing the gloomy newspaper prognostications of English defeat on the morning train from Westcliff-on-Sea. The pair bridged the remaining fifty minutes to lunch, Watson essaying some attractive shots, Bailey wedging his bat incorruptibly next to his front pad and enjoying every second. While Watson drank milk during the adjournment, Bailey ate his normal hearty repast, cleaning several teammates' plates for them.

Hassett had some problems. Johnston, scarcely recovered from his knee strain, had felt the injury give again while fielding on the boundary; Ring and Benaud were proving ineffectual. But Australia's captain did not take the obvious option of uncorking Lindwall and Miller until the new ball fell due at 2.55 p.m. And, by that time, Watson and Bailey were well entrenched: although Lindwall twice hit Bailey across the knuckles, and only six runs accrued in the half an hour, the pair survived.

The ground was filling as news of the resistance spread. 'I cannot remember when a crowd so revelled in defence for defence's sake,' reported E. W. Swanton. 'As Bailey got right behind the ball immediately following those that hit him, the crowd applauded with a fervour that in different circumstances might have greeted a six.' The audience beyond the ground hung on proceedings with equal enthusiasm: newspapers reported that John Christie, the Rillington Place murderer just sentenced to hang, had asked for updates from his cell.

Miller and Davidson bowled at a clip after tea, Bailey weaving from one fierce Miller full-toss, but every over's passing was now greeted with rapture. Not until Ring was employed at the Nursery end from 5.20 p.m., so that his leg-break could turn down the Lord's slope, were the batsmen incommoded. Watson raised his six-hour hundred by swinging Ring just wide of Benaud at square leg. And, twenty minutes later, a Ring leg-break infiltrated Watson's defence and squirted low to Hole at slip. But only forty minutes remained and, though two further wickets fell, the match had been saved.

The local press rejoiced. John Arlott wrote: 'I have seen Test teams with fewer obvious weaknesses, but I have never seen a game more epically, more evenly or more fluctuatingly fought out, nor one which so held the attention and the imagination and the heroic vein'. Neville Cardus's *Manchester Guardian* report was headlined: 'Miracle of Faith at Lord's'. The Australians lamented a lost opportunity, and wondered at its cost.

# Intrigue in Melbourne

## WHO WATERED THE PITCH? (1996)*

The year 1955 would become notable for intrigue: the Petrov Royal Commission, B. A. Santamaria and 'The Movement', the fall of Joe McCarthy, the further fall of Guy Burgess and Donald Maclean. The Third Test at the MCG over the new year threw up a mystery, at least for a time, just as confounding.

The Melbourne Cricket Club's preparations for the match had been fraught. Demolition of the Public Stand ahead of the 1956 Olympics had torn a huge hole in its flank, disturbing its microclimate. Pitches had been so mediocre that secretary Vernon Ransford asked Albert Ground groundsman Jack House to assist groundsman Bill Vanthoff in preparing the square.

When the pitch for the traditional Boxing Day encounter between Victoria and NSW proved sound, Ransford expressed

---

* Part of *The Summer Game* (1996). Percy Beames died on 28 March 2004, aged ninety-two.

optimism about the Test. But House told journalist Dick Whitington the day before the match: 'There should be a packet of runs in it on Friday and Saturday, but I wouldn't go further than that. If conditions are cool over the weekend it may last until Monday. But if they're hot it will crack badly.' And, when Hutton won the toss on Friday, it was stifling hot.

Arguments about the pitch were temporarily eclipsed by the drama of the play, dominated first by Keith Miller and then by Colin Cowdrey. Having missed the previous Test with a sore knee, Miller had not been expected to bowl. Yet on the first morning he told Johnson excitedly: 'I tried the knee in the bedroom this morning. It might be OK.' Finishing his first over and savouring the strong breeze for his outswinger, he was even more excited: 'It's been better than I expected. Gimme another go.' Bowling unchanged until lunch, he extracted Edrich, Hutton and Compton and allowed just two scoring strokes.

When Miller was spelled, though, Cowdrey made a poised hundred. And, happy as they were at rolling England for 191, the Australians were staring daggers at the pitch. The little moisture binding it had disappeared and, without a covering of couch, it was threatening to disintegrate. Harvey muttered to Benaud as they walked off: 'I don't reckon we will be able to play on this on Monday.'

The chances faded further when record temperatures and an infernal northerly wind on New Year's Day baked the pitch to a crumbling crust. Though Victorians Johnson and keeper Len Maddocks saw Australia to within four runs of the lead, the captain grew more anxious by the over. 'We went in on Saturday, the wicket was doing all sorts of things,' says Johnson. 'When I was in with Len toward the end of the day, you could see the ball starting to fly off the cracks.'

Melbourne's hottest night-time temperature of 96 degrees

Fahrenheit was recorded that evening, and players dispersed on the rest day: Harvey had Benaud, Davidson and MCC's Jim McConnon to his home in Heidelberg; Miller and Lindwall played golf with Ossie Pickworth; Johnson spent a fretful day in Middle Park: 'I was thinking: "God! What's this wicket going to look like on Monday?"'

At the Collins Street offices of *The Age*, Percy Beames was filing for Monday's edition when his telephone rang. It was Bill Vanthoff: an old friend, with whom he'd played VFL football for Melbourne twenty years earlier. He sounded distraught. 'Percy, something terrible's happened,' the MCG groundsman said. 'Jack House's flooded the square. He's put too much water on.' Beames was stunned. Such a watering would be completely at odds with Law 10 of MCC's 1947 code: 'Under no circumstances shall the pitch be watered during a match.' He went at once to his editor, Harold Austin.

The story was sensational. But Austin did not want to be the cause of a controversy jeopardizing Anglo-Australian cricketing relations. 'Do you think it will affect the game?' he asked.

'It might,' Beames replied.

'Do you think there was any evil intent involved?' Austin asked.

Beames said honestly: 'No, I don't.'

Austin thought a moment, then proposed: 'Then we won't run the story. What we'll do is black [print in bold] a paragraph saying that watering a pitch during a match is illegal.' Beames was full of admiration: 'I thought to myself that it showed what a great editor Harold Austin was. He was more interested in the game than in a scoop for his newspaper.'

Johnson arrived early on Monday to inspect the wicket. It looked surprisingly firm, and the cracks seemed to have closed. He ran his spikes along it. It was moist. He fetched his deputy Arthur Morris. 'This has been watered,' Johnson said. 'Crikey,'

Morris said. 'So it has.'

As Johnson and Morris went to notify Victorian Cricket Association secretary Jack Ledward, umpires Col Hoy and Mel McInnes arrived from their digs at the Commercial Travellers' Club in Flinders Street. Hoy blanched, and McInnes advised from the corner of his mouth: 'Say nothing to anybody.'

The secret was out, and the press box in pandemonium. Englishwoman Margaret Hughes, writing for Sydney's *Daily Telegraph*, recalled: 'Pressmen could be seen rushing here and there, chatting together in groups, snatching phones – the inexplicable featherbed state of the wicket had been explained – "it had been watered".' Beames knew that there was no holding his story. With the pitch momentarily tamed, Hutton and Edrich mopped up England's arrears themselves. The tourists led by 119 at the close with seven wickets remaining, and all talk centred on the pitch's abruptly reformed character. Next morning, Melburnians awoke to *The Age*'s bold headline 'Test pitch watered during game'.

Tuesday's play furnished further evidence of the pitch's placation. Though Johnston winkled out five in twenty-five overs of probing left-arm spin, May's elegant blade and Bailey's dead one prolonged the English innings. Johnson felt thwarted, especially when tailender Johnny Wardle came in waving his bat like a banner and hit 38 in even time. 'There was nothing we could do,' he says. 'It was like losing the toss twice.'

The Melbourne Cricket Club was in uproar. The story in London's *Daily Telegraph* revealed the unpleasant possibilities facing them: 'Possibility Match May Be Voided.' Secretary Ransford and president William McClelland spent the day collecting statutory declarations from Vanthoff, House and the nightwatchmen denying all knowledge of watering. At the close, Ransford's assistant, Albert Cutriss, entered the press box in the manner of a town crier to proclaim: 'After a searching inquiry, it is emphatically denied that the pitch or any part of the cricket ground has been watered since the commencement of the Third Test match on Friday 31st December.' But, despite two requests, *The Age* declined to withdraw its story. When the newspaper printed the MCC's self-exculpation, it was with the addendum that Beames still believed his information correct. And, without admitting it, VCA president Arnold Seitz dined Beames at the Amateur Sport Club in Little Collins Street in an effort to learn the reporter's sources. 'I wouldn't bite,' says Beames.

Off-field dramas were temporarily suspended when England's last four tumbled in fifty minutes, suggesting that the watering's affect was wearing off. There was, after all, a Test match in session and the Ashes at stake. Johnson requested the heavy roller before Australia began its chase for 240, and it seemed to bind the surface for the balance of the day as Benaud and Harvey saw out proceedings. Australia needed 165 and England eight wickets on the Wednesday for a 2–1 series lead. *The Age* headline forecast: 'Stage is set for great Test finish'.

It was, but hardly one to Australians' liking. When Evans darted to leg to accept Harvey's glance from the day's seventh delivery, it was the first of eight wickets to fall in an hour and a quarter for 34 runs. Statham enlisted Evans in Hole's dismissal and bowled Archer with a full-toss, but the rest bowed before Frank Tyson. The pitch played its part. Inconsistent bounce perplexed all the batsmen. 'It was fast bouncers one-minute, fast grubbers the next,' says Harvey. 'One would go past your ear off a good length, another would go along the deck.' But Tyson would have been fast on mud and, when he ended play on the stroke of lunch, many of the 20,000 who had attended the last day in good faith remained afterwards to hail him outside the players' enclosure. Hutton accepted Menzies's congratulations, then confided in Tyson's mentor, Alf Gover: 'Alfred, there is one thing I'm worried about. The poor caterers now have 20,000 pies and sausage rolls on their hands.'

The only favourable aspect of Australia's defeat was that it appeased many in the public mortified by what Whitington dubbed 'The Great MCG Mirage'. There had been recommendations that the Test be either voided or replayed if Australia won. But the heat remained on the Melbourne Cricket Club. The *Sydney Morning Herald* published a waspish editorial asking why so many officials continued to deny what they knew to be true. No one was convinced when the club produced two experts – G. D. Aitchison, a senior research officer with the Commonwealth Scientific and Industrial Research Organisation, and D. H. Trollope, a civil engineering lecturer at Melbourne University – to explain in abstruse detail how the combination of the hot weather and the tarpaulins could have drawn water from an underground stream. Secretary Ransford took several weeks' leave later in the season to recover from the strain of public odium.

Though the watering's precise nature remains a mystery, Ian Johnson heard some years later a convincing version of events from a ground staff member. Examining the pitch on Saturday, House had apparently been appalled. 'Someone's going to be killed on this wicket,' he told Vanthoff. 'We can't leave it like this.' 'What are you going to do?' Vanthoff asked. House told him: 'Think I'll give it a bit of a fizz.' Vanthoff baulked. 'I'm not in it,' he replied. 'I'm going home.' In leaving, however, Vanthoff would have realized that the operation could not be clandestine: because of the Olympic refurbishments at the MCG, the centre was visible to passersby in Jolimont Park. Which may be why he contacted Beames in the hope that, if details did emerge, at least a responsible journalist would have full possession of the facts.

# Frank Tyson

## TYPHOON REPORT (2004)*

One of the hoariest of cricket's truisms – after the one about it being a funny game and catches winning matches – holds that what happens on tour stays on tour. I'm not sure how well that holds up today. What goes on tour stays there for the time it takes to whip up a tour diary, pose for the cover and get Ricky Ponting to write the introduction. Frank Tyson is more circumspect. He has honoured a stay-on-tour moratorium of fifty years, which gives it a somewhat more stringent security classification than cabinet papers, and a status a little less important than documents covered by the Official Secrets Act – quite right, I think you'll agree.

In Frank's book, he recalls how any player in the England team of his day who found himself being earbashed at a function emitted a mayday signal to teammates by sticking

---

* Speech at the Melbourne launch of Frank Tyson's *In The Eye of the Typhoon*, November 2004.

his fingers in his ear. Should I go on too long, feel free to revive this tradition.

Having Frank write on the 1954–55 tour is like having Spofforth write on the Oval Test of 1882, or Warwick Armstrong talk us through the Ashes of 1921. Ah, let's not undersell him: it's like having Phar Lap confide his impressions of the 1930 Melbourne Cup. And, if Phar Lap has retained his youthful good looks, Frank is a great deal more erudite and informative.

*In The Eye of the Typhoon* is an incalculably valuable book. For one, it's a time capsule. On page eight, in an image from the *Chronicle and Echo*, we see a besuited, betrilbied young Tyson standing solitarily at Northampton station. He could be a young soldier in mufti. He could be a *film noir* gumshoe. But he's a young cricketer waiting for his train to London, without agent, ghost writer, life coach or spiritual guru in sight. Trains figure as prominently in Frank's book as planes would today. Frank tells us that along the train route from St Pancras to Tilbury, supporters had graffitied encouragement: 'Good luck Len' and 'Stick to it, Boil'. Cricket graffiti is, alas, today a thing of the past. The last example I can think of dates from 1989 when, during the Poll Tax riots, someone scrawled on a wall the legend 'Thatcher Out'; another anonymous hand had added 'lbw Alderman'.

To read Frank's book is to be transported back to an era when travellers from Melbourne to Sydney swapped loco-motives at Albury after a midnight meat pie in the refreshment rooms. Nowadays going to Sydney merely entails pretending an IQ fifty points lower. *In The Eye of the Typhoon* is, further-more, not merely the narrative of a cricket tour, but a story about the joy of being part of a hearty, happy and successful team. It proves, if it needed proving, that cricket is the most companionable game of all. Certainly more socially reward-ing than a game of golf involving right-handed Frank and left-handed Brian Statham, whose dialogue, Frank tells us, once they had teed off with their respective slices, consisted of occasional grunts of 'see you on the green' and long solitary walks.

The centre of this unit is Len Hutton: driven, austere, self-sufficient, yet at times strangely vulnerable. Colin Cowdrey told a story about Hutton at his first press conference in Perth, and how his underkill caught the Australian press completely unawares: 'We've got a chap called Tyson. But you won't have 'eard of 'im, 'cos 'e's 'ardly ever played.' Now we learn that while the *Orsova* was en route, Hutton had taken Frank aside, along with Peter Loader, Colin Cowdrey, Jim McConnon and Keith Andrew, and confided that they couldn't expect to play a major role in the series. Have you ever heard of such a thing, consigning five members of a seventeen-man squad to oblivion?

Nowadays, Hutton would probably be sued, or chastised by a sports psychologist for damaging his men's self-esteem even as Frank was sent off for counselling. Frank tells us it redoubled his determination to make a contribution – I wonder whether this wasn't Hutton's intention all along. At perhaps the crucial moment of the tour, immediately after Australia's colossal First Test win, we see Hutton in a different context, calling half a dozen players into his room to tell them that he was completely confident of winning the series. This grand old Duke of York only had seventeen men, but he treated hills with a similar contempt. My favourite Hutton story, however, concerns Frank joining Hutton at Eden Park when England was seven down and still 36 runs in arrears on first innings against New Zealand: 'Stick around for a while, Frank. We may not have to bat again.' The only thing more startling about this assertion is that it was right. England obtained a lead of 42, and bowled NZ out for 16 fewer.

We all know how famously fast Frank was on that tour. Ron Archer once told me that he was caught at slip off Frank in Sydney not because of an edge but because Frank hit his bat so hard that it turned in his hand. For his own part, Frank recalls being clocked by the Royal Aeronautical College at 89mph – this, he modestly adds, was without warming up and while swathed in sweaters; he nobly refrains from adding that it was Wellington where the commonest balls have nothing to do with cricket but are those frozen off brass monkeys.

I dare say Frank bowled about as fast as a man can fifty years ago, but I wouldn't want to overstress the importance of his speed. A 95mph half volley is still a half volley, as anyone who's watched Brett Lee bowl for the past couple of years would tell you. In Len Hutton's *Fifty Years of Cricket* (1984), he startlingly reports that Frank and Brian Statham bowled not a single bouncer in the Adelaide Test. The most important bouncer of the 1954–55 series was bowled at Frank not by him, but by Ray Lindwall, in Sydney. It hit the back of Frank's head, raising an egg-shaped lump. 'When he came out of his concussion I swear there was a new light in his eyes as if a spark had been kindled deep down inside him,' recalled Hutton. 'I am not given to fanciful imagination, and the fact is that when he resumed bowling the next day he was a yard, maybe a yard and a half, faster than before.' What did that feel like? Now, all these years later, Frank is here to tell us. Thanks for keeping your fingers from your ears long enough to hear me out, and I take pleasure in handing over to this remarkable book's remarkable author.

# Laker's Match

## 19 FOR 90 AND ALL THAT (2022)

If Shane Warne perpetrated the ball of the century, Jim Laker, whose centenary falls on 9 February 2022, provided the bowl of the century. Nobody has remotely repeated his near-monopoly on wicket taking in a first-class match, let alone in the Ashes. His analysis of 19 for 90 at Manchester in the Test that became eponymous comes as trippingly from the tongue as it came serially from one direction, the Stretford End, on a dry then a wet pitch.

The other great wicket harvests in Test history have tended to be outliers in the careers of the players concerned: think Massie at Lord's, Hirwani at Chennai; more recently Ajaz Patel in Mumbai. Remarkably, Laker can be seen as working up to his coup. He had transfixed the Australians two months earlier for Surrey, at The Oval, accomplishing a clean sweep: ten for 88. As what favours one slow bowler usually favours another, his county teammate Tony Lock had then spun out seven in the second innings. What, Richie Benaud observed, upgraded Laker from 'the incredible' at The Oval to 'the absolutely incredible' at Old Trafford was that he here shut the light out from not only Lock, who claimed the only other Australian wicket, but every other bowler in the match, who garnered a total of twelve wickets for 724: the next best figures were Australian captain Ian Johnson's 47-10-151-4. Laker, meanwhile, packed into one match two of the five best innings analyses in Test history: 16.4-4-37-9 and 51.2-23-53-10.

Laker was born in Frizinghall, a location that sounds like something from Roald Dahl but is actually 3km north of Bradford. He was raised by his teacher mother after his stonemason father disappeared from his life aged two, leaving no memory. It is possible, without too much of a stretch, to interpret his personality accordingly: he was a self-sufficient, self-taught, dialled-down figure, thrice engaged to be married before he was. 'There can seldom have been a less obviously emotional cricketer than Jim Laker,' said his England captain Peter May. On occasion, though, he kicked against administrative pricks, including at Yorkshire, who let him slip through their net after the war when he took a bank job in London after demobilization from the Army. It was at that point he abandoned batting and medium-pace bowling in favour of off-spin, with an easy lope to the wicket, a high action, and a wicked break that John Arlott evoked.

> Memory will recall him very English-looking, six feet tall, firmly built, fair-haired, fresh-faced, quiet in demeanour, coming up to the bowler's end, his shoulders hunched, cap at a jaunty angle. He moved to his bowling mark at a constabular stroll and with the laconic air of one with his tongue in his cheek pattered along a run of artfully varied short strides. Then, wrist and arm cocked, he swung through a model, high delivery-arc into the positive follow-through that generated so much spin and life.

Still, Laker's record in his first two-dozen Tests was 86 wickets at 28: respectable, but not quite of the front rank. Nor did his bowling averages against Australia (38) and West Indies (33) stand out, and he was overlooked for the Ashes tours of 1950–51 and 1954–55. For Johnson's visiting Australians in 1956 he would have held few terrors . . . until he did. Keith Miller is thought to have, inadvertently, set the scheme in motion by claiming ten wickets on a spicy surface in the Lord's Test. 'Well, Neil,' May told Australia's Neil Harvey afterwards, 'that's the last pitch you'll see like that.' The next Test, at Headingley, was played on a wicket that only rain saved from disintegration: in a dress rehearsal for Old Trafford, Laker bagged 11 for 113. When May swapped Laker from the Warwick Road End just before tea on the second day of the Fourth Test, Australia addressed him like they had never seen an off-break in the wild before. With 459 to defend, Laker picked the visitors off as clinically as an entomologist pinning butterflies to a board, in one twenty-two-ball spell claiming seven wickets for 8 runs.

The critical influence was groundsman Bert Flack's free use of marl – a mixture of clay, sand and limestone sometimes containing shell fragments that was used to bind pitches in England, but that if poured too late became soft and crumbly. The surface spooked the Australians, to such a degree that in hindsight nobody could accurately describe its colour: Miller remembered it as 'reddish', Australia's opening batsman Colin McDonald called it 'yellower', the journalist Jack Fingleton called it 'brown'. All anyone could agree was that the pitch was not green, and that whisk brooms used between innings sent up a dust storm that engulfed Flack's ground staff like a lost desert patrol. Rain subsequently turned the pitch from what McDonald called 'a modified version of Bondi beach in the first innings' to 'a sticky, uncovered mud heap in the second' and the game idled: only 105 minutes' play was possible on the third and fourth days, separated by the rest day Sabbath. Indeed, the Australians were rather shocked to be asked to continue their second innings from two for 84 on Tuesday morning, but as the surface dried went steadily to pieces.

Footage of the game is strangely lulling. Shot from a distance without the benefit of replays or reviews, the players move haltingly, as if they are eyewitnesses rather than participants. Even in his finest hour, Laker remains unemotional, almost detached. Laker's appeals are enquiries not demands; the close catchers, who took ten catches, are sympathetically undemonstrative. This is execution by lethal injection not electric chair. The most vivid figure is Lock, toiling with increasing exasperation at the other end. He had taken his own ten-for against Kent at Blackheath just three weeks earlier and actually claimed more wickets than his partner that summer (155 to 132). Yet on perhaps the friendliest pitch for a spinner ever rolled out, he took a huff-and-puff one for 106 from sixty-nine overs – a reminder for analysts of slow bowling that nothing is preordained even in friendly conditions, and that no bowler can succeed without luck.

The most striking image is the photograph of Laker walking off afterwards, not carried shoulder high, not flashing victory signs or posing for selfies. Hair mussed, jumper over his shoulder, trousers hitched high, he is accepting the applause of his teammates without any visible acknowledgement, a workman satisfied with an honest day's labour. Laker was proudly a professional in cricket's still segregated community: the abolition of the distinction with amateurism, he would later say, was the best thing to happen during his career. There was certainly no Warnesque cavorting from the team balcony: to the crowd, he temperately raised a glass of Lucozade. When he stopped for a pint and a sandwich at a pub on the drive home to Putney, he enjoyed passing unrecognized even when highlights of the day were played on a television in the bar.

'Why only forty-six Tests?' asks a chapter in Don Mosey's *Laker* (1989) without really answering the question, for the bowler's 1944 first-class wickets at 18 seemed to cry out for longer than a decade at the top. In the last twenty-two Tests of Laker's career, he claimed 107 wickets at less than 16, but ended up gaining fewer England caps than Monty Panesar. He foreshadowed his retirement while en route to his only Australian tour, prefiguring the misfortunes that team would suffer. He published a biography, *Over to Me* (1960), trenchant for its time, scolding both May ('aloof and distant' with a 'fear of the press') and Colin Cowdrey ('Does silly things which no Test captain can afford') then wondering at the fuss: 'It's only the truth. What is everyone getting so excited about?' He became a drily humoured, hard-to-please pundit and commentator. He wore his fame lightly, to the point that it barely felt like fame, just something he had done. But what a thing.

# Richie Benaud

## THE GURU (2015)[*]

For most cricketers who transition to the media, it is a stepping back or stepping down. No matter how renowned they have been, or how accomplished they become in discharging their new duties, the glory available to them is now merely reflected, the fame on offer in a diluted form.

This iron law admits of one exception. Richie Benaud was a formidable cricketer and captain – perhaps as admired as any in his era of the late 1950s and 1960s. But his reputation only multiplied when he joined the ranks of cricket's interpreters. In both hemispheres he became the game's default voice, the figure you would want to commentate for your life.

'No man is better prepared,' read the citation for his 2003 lifetime achievement award from the Royal Television Society. 'Never mind the statistician alongside him, providing information – he's already worked out all the information for

---

[*] Written on Richie's death, aged eighty-four, on 10 April 2015.

himself. He also manages to make the modern game as compelling as the old game – every day for this remarkable person is as exciting as the day before.'

Benaud the commentator seldom referred to his on-field achievements – an astute measure which had the effect of making him seem almost ageless. Yet had he retired from the game to join a Trappist monastery he would rank among cricket's wisest captains and shrewdest leg-spinners.

Born in Penrith, Benaud was the son of a schoolmaster father whose career as a leg-spinner was limited by postings to country towns, Koorawatha, Warrandale and Jugiong. Lou Benaud introduced Richie to cricket with great, perhaps quietly vicarious, hopes, gifting him a first bat at the age of four, cut from the timber of a packing case, and overseeing his first competitive game at the age of six, on a coir mat pitch with a compressed cork ball. 'Cricket,' Benaud recalled, 'was talked breakfast, lunch and dinner in the Benaud household, every day I can remember.' Playing and talking: the successive careers were in outline long before their filling in.

When his family returned to Sydney, Benaud became a prodigious junior cricketer, a spinner of leg-breaks and a dashing bat, although he was a starstruck teenager when first chosen for New South Wales, and a callow twenty-one-year-old when picked for his debut Test in February 1952. For much of his first five years as a Test cricketer, he fluctuated like a barometer in stormy weather. He surged to 121 in ninety-eight minutes against the West Indies at Sabina Park in June 1955, turned India inside out at Kolkata just over a year later with 11 for 105. But his first twenty-seven matches yielded 73 wickets at 28.9 and 868 runs at 20.7. Neville Cardus accounted him 'inexplicable', capable of deeds 'which nobody merely talented is able to do', then guilty of 'gross and elementary errors'.

With the retirement of Australian captain Ian Johnson, however, Benaud abruptly fell upwards into the role of first-choice spinner. Seniority, said his biographer Johnny Moyes, suited him: 'Often in life and in cricket we see the man who has true substance in him burst forth into stardom when his walk-on part is changed for one demanding personality and a degree of leadership. I believe that this is what happened to Benaud.' Under Johnson's successor Ian Craig in South Africa in 1957–58, Benaud ripened suddenly and fruitfully, taking 106 wickets at 19 and scoring 817 runs at 50 in eighteen first-class matches on tour. When Craig contracted hepatitis on the eve of the 1958–59 Ashes series, Benaud filled the leadership breach as to the manner born.

Before the Tests, it was rumoured that England's captain Peter May had advised his players: 'Play Benaud down the line. He won't worry you.' He had been thinking of the old Benaud not the new; Australia's captain claimed 31 wickets at 18 in the 4–0 series victory. His strengths as a captain extended beyond all-round virtuosity and tactical acumen. Benaud led by both example and empathy, arguing that 'cricketers are intelligent people and must be treated as such', and recommending 'an elastic but realistic sense of self-discipline'. His team was blessed with one great player, Neil Harvey, and two greats in the making, Alan Davidson and Wally Grout. But Benaud's knack was for drawing the best from the most: on the 1961 Ashes tour, eight players made at least two hundreds, while nine took 40 wickets or more.

Benaud's other success was public. Head uncapped, shirt unbuttoned, he stood out in this short-back-and-sides era, a continuation of the spirit of his idol Keith Miller. A journalist himself – for some years, he worked as an ambulance-chasing police roundsman on Sydney's *Sun* – Benaud was also masterful in the presence of the media, to the extent of hosting them in the Australian dressing room. 'In public relations to benefit the game,' wrote Ray Robinson, 'Benaud was so far ahead of predecessors that race-glasses would have been needed to see who was at the head of the others.'

Benaud combined cricket and public relations most effectively during Australia's 1960–61 series against Frank Worrell's West Indians, which began with Test cricket's first tie, involved perhaps its tensest draw, and was played with an enterprise and generosity out of keeping with the austere times. Benaud and Worrell, wrote Jack Fingleton, 'set an example which other cricket countries will ignore at their peril'.

If other countries *did* largely ignore it, the trend at least rekindled the Ashes, whose 1961 instalment proved one of the best, Australia prevailing 2–1 after a stirring fightback at Old Trafford. England were 2–150 on the last day requiring only 106 to win at not quite a run a minute when Benaud, having taken 0–40 from seventeen overs, told his vice-captain Harvey: 'We've had it as far as saving this, Ninna. The only way we're going to get out of it is to win.' Indulging a hunch by coming round the wicket to target rough outside the right-hander's leg stump, Benaud took a match-winning 5–13 from twenty-five deliveries – one of nine five-fors during his twenty-eight Tests as captain, only four of which were lost. For teams he led, Benaud claimed 138 wickets at 25.7.

Benaud was above all shrewd. 'As a person,' commented his successor Bob Simpson, 'I think he planned every move from the time he got up to the time he went to bed.' This seemed truest of all in his choice of post-career media vocation. Not only had he already worked as a journalist and fraternized freely with them, but he had spent two weeks in London after the Ashes of 1956 studying television production, especially outside broadcast, at the BBC. After early dabblings in radio, Benaud settled into a role as an expert summarizer on

BBC Television's Test match coverage, while also writing columns for Sydney's *Sun* and London's *News of the World*.

As a commentator, Benaud had first the advantage of his own reputation and knowhow. But it was as much his manner that endeared him to the public: gnomic but undogmatic, cool but not humourless, dignified but not stuffy. 'If you can add to the picture, do so,' was his maxim. He stuck to it fastidiously. Benaud also harboured strongly held beliefs about the cricket labourer being worthy of his hire. He never forgot his own father's sacrificing of his cricket to keep his family; he asserted, as far back as 1960, that 'some players – made nothing out of tours', and opined that 'cricket is now a business'. In 1969 he published the wide-ranging *Willow Patterns*, and left the *Sun* to form a sports marketing consultancy with second wife Daphne (cricket writer E. W. Swanton's secretary, whom Benaud married in July 1967).

In this sense he made a natural fit with World Series Cricket, the brainchild of Channel 9 mogul Kerry Packer, when it was mooted in April 1977. A breakaway professional circuit, wrote Benaud, 'ran alongside my ideas about Australian cricketers currently being paid far too little and having virtually no input into the game in Australia'. And as consultant and commentator, he contributed inestimably. To the organization, he brought sporting savvy; to the presentation, he added a veneer of respectability. As Nine's front man, he provided the continuity amid two years of restless change and experimentation – night play, coloured clothing, the white ball, field restriction circles, television coverage from both ends of grounds with replays aplenty. He was present at its vindication, when a crowd in excess of 50,000 attended the SCG's first night match in November 1978 – something he said he'd not forget 'until the moment comes to make my way to that great vineyard cum cricket ground in the sky'.

When the cricket establishment sued for peace in April 1979, Benaud bridged that gap too. For the next quarter of a century, he was the television commentator of most people's choice on both sides of the globe, always spruce, never jaded, whether it was the first Test of an Ashes series, or the seventeenth one-day international in an interminable tri-series. Surrounded by increasingly garrulous colleagues, he maintained standards of economy and restraint. An audit of his commentary stints down the years would reveal a word ratio growingly in favour of the colleagues with whom he shared a microphone.

In fact, Benaud's natural vein made him the perfect commentator for the new order. Under the Nine regime, commentators had less time: commercial breaks deprived them of twenty-five seconds every over; the previous convention of the forty-minute stint was shortened to half an hour. The subtly smaller canvas played to Benaud's strengths. Nine also gradually relieved commentators of mundanities like repeating the score or reciting statistics by presenting these on-screen. Benaud could confine his scrupulously rationed remarks to what mattered, which probably no commentator has done so well.

Channel Four changed many aspects of cricket coverage in England when it replaced the BBC in 2000, but was compelled to recruit Benaud almost by popular demand. When he at last took his leave, in the Oval Test of 2005, the crowd and the players of both sides marked the end of his final stint by standing as one to salute him. In Australia, Benaud seemed to be continuing into perpetuity when his half-century of television was curtailed by an accident. In October 2013, aged eighty-three, he crashed his 1963 Sunbeam Alpine into a wall near his Coogee home, sustaining painful breakages.

His lengthy convalescence was punctuated by talk of

comebacks that never eventuated. His voice was last heard in an Australian cricket ground at Adelaide Oval in December: a moving recorded recitation of a tribute to the late Phillip Hughes. Another Benaud mot was that no commentator should ever reach for the word 'tragedy': the *Titanic* was a tragedy, he would say; what befell cricketers were, in the main, setbacks. Now the word was fitting, and Benaud proved that such events lay within his emotional register. The last words heard from him by a cricket audience were a gentle benediction: 'Rest in peace, son.'

# Alan Davidson

## 90 NOT OUT

The man on the mobility frame in the forecourt of Strathfield Plaza might be Alan Davidson. Another look. It's fifty-six years since he was perhaps Australia's finest all-rounder. It's half an hour before our scheduled meeting. But still the hawkish profile and crinkly hair give him away.

Alan turns ninety on Friday [14 June 2019]. His health hasn't been great. Late one night last year he slipped on a bathroom floor, fractured a knee cap and was confined to bed for three months as a surgeon's pins knitted him back together – he has a photo on his phone of the condition in which the ambulance men found him, his right leg twisted at a crazy angle, like a puppet whose strings have been cut. Trouble coming in threes, Alan, wife Betty (back trouble) and son Ian (cellulitis) were at one stage all in Concord Repatriation Hospital together.

What's worth noting about Alan's injury is that it wasn't part of a slide down, but the interruption of a busy life that has since resumed. He remains an advertisement for the health-giving properties of a full diary. Alan's *Who's Who in Australia* entry runs to fifty lines, full of board positions, voluntary roles and life memberships. He continues as chairman of Fresh Foods Australia and patron of Cricket New South Wales, of which he was president for thirty-three years. The Alan Davidson Shield, which involves 400 schools across New South Wales, lays claim to being the largest competition of its kind in the world.

Alan has lived in these parts seventy years, since 1957 in the same house. He's from an old Australia but comfortable in the new. What used to be Anglo is now decidedly not: in the last census, only thirty-five per cent of Strathfield residents were Australian-born. Still, everyone responds to a smile, don't they? His street is full of Indians and Sri Lankans, but the other night when he was struggling with his bins hands came from everywhere to help.

Plus there's cricket to draw people together. On the subject, he lights up. The shoulders are still broad. The left hand with which he demonstrates grips and variations is still massive – the middle finger that guided his lethal in-ducker and finessed his changes of pace resembles a raptor's talon. Alan will never do cricket or cricketers down, but he has his pet peeves. Why do they bowl round the wicket so much these days? He only ever did it once, and that was bowling slow stuff. And why don't they bowl more? The workload restrictions on bowlers these days – they're crazy. He invokes the great English seamer Alec Bedser: 'The way you become a great bowler is by bowling.'

Among Australia's current crop he likes Pat Cummins and Peter Siddle, who are at the batsmen morning til night. If Alan had a cardinal principle, it was that he never gave batsmen a sighter: half his 186 Test wickets at 20 were of batsmen in single figures, a third were bowled or lbw, and he conceded fewer than two runs an over.

It's on the matter of culture that Alan is most unconsciously revealing – unconsciously because Alan's generation did not think of it as 'culture' so much as of 'character'. His upbringing was simple, in farming country near Gosford since swamped by housing. 'I didn't know what a steak was until I got to Sydney,' he recalls. 'My mother knew how to cook rabbit ten different ways.'

Alan's first mentor was his maternal grandfather, Paddy Clifton, born in 1878, who electrified his grandson with tales of Victor Trumper and Drewy Stoddart. 'He was one who told me what the game was about, and what it represented,' Alan says. Paddy yoked bullocks and cut timber during the week, pillaged bowlers at weekends. Alan still has some of the scoring sheets, recording hundred after hundred. Paddy was strict, sparing in his praise. 'When are you going to learn to play a straight bat?' he would scold Alan, well into his Test career.

All the same, Paddy would stand no bullying. Alan remembers as a boy having to duck beneath a speedy bouncer from Billy Rogers, grandfather of the Australian opener Chris. Non-striker Paddy fastened the bowler with a basilisk stare: 'Do that again and I'll wrap this bat around your head.' Rogers desisted.

When Alan matured into a new-ball bowler, for Lisarow, he came up against his grandfather, for Ourimbah. 'That last summer in the bush, I took a hundred wickets at 6,' Alan remembers. 'The old man was sixty-seven. And guess what. He finished the day on 80 not out. I was good: the next summer I topped the averages in Sydney grade cricket. But how good was my grandfather?'

At Gosford Boys' High, Alan came under the influence of a stern headmaster in Jack Gibson, who insisted he view sport in proper proportion. 'Thanks to Jack Gibson, I took a book home every night,' Alan remembers. He recalls taking an encyclopedia home, and learning the word 'magnanimous' – it rather suits him.

Under family pressure to do otherwise, Alan stayed to complete his leaving certificate. The choice changed his life – he successfully sat an exam for the Commonwealth Bank, where he worked for twenty-six years. Alan still cherishes the congratulatory letter he received from Gibson when he was chosen for the NSW second XI in November 1949. 'I feel sure you have enough balance in your make-up not to allow success to go to your head and turn you into that most hateful of all things – a sporting snob,' wrote Gibson. 'He who bears his honours with modesty, and behaves himself as a good sportsman should is the one whom we admire.'

So modest was Alan that it took him ages to summon the courage to speak to a girl he liked who worked in the chemist shop near the Commonwealth Bank branch in Strathfield. He broke the ice in January 1950 by asking if Betty McKinley could recommend some seasickness tablets, although he did not divulge the reason – that he had been chosen for his first Australian tour, to New Zealand. He remembers the severe words of her protective brother Stanley: 'Alan, are your intentions honourable?'

Alan and Betty celebrated their sixty-seventh anniversary in May, and Alan describes her in the same terms as when they first met: 'Great dancer. Great swimmer, like Esther Williams. Go to the beach and she'd be further out than the lifesavers. Great support, always. Whatever I wanted to do, she backed me a hundred per cent.'

That guaranteed Betty some lonely, penurious times during Alan's career, which is why he remembers another figure, in an improbable role. Sid Barnes was Australian cricket's great controversialist of the 1950s: a superb opening batsman who played only thirteen Tests because of his regular rows with the establishment, which included effectively sueing the Australian Board of Control for defamation, and a newspaper column provocatively entitled 'Like it or Lump it'.

Yet Barnes took a warm and paternal interest in Alan. On the night in 1953 that Alan learned he was to tour England for the first time, Barnes knocked on his door in Strathfield. 'I've got a few bob and I know you've only got pennies,' Barnes said, giving the youngster his own cricket bag and cabin trunk. Observing that Betty was pregnant, Barnes promised to look after her while Alan was away, and did so. When their son Neil was born, Barnes covered the family's hospital expenses. Arriving home, Alan tried paying him back. 'You've got to be joking,' said Barnes and tore the cheque up.

Alan's captain on that first tour was Lindsay Hassett, Bradman's successor, wise and whimsical. Alan remembers his management of him as a cricketer and as a man. A tailender in his first match, at Leicester, Alan made a breezy 63 in an hour. 'You didn't tell me you could bat like that,' said Hassett. 'From now on, you're batting at seven.'

In that role, Alan made his maiden first-class hundred at Somerset. But when Australia bowled, Hassett whipped him off after a single over, let the spinners do the bulk of the bowling, and only spoke to him again at close of play. 'You probably think I was tough today,' the captain told him. 'You made your first hundred today. I just wanted to make sure you kept your feet on the ground.'

Does anything dismay Alan about modern cricket 'culture'? He won't be so outspoken, but addresses it indirectly: that is, the attitude to opponents. Alan knew all his opponents. Many of them ended up becoming friends. Codes of hospitality could almost be comical.

The first season Alan came to Melbourne to represent NSW against Victoria in the Boxing Day Sheffield Shield derby, the team were invited to spend Christmas Eve at the family home of the local champion Neil Harvey. First, though, Neil's father Horace had plans, and put these strong young men to work in his garden for some hours. Finally, one of Alan's teammates summoned the nerve to ask: 'Errrr, when do we eat?' Horace replied gruffly: 'When you've finished.'

After play on the third evening of the last Test of the 1961 Ashes, Alan was having a drink with Ken Barrington, England's ruggedly dependable number five. What was Alan doing the following night? Would he come along to help at a junior presentation night? They agreed to rendezvous at 6.30 p.m. It happened that Alan was bowling the last over of the day's play to Barrington, stubbornly ensconsed on 33. He finished the over with a fierce bouncer; rather than hook, Barrington stopped it with his chest. As stumps was called, spectators saw Barrington gesturing towards Alan with his bat, seemingly in remonstrance. In fact, he was saying: 'Remember! 6.30!'

Familiarity maintained behavioural bounds in play as well. During the Headingley Test, Barrington's teammate Colin Cowdrey was 93 when he gloved a ball down the leg side but looked like getting away with it when the umpire's finger stayed down. Cowdrey's reputation as a 'walker', even as a man of piety, was briefly jeopardized by the scent of a hard-won hundred. From Alan's wicketkeeper Wally Grout emanated a delicious sledge: 'Are you reading the lesson this Sunday, Colin?' Cowdrey hastily tucked the bat beneath his arm and departed.

Alan was content when he was done. He cherishes the compliment he received on retirement from Sir Donald Bradman, that he had 'played the game with integrity'. Mention of his grandfather brings to mind another vignette, of when Alan and Betty had grandpa Paddy to stay during the Sydney Test of 1961. Paddy enjoyed the match, the occasion, the comfortable home, the company of his grandsons. Not one to bestow praise lightly, he at last said quietly: 'You've done good, Alan.' So he has. So he has.*

---

* Alan died on 30 October 2021. He was ninety-two.

# Norm O'Neill

## WONDER BOY (2008)*

Fifty years ago no cricketer on earth excited such anticipation as Norman O'Neill, a powerful batsman and a superb cover fielder glowing with strength and health whose record breaking earned him hushed, then not-so-hushed, comparisons with Sir Donald Bradman. These were expectations that O'Neill, who has died aged seventy-one, could not fulfil – indeed, they would have overtaxed almost anyone. His Test career ended when he should have been entering his prime, and his six centuries now seem inconspicuous among modern statistics, inflated by the surfeit of international cricket.

O'Neill's flair and daring nonetheless won him fans and friends around the world. 'One of the greatest entertainers we've had in Australian cricket,' said his captain Richie Benaud. 'The art of batting, he reminded us, was not dead, merely inexplicably dormant,' decreed his era's leading critic,

---

* Written on the death of Norm O'Neill, 3 March 2008, aged seventy-one.

E. W. Swanton. So popular was O'Neill in the subcontinent that the parents in one cricket-crazy Karachi family named their new son for him: wicketkeeper Anil Dalpat became the first Hindu to represent Pakistan when he played nine Tests in the early 1980s.

The son of a builder from the Sydney suburb of Carlton, O'Neill was dismissed without scoring on his debut for New South Wales, aged eighteen, but his formative years were otherwise a pageant of successes. He topped the averages in the Australian summer of 1957–58 with 1005 runs at 83.75, needing just four hours to score 233 against Victoria, including thirty-eight fours; he also claimed 26 wickets at 20 with quickish leg-breaks.

English bowlers were eager to test him out when he represented the Combined XI against the MCC in a tour match at Perth in November 1958, and he showed an unsuspected steeliness in spending four and a half hours over 104, even eschewing the hook shot that usually brought him many runs. 'I was under t'impression thee 'ooked bloody bumpers,' Fred Trueman chided him. O'Neill stared back inscrutably, and instead showed off his arsenal of offside shots, including a backfoot cover drive that became his signature.

The Englishmen elected to nag away at leg stump when O'Neill made his Test debut at Brisbane, but he enlivened the last two hours of a funereal game with an unbeaten 71 out of 89 added while he was at the wicket. 'Although O'Neill is in the very early stages of his career,' noted Ian Peebles of the *Sunday Times*, 'it is already something of an occasion when he comes to the wicket, and one can sense the expectancy of the crowd and the heightened tension of the opposition.' This never changed.

O'Neill presently found himself in demand. Not only was he courted by South Australia, where a grocery magnate offered him a hearty inducement to move, but he was invited to train with the New York Yankees. A talented pitcher and short stop, he had emulated his uncle in representing his state, and been named the utility player in the 1957 All-Australian team. The sports-mad chairman of the local arm of the tobacco giant Rothmans of Pall Mall, Sir Ronald Irish, persuaded the young man to stick to cricket with the offer of a job, and O'Neill bolted to 1000 runs in his fourteenth Test, at which stage his average was 68.

Thereafter, however, O'Neill's form fluctuated. For a batsman so instinctively aggressive, he suffered badly from nerves and was acutely superstitious. 'Batting is a lonely business,' he noted in his 1964 autobiography *Ins and Outs*, admitting that he sometimes found cricket at the top level to be 'depressing and lonely'. An admirer gave him a 'lucky coin' before the Oval Test of August 1961 and, dropped at 19, he bludgeoned 117. He scored 1981 runs on that Ashes tour and was named one of *Wisden*'s Five Cricketers of the Year. His wife Gwen, who had won relay gold in the 1954 Empire Games, prepared him a pair of 'lucky lemon socks' before the Adelaide Test of January 1963 and he compiled a much-needed hundred. But he then went fifteen innings without a half-century before making 51 and 74 not out in what proved his last Test, at Bridgetown, Barbados, in May 1965, and his international career ended soon after in some ignominy.

One of several Australian players infuriated by the bowling action of the West Indian Charlie Griffith, O'Neill agreed to put his name to a series of feature articles in Sydney's *Daily Mirror* branding Griffith 'an obvious chucker' whom the hosts had been 'wrong to play'. He stated: 'If he is allowed to continue throwing, he could kill someone.'

When the *Mirror* syndicated the articles, London's *Daily Mail* ignored an embargo and put O'Neill in breach of his tour contract by making a comment in the media before the end of the tour. He was never sure if the misdemeanour marked his card, but O'Neill had represented Australia for the last time at Test level. He remained at Rothmans, at probable cost to his health, being dogged in his last years by throat cancer. O'Neill's 13,805 first-class runs at 51.51, including forty-five centuries, suggest that he was shortchanged by his forty-two Tests. The reflections of contemporaries imply that he has been historically underestimated. 'A disappointment he was, perhaps,' concluded Swanton, 'but his cricket will be recalled when those of lesser gifts are forgotten.'

# Bob Cowper

## THE 307 (2016)

Test match triple-centuries have become a little passé, with fifteen in the last twenty years, but there have still been only three in Australia. This weekend sees the fiftieth anniversary of the first of these, which remains the only one in Ashes Test matches here: 307 at the MCG by local boy Bob Cowper – known universally as Wallaby, for his father's having captained Australia at rugby union.

This was an innings notable for scale rather than event, a sort of statistical Ayers Rock: it spanned 727 minutes and 590 balls in a drawn Test ending the drawn 1965–66 series. The duration was further exaggerated still. Cowper went in at 4.22 p.m. on Saturday 12 February, the second day, and was 32 not out at the close. After a rest day Sabbath, he proceeded on Monday to 159 not out, whereupon rain blotted out the whole of Tuesday, and it took a lovely ball from Barry Knight to bowl him at 4.34 p.m. on Wednesday.

'Immediately Cowper was dismissed, Bobby Simpson declared,' reported Ken Mackay in his tour book *In Quest of the Ashes* (1966). 'And as the young Victorian walked into the shadows of the MCG, proud Melbourne folk rose to receive him. He looked surprisingly fresh as he came through the players' gate past cheering, back-slapping grounds members.' That he looked fresh was surprising indeed: thanks to the waterlogged outfield and the immensity of the unrestricted MCG, Cowper had had to run no fewer than twenty-six threes. Records at such a granular level can be hard to obtain, but this must surely be unique. For comparative purposes, Don Bradman hit six threes in his 334, Len Hutton fifteen threes in his 364, Hanif Mohammad sixteen threes in his 337. There is a whole tale to tell here, by the by, about the decline of the three: Brian Lara hit only four threes in his 400 not out at Antigua, Matthew Hayden only one in his 380 not out in Perth. Their decline, of course, comes in inverse proportion to the weight of fours and sixes. Cowper scored twenty-six per cent of his runs in boundaries; in Ben Stokes's 258 a month ago in Cape Town, the ratio was seventy-two per cent.

The span of Cowper's innings is further uniquely evoked by its beginning with his country using one currency and ending with it using another. As he wandered to the crease on Saturday, Australians were preparing to trade their pounds in for dollars. *The Age*'s vital statistics for play on Saturday document a record gate taking in pounds, with the putative sum in dollars in brackets. *The Age*'s board for play on Monday, the first day of decimal currency, report the takings in reverse, with dollars out front, and the obsolete pounds equivalent in brackets. Test matches, eh? What other game can toddle along at its own pace while wholesale national change takes place, and accommodate it effortlessly? Hats off to Wallaby, then, for a curious landmark, but a very cricket-y one all the same.

# Doug Walters
## STRAIGHT OUTTA DUNGOG (2015)

In his lovely chapter in *Australia: Story of a Cricket Country* (2011), musician Robert Forster (b.1957) describes Doug Walters as Australia's 'first "Sixties" cricketer', being 'to my amazed calculation only eleven years older than me': 'Walters instantly felt close, and suddenly the Australian cricket team (and life itself) didn't seem so far off either, and to be staffed by older men such as Brylcreemed Bob Simpson or Bill Lawry, or my male teachers at school or even my father.' Walters was nineteen on the occasion of that debut century in Forster's home town of Brisbane, lean and fresh-faced beneath a cap that seemed too big for him: the England players who shook his hands on the achievement of the milestone looked like the indulgent parental opponents in a fathers versus sons game.

It comes as a slight shock that Walters today [21 December 2015] turns seventy. The arc of his career was flatter than most. Precociously mature as a youngster, he never seemed to change much, in features, in style, in role. Nobody ever promoted Walters as a candidate to captain Australia; nobody has ever suggested he would make a great coach, commentator or selector; he has gone his whole life being Dougie, crowd pleaser, team favourite, anecdote machine, most of the stories evoking his nonchalance. In *Passing Tests* (1973), for example, Ian Chappell recalled Walters announcing before an Australian tour match that he needed some practice. Shock was expressed, glances exchanged. Walters picked up a dart and threw it at a board on the dressing room wall. 'I'm loose,' he said, deadpan.

The statistical expression of Walters's enigma is undoubtedly his record in England, which he toured four times without a Test hundred. On his debut in England at Manchester, Walters scored an accomplished 81 and 86 in an Australian victory. In seventeen further Tests on English soil across four tours he averaged 21.4. Yet in every other country round the world – Australia, West Indies, India, South Africa – he averaged 56.24. Perhaps it was the success elsewhere that made for the underachievement in England: the determination to play his natural game which made him so formidable elsewhere discouraged remedial technical action necessary in England – the case of a strength become a weakness. Mind you, he may have been more capable of change than imagined: after all, the man who used to try to smuggle a packet of Rothmans Filters into team photographs gave up smoking five years ago.

Anyway, no mention of Walters is complete without the tale of his 103 at the WACA in December 1974, which in highlights packages is one imperious pull shot after another – played the old-fashioned way, with the back foot going across, a roll of the wrist and a battle-axe swipe of the bat. The penultimate ball, we can see, almost produced a single off a misfield. Thank goodness it did not, given the superbly defiant denouement – that immortal pull shot off Bob Willis, in front of square, for six, completing his century in a session. Walters seems to be halfway off by the time the ball lands, as though he has just disposed of a pressing and irksome chore. Happy birthday KDW, once glimpsed, not forgotten.

# THE INSTANT AGE

*The year 1972 is a neglected hinge point in Ashes history. Not only did it presage the rise of a great Australian team, led by the Chappells, and including Dennis Lillee and Rod Marsh, but it involved the first Test seen via satellite on the other side of the world – something we now take for granted, but which, also in an Olympiad, heightened sport's immediacy of impact and instancy of judgement. You had seen it. Everyone had seen it. How did your impression compare? And who were these men, suddenly so visible, so familiar? Participants in the Ashes now loomed larger than ever. They became, in fact, valuable, commercially as well as culturally, as Kerry Packer would be first to realize, disrupting an Ashes year when he made his play in World Series Cricket. The balance of global cricket power was shifting also: South Africa were in extended exile, West Indies at their long peak, Asia was rising. But, notably in 1981, Anglo-Australian cricket achieved new peaks of glamour and drama.*

# The 1972 Ashes

## EVEN, TEMPERED (2016)

ive being an odd number, Ashes series are implicitly directed towards a decisive outcome. Yet every so often, one has finished with honours even, including consecutively in 1965–66 and 1968, each featuring three rather wearying draws. The Ashes of 1972 belongs in a subtly different category, the touring team having been uniquely compelled to come back twice from deficits: played out, as John Arlott put it, 'at full competition without acrimony' and providing 'constant surprise and suspense', it is in some respects a forgotten classic of the Test genre, owned by nobody. And although Ian Chappell's team were to leave the trophy behind, their spirit and skill heralded a resurgence in Australian cricket after a period of austerity. With the addition of a few moustaches and the exposure of a little more chest hair, this was the team that would lead the decade, the names of Chappell, Lillee, Marsh, Stackpole, Edwards, Walters and Mallett et al. coming trippingly from the tongue.

In advance of the tour, Australian Test selector Neil Harvey told Chappell that he had been charged with 'a team of goers'

– this was by way of consoling him for the non-selection of Australia's most experienced batsman, Bill Lawry, and pace bowler, Graham McKenzie. If some choices yielded little, they were all decisively forward-looking, and on which the captain was free to place his stamp. Just as well, perhaps, that he had one. Grandsons of a former Australian captain, Victor Richardson, Ian and his brother Greg liked their cricket with a touch of flair and a philosophy of selflessness. England, meanwhile, was cannily captained by Ray Illingworth, and contained many of the players he had led successfully while recapturing the Ashes eighteen months earlier. After 31 wickets at 23 against Australia away, John Snow would take 24 wickets at 23 against them at home, a noteworthy double.

The Australian campaign began inauspiciously. At Old Trafford, they extended to twelve their streak without an Ashes victory, suffering an 89-run defeat, mainly by losing all ten first-innings wickets for 74. The twenty-five-year-old South African émigré Tony Greig marked his Test debut with 57 and 62, five wickets for 74 and a crucial slip catch. But Snow's eight for 128 was matched by Lillee's eight for 106, and the game's highest scorer, with 91 from 111 balls to complement six catches, was the pugnacious Rod Marsh. The emerging dynamic was of experience versus energy, and at Lord's it veered back violently.

The Second Test ranks as one of the most extraordinary of all. In 1970, West Australian Bob Massie had come to England to try his luck, taken three expensive second XI wickets at Northants, and not been offered a contract. Now, in dim and muggy conditions, he swung, swerved and slanted the ball every which way, transfixing batsman after batsman from the Nursery End, from round the wicket as well as over: by early on the second day, he had become only the third bowler to claim eight Test wickets on debut.

In defiance of Snow, Ian Chappell made a militant half-century and Greg Chappell a poised and controlled century, with their parents, brother Trevor and long-time coach Chester Bennett in the crowd. Greg would regard his 131 in 373 minutes as the best innings of his career: in conditions demanding vigilance in the 'V', it took him three hours to strike the first of his fourteen boundaries. In the middle, he counted his runs in silent 10s; at intervals, he would sit away from his teammates so as not to let his concentration slip. In more light-hearted but hardly less crucial vein, Marsh hit two sixes and six fours in 50.

Massie then proved even more effective and hypnotic in the second innings, breaking through every time Ian Chappell was on the point of resting him. All sixteen of his wickets, for 137 in sixty overs, were bowled, lbw or caught behind the wicket. Never again would Massie obtain such parabolic movement – he would play five more Tests for only fifteen further victims. But his figures at Lord's remain the best by a pace bowler in Anglo-Australian annals. Just as amazingly, Australia's eight-wicket victory was its first Test win of the decade. It was celebrated with such gusto that Lillee at a royal reception a few hours later introduced himself to the Queen with a timeless 'G'day.'

Still slightly spooked by Lillee and Massie when the Third Test began at Trent Bridge two weeks later, Illingworth responded to another overcast morning by sending the visitors in, only for hundreds by Keith Stackpole and Ross Edwards to build Australia an unassailable advantage. Eventually, Australia set England 451 to win in 561 minutes in the final innings. 'Outplayed, outmanoeuvred and outclassed,' as Arlott put it in *The Guardian*, the hosts needed all their professional aplomb to ensure a stalemate.

Reporting for *The Cricketer*, John Woodcock described the

Fourth Test at Headingley as 'one of the most controversial Test matches of recent times'. If anything, this was an understatement. In freezing damp before the match, grounds-man George Cawthray's alarmingly piebald pitch was stricken with a fungus called fuserium. The result was a surface that every so often produced something unplayable and otherwise generated the mainly untimeable. Not since Old Trafford in 1956 had slow bowlers exerted such a thrall, 22 of 31 wickets falling to spin over the game's eight hectic sessions. Illingworth's first-innings 57 was the match's only half-century, the 104 he added with Snow for England's eighth wicket one of only two partnerships worth more than 50. Derek Underwood, in conditions tailored to his insidious left-arm deceptions, claimed ten for 82 from 51 overs, ensuring that the Ashes remained in English custody. After the match, Cawthray's dubious surface was lugubriously dug up – as far as Australians were concerned, one game too late.

Beginning on 10 August, the Fifth Test at The Oval was the first in England to be televised live in Australia; it would round out, too, the first Ashes captain's diary, being kept by Ian Chappell for publication as *Tigers Among The Lions* (1972). The cricket fully lived up to its expanded global audience. Lillee, his walk back a hearty forty-four paces, his run-up as untamed as his hair, hurled himself into the fray on the first day, and with three wickets in four balls reduced England to seven for 159. They were revived by an irreverent partnership between Alan Knott and Geoff Arnold of 81 in sixty-nine minutes, but Australia after two early losses took control, in the person of the brothers Chappell. For the first time in a series dominated by the ball, a session passed without a wicket; for the first time in history, brothers each scored a century in the same innings of a Test match. In six years of first-class cricket, the pair had only once added a hundred; now they added twice that, in just over four hours, and Australia secured the lead for the loss of three wickets. Underwood kept England's arrears to 115, but England then lost three wickets in erasing it.

With the match to be played to a completion, the fluctuations never ceased. Dropped catches impeded Australia's progress; the second new ball expedited it; Knott and the tail again proved hard to remove. With ten for 181, Lillee's series record grew to 31 wickets at 17.7, an Australian record to that time; gate receipts, meanwhile, swelled to a world record of more than £250,000. Australia began the sixth morning, the last of the series, needing 126 with nine wickets in hand – on a wearing wicket against Underwood, harder than it sounded. They lost three for 5 in twenty-five minutes; they went a quarter of an hour without a run; another wicket at this point and a 1–3 defeat would have been distinctly possible. Injuries to Illingworth and Snow tilted the balance back. With positive, perky strokes either side of lunch, Marsh and Paul Sheahan put on the 71 necessary to square the series, a widely published photograph of their excited, arm-in-arm dash for the pavilion at the end symbolizing the strides their cricket had taken.

If later Australian cricket sides would at times invest too much in machismo, this one, as Woodcock noted in *The Cricketer*, was respected for courtesy as well as competitiveness; it even got on with its manager Ray Steele, who admired the captain's 'basic down-to-earth attitude and freedom from humbug'. 'We're a young team and this tour has done a great deal to teach us how to play under variable conditions,' said Ian Chappell after the series. 'The team should be better the next time we meet England in our own country in 1974–75.' By then they were without the retired Stackpole and the faded Massie, but the volatile Jeff Thomson and the reliable Max Walker had joined Lillee in a to-die-for pace unit. England were also sans Illingworth, curtly sacked in September 1973 despite a record of twelve Test wins and only five defeats. Two-all, then, belied the teams' funicular fates: well-matched as they were for the summer, they were trending in opposite directions.

# Greg Chappell

## THE GOLD STANDARD (2011)

Australian cricket doesn't have much time for elegance. It looks unserious, brittle, even a little effete. Australians favour aggression – bustling, bristling, business-like. They like to think of themselves as all about effect and output; it's not how but how many. For Greg Chappell, they made an exception.

The elegance did not, of course, come first. For more than a decade Chappell was the gold standard of Australian batting. He was like bullion in the vaults: the reserve currency. In the speculative side you chose at the pub, you put down his name at number four, then started on the rest. I dare say Australia's selectors were the same. So Chappell did what was in him, and it *happened* to be beautiful. He set himself high standards by scoring a hundred on debut in Perth's inaugural Test match, against England, in December 1970, and fastidiously maintained them.

Yet it *did* matter that he achieved this by looking a treat. After an early tightening of his technique, there was no stage in Chappell's career when he was not a dazzling strokemaker.

Nobody ever enjoined him to 'bat ugly'; it would hardly have been possible. He had a bearing, a majesty, even in repose. He might have played three maidens, but if one dropped into the slot you knew it would be on-driven for four; he might take three hours over the first 50, but the second 50 would take forty-five minutes with barely a hint of extra effort.

Chappell was a tall, taut, lean man – even a little austere. He played his cover drive from full height. The bat came down straight. The weight surged through the ball. It looked imperious. It *was* imperious. As a spectator, you felt the wash of disdain – how it must have felt to bowlers. As for the leg side, you sensed he could have nominated any of its 180 degrees and hit it there, particularly behind square, the quadrant into which he directed his signature, wristy, upright flick. He never hurried, never seemed to push too hard, never thrashed or slogged when a stroke would do – he just made up his own rules and followed them, without deviation.

Between balls and times, Chappell looked a little uptight, his pipe-cleaner man's physique emphasized by a shirt buttoned to the neck, sleeves always to the wrist. His stance was stiff-legged, over-topped by a stoop. The bat made a rhythmic tap, before one final, faintly voluptuous loop to-wards gully. Then, with the ball in flight, everything changed. The bat and body snapped into line. The hands aligned perfectly at slip. Chappell didn't take spectacular catches, fumbles or rebounds – his anticipation was too good to need to. The ball simply vanished and never reappeared. When the Ashes returned to Perth in December 1974, he took no fewer than seven catches, and with notable ease.

The effect was strangely humbling. When Chappell reached 200 at the Gabba in December 1981, a spectator bounced off the old Hill there and began haring for the centre, pursued at the plod by security – a year before the misfortune of Terry Alderman, such invaders were an annoyance rather than a threat. It wasn't to slap Chappell on the back or obtain his autograph that this man came either: he took the batsman's gloved hand, went down on one knee and bowed his head, as if genuflecting to royalty. Watching Chappell put John Arlott in mind of William Clarke's description of Joe Guy: 'All ease and elegance, fit to play before the Queen in Her Majesty's parlour.' It was something to provoke similar spontaneous homage from the Aussie egalitariat.

It was not all patrician airs and drawing-room decorum, of course. Most people know that Chappell scored a century in his first Test. Not everyone remembers that he did so batting at number seven, bowling his medium pace as the first-change bowler. He was joining a rather embattled team, recently mauled in South Africa and about to lose the Ashes, too. Nor did he immediately impress as a permanent fixture. A couple of months before the Australian team to tour England in 1972 was chosen, his place was uncertain.

Chappell's batting crystallized when abundant natural talent was harnessed by an anchorite's self-control. Early in his career he played his shots with a generous abandon. His biographer Adrian McGregor explains that the admonitions of Chappell's father, and of the respected Adelaide journalist Keith Butler, caused him to undergo some soul-searching. Nine times out of ten, Chappell reasoned, a batsman blew himself up. He must not indulge bowlers so. He sacrificed none of his strokes – Richie Benaud had enjoined him not to. He simply developed a mental self-discipline more severe than any contemporary's: his 131 at Lord's in 1972 made a mockery of conditions in which others floundered. Chappell's was the first generation to take the mental side of cricket in earnest, reading Rudi Webster's *Winning Ways* (1984), visiting the hypnotherapist Arthur Jackson, invoking the 'flow' of psychologist Mihaly Czikszentmihalyi. They were lucky in already having good techniques – later players thought positive thinking could do the work for them. Chappell, however, was a class apart. He may even have imparted some of his drive to brother Ian, whose average after Greg joined him in the Test team was 12 runs higher than before.

There was something slightly forbidding about this. In contrast to Ian, a natural leader of men, Greg confessed himself only a 'workmanlike' captain. Even to teammates he could look stern, schoolmasterly. Geoff Lawson has described the agonies of entering the Australia team in 1980, of Chappell with hands on hips at slip 'as if to say, "Don't bowl that crap, son," every time I bowled a half-volley or got hit for a boundary': he deemed Chappell 'one of the poorest captains that I had ever played under'. His confrères Dennis Lillee and Rod Marsh found Chappell a more communicative and empathic captain after he had tasted ruinous failure in the summer of 1981–82. The struggles of others became more explicable in terms of his own.

Chappell's great indiscretion was the underarm delivery. Most cricket conflicts arise from adrenaline, anger, petulance. Here was a rare counter-example, originating in the opposite state of mind, from a coldly rational assessment of problem and of probabilities, involving a solution on Chappell's mind since a one-day match during World Series Cricket had been won off the last ball by a tailender's six. Chappell's decision is generally construed as a momentary lapse, an instance of judgement impaired by tiredness. Yet it might also be seen as one of Chappell's truest actions – evidence of his analytical mind and unsentimental nature. Producers in Channel 9's commentary position used to direct cameramen to vision of Chappell with a terse instruction: 'Give us a shot of Killer.' Killers are as killers do.

Chappell's self-mastery might have come harder than it appears. He retired twice in his career, once publicly in 1977, once privately in 1982, when his form was at its worst, before reconsidering. When he came back to lead Australia to victory in the Ashes of 1982–83, his 114 at Adelaide Oval showed all his old severity. He also developed considerable business interests, as though he aspired to leave cricket behind. When they did not fructify, he remained in the game with a seeming ambivalence. Few men know batting better, but his coaching record is indifferent. He commentates knowledgeably though without much enthusiasm. He quit noisily as an Australian selector in the 1980s, and has returned more than twenty years later, this time in the created role of national talent manager. He is not the only cricketer, of course, unable to find a place in life as conducive as the crease. Nor in art is it rare for beauty to arise from hidden struggle.

# Dennis Lillee

## THE MAN WHO NEEDS NO INTRODUCTION (2011)

D ennis Lillee still does television advertisements in Australia. There's more hair under his lip than on his head these days, and it's decidedly grey. He also has this signature gesture of pointing to the camera no matter what he's promoting, which he's been doing at least twenty years. But what's interesting about Lillee's ads is that his provenance is never explained. There's no: 'Back in the days when I was bowling to Viv . . .' Nor is there any attempt at an expository caption: 'D. K. Lillee, 355 wickets at 23.92.' Nope: here is a man who needs no introduction, and won't be getting one.

Maybe explanation is just too hard. This is the era of the speed gun, yet Lillee wasn't the fastest of his era by a long way. This is the age of getting it in 'good areas', of just nagging away, of waiting for the batsmen to make a mistake, yet Lillee reminded you always why it is a 'bowling attack', not a 'bowling defence'. This is a time of instant and perishable celebrity, yet more than twenty-seven years after bowling his last delivery in Test cricket, Dennis Lillee remains one of his country's most recognizable cricket faces, despite his having remained a stranger to commentary, and making comparatively few public pronouncements – the ones he does make, like lauding Mitchell Johnson to the skies or calling the Australian top order 'Dad's Army', tend accordingly to be treated as *ex cathedra* truths.

So why did Lillee capture Australian imagination – and then not give it back? Firstly, he emerged in barren years. For most of the 1960s, Australia got by on the smooth control of Garth McKenzie, with a bit of brawn from Neil Hawke and some solid persistence from Alan Connolly. The most menacing bowler around was Ian Meckiff, famous for all the wrong reasons. Lillee's hero growing up was not Australian at all. Just as Ray Lindwall first thrilled to Harold Larwood, so Lillee was inspired by watching Wes Hall bowl for West Indies at the WACA Ground in November 1960. He emerged as a teenager with a marathon run and wild eyes. To watch footage of Lillee in England in 1972 is to see fast bowling at its raw, riotous best. The legs pump, the arms are everywhere, the mane flows. It looks like a brilliant and crazy machine bound sooner or later to disintegrate – which it duly did.

This leads to the second aspect of Lillee's greatness. For fast bowlers these days, stress fractures are almost as hip as tattoos. In those days, they went undiagnosed, usually until it was too late, and when Lillee's back gave way his spine was fractured in three places. In those days, too, a cricketer's physicality was his own affair. There was little or no support from the game's administration. Lillee's recovery came under his own steam, and by his own resources, thanks to a doctor, Frank Pyke, who had been Lillee's physical education instructor at Belmont High School.

Pyke was a top-class Australian rules footballer, a runner-up in his league's Sandover Medal, and a first-grade opening bowler at Lillee's club, Perth. This was important. The treatment and exercise programme Pyke devised was specifically with cricket in mind. It was about rejuvenation as well as healing. It left Lillee aware as perhaps no bowler before him of his body, of its limits and of how to extend them; it contributed also to Lillee's sense of individuality, and mistrust of authority. Which leads to the third and fourth aspects of Lillee's significance.

In coming back from being perhaps as far gone as a bowler has been without actually quitting, Lillee worked his way towards what he condensed in the title of his second book, *The Art of Fast Bowling* (1977). Bradman had defined *The Art of Cricket* (1960), but his were batsmen's parameters. Bowling fast was commonly seen as an act of brute force and ignorance; in writing their book, Lillee, with Pyke's assistance, was crafting something as improbable as *The Art of Bulldozing*.

In the second half of Lillee's career, he did more than any other to expand the grammar of fast bowling. Having started his career simply with an outswinger, Lillee developed a change of pace, a yorker, leg and offcutters, a fast bouncer and slower bouncer. He perfected a shorter run. He experimented with different angles at the crease. Perhaps the definitive essay in Lillee's transformation was a Test in February 1980 on a low and pebbly Melbourne pitch, on which he would not have known how to bowl five years earlier, but on which he now obtained 11 English wickets for 138 bowling impossibly accurate cutters. Geoff Boycott, in prime form, shouldered arms to a ball two feet wide of off stump, only to see the width of Lillee's angle and the wickedness of his cut drag it back to kiss the timber.

For fast bowlers the world over, Lillee became a touchstone, in temperament as well as technique. 'As far as I am concerned, the sign of an outstanding player is his ability to perform well constantly under pressure,' said Imran Khan. 'He must always be a complete team man. The bowler who stands out is Dennis Lillee.' He remembered Lillee coming over to sympathize with and encourage him after a Melbourne Test in which Lillee had bagged ten for 135 and Imran five for 237; Imran bagged a dozen in the next game. For Richard Hadlee, it was a case of WWLD: 'When things are going badly I often think, "What would Lillee do?" And the answer is: "He would not give up."'

Most interestingly, Lillee became a master of concentration, often discussed in the context of batting, almost never as a factor in bowling. He called his first autobiography *Back to the Mark* (1975), and always made this walk a fascinating sight, headed back straight, unsmiling, eyes ahead, gazing into a middle distance. He had this characteristic gesture: a single finger to the forehead. It went from the centre to his left, then back to the right, flicking off sweat like a windscreen wiper. The ball by this stage would have been conveyed round the Australian infield to mid-off, who would be polishing it furiously. Lillee would turn his head just slightly right, and extend his arm just above shoulder height. Mid-off's throw would have to be timed precisely so that Lillee did not have to alter his stride, and could catch the ball in one hand. The ball would then continue with Lillee the length of his run, being shone meditatively the rest of the way. As he turned at his bowling marker, all was genuinely in readiness. The cricket spoke for itself and still does.

# Rod Marsh

## PEOPLE'S CHAMPION (2022)[*]

There is a wonderful photograph of Rod Marsh accompanying Dennis Lillee on a walk to fine leg at the MCG in 1975. Lillee is staring ahead, sweat-soaked and seething, at odds with his captain Greg Chappell about field placements. Marsh, shaggy hair protruding from beneath his baggy cap, is walking in step with and looking upwards at his mate, solicitous and attentive; you can see his gloved hand patting Lillee's backside.

I once asked Rod, who has died aged seventy-four, to talk me through what was happening. Was he agreeing with Lillee or Chappell? 'I disagreed with Dennis on a few things, but I never let him know,' Rod chuckled confidentially. 'And I could get him to change his mind without him being aware of it.' Rod paused. 'The best I could.' Then he laughed

---

* Written on the death of Rod Marsh, 4 March 2022, aged seventy-four. Little did I know when I commented they were 'starting to go now' that I would be writing about Shane Warne in the past tense within twenty-four hours.

224

again: 'He could have been double-bluffing me.'

I loved the respect, affection and shrewdness of that answer. Rod knew cricket, of course, but he also knew people, and that combination made him perhaps the definitive Australian cricketer of the 1970s and 1980s. Others led; others starred; but, day-in, day-out, Rod personified the game in this country as perhaps no other player: aggressive, rugged and bristlingly competitive, but also democratic and companionable.

The people's star. The man of partnerships, of which 'caught Marsh bowled Lillee' was cricket's greatest catechism. Those stocky legs; those hairy forearms; the definitive moustache; the growl of his appeal, usually one arm raised. Above all, of course, his job. Nobody in his era felt cricket more than Rod, through his hands, and into his heart. In some ways, I suspect that Rod subtly invented that idea of the wicketkeeper being a team's unifier, rather than merely functional or auxiliary.

I remember Alan Crompton, an administrator who managed many an Australian team on tour, saying that Rod was the centre of every XI he formed part of. The noise, the chatter and the laughter that is the soundtrack of every successful and harmonious side, came unfailingly from Rod's corner of the dressing room.

Ian Chappell tells another story. At the time there was a superb but ageing writer, Ray Robinson – one the players read avidly and trusted to sit in their dressing room at close of play. But Robbie suffered gravely from ulcers, and could not stomach frothy beer. So, at tea every day, Rod would take the top off a long neck so that it was flat by stumps for Robbie to partake of.

Lest we forget, Rod was a genuinely great cricketer – greater than was recognised at the time maybe. Keepers' statistics are difficult to interpret. Their chief attributes are reliability and unobtrusiveness. Rod's metier was keeping to fast bowling, throwing himself for catches, diving after wides, leaping for bouncers. For such a seemingly earthbound figure, he was remarkably agile, sometimes seemingly weightless. There would be more photographs of Rod airborne than almost any other keeper in history. There are also those catches you simply remember.

Here's mine: second International Cup final, 28 January 1979, VFL Park. Lawrence Rowe top-edged Greg Chappell towards fine leg, where it looked like falling short of Lillee, sprinting off the boundary. Rod ran thirty metres, twisting and turning, but never losing sight of the ball over his shoulder, like a butterfly collector chasing a precious specimen, finally diving to complete the catch. I saw it once. I have never seen a replay, but don't need to – I remember it clear as day.

But if he sometimes looked like clothes had been pitch-forked onto him, Rod was also a deceptively tidy keeper. He would lightly push his gloves on before descending into his crouch; he would take the ball neatly on the inside of his body; the nickname 'Iron Gloves' was bestowed on him after some faulty early performances, but gradually became a sort of endearment, signifying resilience and dependability.

As a coach at the AIS Cricket Academy, Rod was almost, if not quite, a martinet. He had high standards. He was tough, and caring; he was harsh, and forgiving. He welcomed Ricky Ponting and Glenn McGrath; he welcomed Shane Warne back; he enlisted his own generation in the making of the new.

In 1993, I went to interview Rod at the academy. We walked around, bumping into its people: young cricketers, assistant coaches, ground staff. He had that fascinating capacity for seeming to find the right chord with everyone, alternately gruff, direct, mellow, humorous. It was as though he had brought his understanding of dressing room dynamics to life. We stopped to watch Dennis coaching the young fast bowlers. You felt that effortless continuity between past and present.

When the academy wound up, Rod was recruited by England's counterpart, and proved instrumental in the rise of cricketers as diverse as roommates Andrew Strauss and Graeme Swann. Rod told Strauss he didn't think he'd make it; it motivated Strauss to prove he could. Swann tells a story of his introduction, which involved the cheeky young Englishman calling Rod 'an ignorant cunt' to his face in a jest he suddenly repented. 'You know when you've totally misread a situation,' Swann recalled. For the next three years Swann chafed against the discipline, but gradually honed his abilities and ambitions.

Rod finally called Swann to his office, and asked the spinner what he wanted from the game. Swann said he wanted to play for England. Rod said he could: 'I've spent the summer watching county cricket and you are the best spinner. Full stop.' Then: 'I'm not a man to hold a grudge. Even against someone who calls me an ignorant cunt . . .'

Swann cringed. A belated and craven apology spilled out. Rod offered a laughing handshake: 'Go and take some wickets!' For England, Swann would take 410.

They're starting to go now. David Hookes, of course, tragically predeceased them all. But last October's passing of Ashley Mallett heralded the twilight of the generation who excited and awed those of us now in middle age, and who in some ways stayed our heroes and benchmarks. In their feats and their attitudes, though, you can still see all of cricket, what's changed and what remains the same.

# John Edrich

## FIGHTING CRICKETER (1995)[*]

S ome English captains step in as though assuming an
ancestral seat; others a professorial chair, or a family
heirloom. John Edrich fell like a penny into the slot.
Despite two decades' preparation as a professional cricketer,
the Surrey left-hander had less than half an hour's notice that
he and not the designated Mike Denness would toss with Ian
Chappell on 4 January 1975 in what shaped as the series'
deciding game. Suspicions had been aroused that the pilot,
with 65 runs in six innings on tour, would drop himself, and
Edrich, sympathetically pragmatic, made no attempt to
dissuade him. 'Mike was having a bad run at the time, not
making runs, and decided not to play when we went to the
nets,' he recalls. 'If you don't feel like you should be playing,
you can hardly lead a side.'

It was hardly fair weather in which to take the helm, with
England in the teeth of a 0–2 gale blown by Lillee and

---

[*] From *One Summer, Every Summer: An Ashes Journal* (1995).

Thomson, Edrich and Dennis Amiss having barely recovered from broken fingers, pace bowlers Mike Hendrick and Chris Old lame. Losing the toss then condemned the team to a long spell in the field, with ever diminishing resources.

'I don't think we saw Hendo for six weeks on that tour,' Edrich says. 'And after about five or six overs, Bob [Willis] broke down, and had two needles stuck on his knees at lunch, so it was clear he wasn't going to be bowling much more. Derek Underwood was short of confidence at the time and Fred Titmus hadn't played a lot, so I was left with 'Orse [Geoff Arnold] and he bowled well. But it was a game we should have drawn.'

Arnold did bowl well – more packhorse than thoroughbred as he shouldered twenty-nine eight-ball overs in taking five for 86 – but Australia passed 400 and secured a commanding lead before Ian Redpath and Greg Chappell made second innings hundreds. That left the Edrich XI to bat through 9 January to keep the series ajar, and the leader was the key to survival when he entered to face Lillee at 2 for 70.

Photographs of his first delivery show Edrich curling foetally as the ball rolls away. Teammates discovered a weal in his side like a hot poker had been plunged between his ribs. Edrich felt to blame: 'Dennis always bowled me a bouncer first ball. I got down too early and it never bounced. If I'd stood up and played it I'd have been fine and we'd have drawn it.' There was actually still a chance when, X-rays having suggested no break, Edrich resumed at 6 for 156 to an enfilade of bouncers from Lillee, but stuck fast, until he had batted more than six hours in the match. Trouble was at the other end, about which you sense he still feels keenly. 'We could have drawn it, you know. There were some others in the side who never applied themselves. Greig was stumped four yards down the wicket and you don't do that if you're trying to save a match. We only lost with four overs to go and that was the problem throughout.' Edrich was frowningly unbeaten on 33 when the innings expired and the Ashes were conceded.

The addendum and erratum were that Edrich's ribs *were* fractured. He batted in Tasmania, had to retire at 35 when he realised he couldn't bend down, and after several sleepless nights was X-rayed again in Adelaide, which sidelined him from the Test. 'I've still got the indent in my side where Dennis hit me, actually, and a bit of bone sticking up in my arm where Thommo hit me,' he says. Pause: 'Adelaide was a match we should have won . . .'

This is a series Edrich had obviously relived often and, granted a side of Edriches, England would certainly have been a sterner opponent for Ian Chappell's men. Edrich's 5138 Test runs at 44 oozed obstinacy, his bottom hand coming through like a clenched fist. Lillee actually nominated Edrich the hardest Englishman of his time to dismiss – indeed, in 1974–75, he did not get him once.

Edrich's experience of pre-Warne Aussie leg-spin, meanwhile, spans three decades: in his first Championship hundred for Surrey at the Oval in 1959, Somerset's Colin McCool was in the opposition. 'Kept slogging the goog over mid-wicket that day,' he laughs. 'And did it a few times after that.' His method of playing from the pitch not the hand was disarmingly successful.

'The Aussie guys in county cricket – McCool, Tribe, Walsh, McMahon, Dooland – they gave it a fair bit of air so my theory worked,' Edrich explains. 'I'd plant my foot straight, so if it was the goog I missed it and the leggie hit my pad. Otherwise I'd work at getting them on the full. Johnny Gleeson was a good bowler, but he did far too much to get the edge so I concentrated on playing every ball as a straight one. Percy Philpott was a useful spinner too, and got players who pushed into trouble. So I relied on the theory that if it was up it had to go, and I remember hitting him over the sight screen at Sydney to get my hundred.'

That was twenty-nine years ago on Edrich's first Ashes tour, a trip he'd secured after hovering at the periphery of English selection for a few years by creating a record few Australians can believe he holds: the greatest number of boundaries in a Test innings (fifty-two fours and five sixes) in an undefeated 310 at Leeds in nine hours in 1965 against New Zealand. 'I made about ten comebacks in my career and there were a lot of good players around,' Edrich says. 'But in the winter I'd gone to South Africa coaching and it was really the first time I'd played on really good wickets. I found out that I had to score quite quickly in the weekend club cricket, so I perfected playing the off and on drives on the up and kept on doing it when I got back to England.'

His Surrey colleague Ken Barrington shepherded Edrich through half an hour chasing his first run, telling him to look forward to batting in the afternoon, and so the pair did in a six-hour stand of 369. 'Kenny was always good when you were struggling a bit,' Edrich says. 'And he was such a good player of fast bowling, 'cos he said you should never make a quickie angry. He'd say: "Don't hit 'em for four, just take ones and twos, say 'well bowled' occasionally, keep it nice and friendly."'

It was a South African who curtailed Edrich's rich vein of form at Lord's three weeks later, Peter Pollock leaving a cricket ball-size lump in the batter's temple in knocking him senseless. 'My fault again,' says Edrich. 'Took my eye off it. But looking back it was quite good for my career. I never took my eye off it again. I had terrible headaches for ten days, but then they cleared up.' Pause. 'Lucky to be here, aren't I?'

On his first visit to Sydney, Edrich remembers finding it hard to see an eye on anything. At number three behind Bob

Barber and Geoff Boycott he kept a restless vigil throughout their heady first-day stand of 234 in four hours. 'The SCG dressing room in those days, you couldn't see where the ball was landing,' Edrich explains. 'I got up half a dozen times when I saw Bob pick up his bat and make these huge drives, and I'd have to ask: "Is he out? Is he out?" When they said no I'd have to put the old gloves down again and keep waiting.'

Australians bracket Edrich mentally with Boycott, for it was alongside the archetypal Yorkshireman that he plundered Bill Lawry's bowlers with Illy twenty-four years ago. Edrich made a century in the inaugural WACA Test, and shared consecutive opening stands with Boycott of 161 unbeaten, 103 and 107. He even survived being the first Englishman to fall to Lillee and Thomson – though a debutant Dennis and 'Froggy' of Victoria were a good deal easier than the second edition.

I asked Edrich his views on the current series, and his main bother is not the batting but the way England's seamers have slumped by the wayside. 'When I was in the Surrey dressing room, you had Tony Lock just covered in bandages and Alec Bedser always strapped up, because they always played through niggles,' says Edrich. 'Otherwise, because you were on basic match payments with a very low base wage, you really didn't get paid if you didn't play.' I suspect he'd like to say more but is restraining himself. He tells me instead he quite fancies settling in Australia, bringing his wife back to her home country. 'Australia's a good place to live,' Edrich avers. 'I might have made a few more runs if I'd grown up here.' It'd just be good if England could put up a bit more of a show in Sydney, at least hold out for a draw. One more time, John Edrich observes that they should have done so twenty years ago.

# Australians v Boycott
## ABOMINABLE SLOW MAN (2005)

ustralians and Yorkshiremen are meant to have a strange affinity, both calling a spade a bloody shovel, equally contemptuous of traditional hoity-toity, plum-in-the-mouth pomminess. Hutton, Leyland, Trueman, Illingworth: bonny fighters all, and straight talkers, too.

Where Geoff Boycott was concerned, however, Australians made an exception. Granted, he could play a bit. But about his version of that particular northern obduracy, there seemed to lurk personal rather than communal ambition. Hell, let's call that shovel by its name: Boycott's batting had a broad streak of monomania. Even in his finest hour, his return to the colours amid England's 1977 Ashes win, Boycott lime-lighted unashamedly, being seen so frequently with his arms aloft that he should almost have glued on his bat labels upside down.

In great sportsmen, of course, often lurks a streak of selfishness – it is a dimension of that self-mastery they today call 'focus'. And Boycott the batsman was nothing if not focused. Over two months I spent following county cricket in

1985, mainly in the north, I watched him for what seemed like days. His batting, rationalized and regimented to the brink of automation, had by then a kind of icy beauty.

I recall with particular vividness his last innings against Australia: an unbeaten 52 in a rain-ruined game for Yorkshire. I arrived early to find Boycott finishing a lap of Headingley, in his whites, wearing his cap. He then drafted two young seamers to bowl to him, not in the nets, but on an old pitch on the square. He regularly left wide deliveries which because he was in the open he had then to chase and retrieve. Not the slightest effort did he expend sticking his bat out to stop them; one wouldn't perpetrate such a solecism in a match, so why do so when training?

As he came out to bat, he withdrew a handkerchief from his pocket, and dangled it between thumb and forefinger to ascertain the wind direction. One half imagined that, like Arthur Shrewsbury, he had already ordered his seltzers for the next two drinks breaks; certainly, he batted like a man who had already played the innings in his mind. It was a cold, still, quiet day, with so little crowd noise that one could hear the Australians chivvying and gingering one another in the field – 'C'mon, digger!'; 'Let's get up 'im, Billy!' But they were like bursts of disapproved noise in a library, in which Boycott went on peacefully swotting.

Australian objections to Boycott, though, did not really originate in his style; after all, Australians esteemed Ken Barrington, who shares with Boycott the ignominy of being dropped from a Test for slow scoring. Like his countrymen, if not perhaps his Yorkshire countymen, we were baffled by his thirty-month sulk in the 1970s, which meant, among other things, that he avoided Lillee and Thomson in harness. Boycott's disgruntlement arose from the spectacle of England being led by a Welshman (Lewis), Scot (Mike Denness) and

South African (Greig), but that elicited little sympathy in these parts. Australians can actually condone selfishness – providing one's country shares any benefits.

# Alan Knott
## KNOTT CRICKET (2022)

In her book *English Eccentrics* (1933), Edith Sitwell described their condition as 'some exaggeration of the attitudes to life' arising from the 'ordinary carried to a high degree of pictorial perfection'. No English cricketer has been so ordinarily exaggerated to such a pitch of perfection as Alan Knott, still perhaps the finest keeper of all time, and the most legendarily extreme in his fastidiousness and superstition. Compacted of ritual and idiosyncrasy, he thought more deeply and laterally about his craft than perhaps anyone before or since, from his custom of warming his hands in a basin of water before a day's play to roughing his gloves with a penknife and sandpaper.

In certain respects, Knott was way ahead of his time: his early morning calisthenics to ward off stiffness anticipate the yoga and pilates of modernity. In others, he stayed resolutely out of step. He disliked late nights. He was fearful of drafts. That evolving custom of verbal geeing-up which he noticed towards the end of his career – what, he complained, was that about?

'It seemed out of place after a batsman had played forward and middled the ball to hear the cry, "Well bowled,"' he cavilled. 'It would not have encouraged me if I had been the bowler – quite the opposite: I would have felt that my colleagues were trying to encourage me because I was not bowling well . . . All this shouting seemed rather false, and I found it very difficult to get used to.'

For his eccentricity, excellence made a space. The practice rituals in the hallway of his home; the upturned hat brim and collar to guard against sunburn, the elastoplast on the junior-sized pads to ease the bending of the legs; even, in his private life, the piety and uxoriousness: there was no challenging or doubting any of these singly because they formed such a comprehensive package with the quicksilver reflexes, the dainty footwork and the smiling appeals. Whether it was anticipating the vagaries of Derek Underwood or maintaining perfect understanding with first slips Colin Cowdrey, Basil D'Oliveira and Mike Brearley, he made a team feel more than its cumulative manpower. Once when Knott dropped a rare catch in Australia, Ray Illingworth grunted: 'At least now we know you're human.' It was a wink at the otherworldliness of his keeper's obsessional genius.

Plus the batting. Knott wasn't the first keeper whose batting was a factor in their selection: Jim Parks had edged superior glovemen in John Murray and Alan Smith before him. But Knott was inclined to make a selector feel trebly blessed – not only the best keeper and the fittest man but also among the most effective batsmen in the teams of his time, good enough to play in the top six, but licensed by his slot at number seven to go his own front-on, back-leaning, hard-slashing way. The Knott upper cut and the Knott sweep – these were chafing against orthodoxy, revolution from below, from a particular strand of Englishness.

# The Centenary Test

## HINDSIGHT ON HINDSIGHT (2017)*

Test matches present have a way of inciting memory of Test matches past. In the case of the Boxing Day Test, memories are being channelled formally to the Centenary Test, four decades ago.

The Centenary Test was itself an anniversary, a hundred years to the week of the inaugural Test match, on the same ground, between the same countries – by freak circumstances, Australia's margin of victory, 45 runs, was likewise repeated.

So it is that Cricket Australia will fete the surviving members of the home team, Bob Willis as a representative of the visitors, and umpire Max O'Connell, at a dinner tomorrow evening at the Pullman Melbourne on the Park – which, back in the day when it was the Hilton, was the Centenary Test's staging post.

It was O'Connell, eighty-one, who started the ball rolling on the event a year ago, pointing out to CA the passing of

---

* Written on the fortieth anniversary of the Centenary Test.

forty seasons. Asked about the urgency for such a function, he replied: 'Wait for the fiftieth anniversary and a few of us might not be around.' As it is, three of Greg Chappell's Australian team have passed away: Gary Gilmour, Max Walker and David Hookes, plus England's captain Tony Greig and O'Connell's umpiring partner Tom Brooks.

Among participants, however, memory of the game seems remarkably fresh and vivid: the tenacious centuries of Derek Randall and Rod Marsh; the leonine fast bowling of Dennis Lillee; Hookes's five flourishing fours from Greig's bowling; the bravery of wounded Rick McCosker in batting swathed in bandages in the second innings. It's also interesting to contemplate how different Test cricket was in that era. The Test, summer's second at the MCG, began on a Saturday, and had a rest day on the Tuesday. It was broadcast on television by the ABC, featuring Keith Miller and Frank Tyson, and by Channel 0/10, featuring Richie Benaud and Geoff Boycott; the latter's coverage was interrupted by advertisements, the ABC's by horse racing. Melbourne stations carried only the final session.

There were no coaches; no support staff; no days of press conferences and preparatory rituals. The teams had one preliminary session in nets erected over pitches on the outfield in the ground's south-east corner. Batsmen sported no body armour or helmets, which might have spared McCosker the broken jaw inflicted by Willis on the first morning. Not a single six was hit, despite some superb attacking batsmanship; nobody worried about 'loads', Lillee bowling the equivalent of sixty-four six-ball overs, and completing 2832 deliveries in his first-class season of fifteen matches. 'Once he was bowling, captains knew it was impossible to get the ball out of Dennis's hand,' recalls his old confrère Marsh. 'His theory was that if you bowled all day from one end, then you would take five wickets.' Lillee slightly outperformed his own expectations, taking eleven wickets for 165.

Security was negligible. Gary Cosier recalls toddling down to the ground from the Hilton each morning in his trackies hoping he had the right pass – the gatekeepers were gimlet-eyed. Security of tenure was limited, too: Cosier found out only on the first morning that he would be batting at first wicket down, and was taking guard in the first half hour.

On the players, the game's significance dawned only slowly. Chappell recalls the jolt he experienced in encountering the scoreboard name boards in and around the players' entranceway. 'The closer you got to the occasion, the more important you realized it was,' he says. Intimations grew as the players circulated at the Hilton with more than 200 ex-Test players gathered from Australia and England. That little chap, nearly blind, was Percy Fender. That tall chap, still elegant, was Frank Woolley. At a banquet on Monday night, Sir Donald Bradman gave a speech referring to his having met the scorer of the first Test century, Charles Bannerman. Harold Larwood posed with Lillee on the front page of *The Age*. Standing tall at the parade of captains was eighty-seven-year-old Jack Ryder, who before the First World War had bowled to Victor Trumper (who died of Bright's Disease in 1915) and faced Tibby Cotter (killed in action in 1917). 'It got a bit difficult not to get caught up in the hype, with so many ex-players around,' recalls McCosker. 'You wanted to show all these old guys that you could play a bit.'

At least at first, this was made more difficult by grounds-man Bill Watt's green-tinged pitch, prepared in an overcast February and March, long before the superlative systems of modern drainage that dry rain-affected outfields so quickly but also have the effect of sapping moisture from squares. Greig sending the hosts in made for a match of two halves,

Australia making 138 and England replying with 95. O'Connell was then privy to an intriguing conversation.

Umpires were then cricket's menials. The Friday before the Test, O'Connell had been at work as an accountant in Adelaide when advised by Australian Cricket Board secretary Alan Barnes of his appointment, subject to the approval of Greig, who was unfortunately in transit with his team from India and running late. That delayed confirmation until 9.30 p.m. that night, and O'Connell's application for ten days' leave until Monday – two days' notice. Lucky his ultimate boss was an ex-League footballer, and so was the local manager of TAA, or he mightn't have made it to Melbourne in that DC-9's jump seat.

O'Connell has the unique distinction, in fact, of umpiring Test cricket and Australian rules on the MCG, having presided in two State of Origin games. He notes that he umpired twenty Tests with thirteen other umpires, eight of whom never did another game. 'They'd crack under pressure,' he says. 'Pressure didn't bother me. I'd been abused by Barassi.'*

Now it was the organizers who were under pressure, with the game more than half over at the end of day two. O'Connell and Brooks sat down in the umpires' room that evening with Barnes and his chairman Bob Parish discussing how to ensure that there was cricket at tea on the final day when Her Majesty the Queen was scheduled to visit. If worst came to the worst, it was agreed, a one-day international would be played. Fortunately, the pitch flattened out, and Australia extended its second innings to nine for 419, thanks to Marsh's unbeaten 128, half-centuries from Hookes, Ian Davis and Doug Walters,

---

* At Melbourne FC, Walker played for two years alongside Australian rules football champion Ron Barassi, later a famously ruthless and demanding coach.

and tailend contributions from the indefatigable Lillee and the stoic McCosker.

McCosker prefers not to discuss his legendary reappearance that day. I chatted to this most unassuming of men while he was mowing his lawn – a far cry from the day his battered and distended features were emblazoned across the front page of the day's *Sun News-Pictorial*, with the headline: 'COURAGE: THAT'S MCCOSKER'.

Others speak for him. Cosier remembers the dressing room windows being flung open so that colleagues could hear the crowd's spontaneous rendition of 'Waltzing Matilda'. Marsh remembers greeting him in the middle: 'I might have said: "What the hell are you doing out here"?' O'Connell recalls overhearing Greig instruct bowler Chris Old to give McCosker a gentle half-volley on leg stump to get off the mark. Nowadays, perhaps, McCosker would have been advised to 'suck it up'.

The 54 runs that McCosker added with Marsh, Chappell recalls, were hugely important, more or less the difference between victory and defeat: the surface, by day four and five, was just about perfect. 'In fact,' he says, 'it was the last good pitch I played on in Melbourne.'

England batted so well that even Lillee wondered if Australia, having set England 463 to win, would 'get out of this'. Randall batted seven and a half hours for 174, stirringly reprieved on 161 when Marsh disclaimed a catch at the wicket from Chappell's bowling. O'Connell at square leg also saw it bounce first, and was about to query Brooks's decision when Marsh did the job for him.

The fourth night, Cosier watched highlights of that day's play, during which he had missed a couple of half-chances at short leg. He noticed that he had had his weight on his left leg, and resolved to change his stance the next day: 'I wanted to be on my toes more. If a chance came I was just going to go for it.' Short leg stood far closer and was far less well protected than today. But when Randall gave the hint of a bat-pad chance from Kerry O'Keeffe just before tea on the last day, a diving Cosier caught it virtually at his feet. That and a similar catch of Greig after tea were crucial intercessions.

Cosier recalls something else now of only hindsight significance. The Centenary Test was Janus-faced. It looked back over the vista of a century; it also became the focus of Kerry Packer, whose made-for-television World Series Cricket was taking shape, and whose recruiting agent Austin Robertson mingled freely with the players. Cosier remembers at the pre-match meeting how vehemently senior players disparaged Bradman. 'Gee, we're playing against England, not Bradman,' he thought.

Marsh had been leading a campaign for improved terms in the players' superannuation, the so-called Provident Fund, to which Bradman was widely seen as opposed. The Australian keeper actually received his Packer offer from Robertson, even as the Queen was arriving, at tea time on the final day, and needed no persuading to sign. 'Austin was always in the dressing room,' Marsh laughs. 'It would never be allowed in this day and age.' Afterwards, right under the noses of officialdom, Robertson distributed the players' sign-on cheques in plain envelopes, with the immortal words: 'Here are your theatre tickets, fellas.'

Cosier wondered why he did not receive an envelope: 'I always liked to be in on the things the team was doing.' In fact, as would become clear a month later on Australia's Ashes tour, he was the only member of the thirteen-man Australian squad to whom Packer had not offered a contract. Memories: they come in all shades.

# Bob Willis

## BUSTLING BOB (2019)[*]

Austral ians called him 'Bustling Bob', from years of
watching Bob Willis shear in from his long, curving
run, and bang the ball in on that length no batsman
likes.

Willis, who has died at the age of seventy, took 128 wickets
at 26 in thirty-five Ashes Tests, 72 of them in Australia at 29.8
on hard pitches that often turned his pounding feet bloody
and caused his wonky knees to ache. Eight of them, of course,
he took for 43 on a celebrated afternoon at Headingley in
1981 when he seemed involved in a game within a game,
treating the batsmen as undifferentiated targets, achieving lift
that to the naked eye appeared almost vertical.

Australians had long respected him; from then they
looked on Willis with, if not fear, certainly new deference. 'He
had been a lion-hearted performer for England for a lot of

---

[*] Written on the death of Bob Willis, on 4 December 2019, aged seventy.

years and this was his moment of glory,' wrote Allan Border. 'He richly deserved it. I just wish he'd saved the most devastating performance of his career for some other team. Why pick on us?'

The answer was that Ashes cricket was then the acid test of a cricketer and of a character. Willis had first been summoned in the Australian summer of 1970–71, when he was whisked to Australia, aged twenty-one, to replace an injured Alan Ward. Tall, raw and ungainly with an unruly mop of hair, Willis was so unlike the standard English seamer that the normally conservative *Sydney Morning Herald* rhapsodized of him as '6ft 6in of blue flame'.

He had an uncredited cameo on his debut in the Sydney Test when John Snow knocked the Australian tailender Terry Jenner senseless and was then manhandled by a spectator on the fine leg fence. After the England team returned from a temporary evacuation and Snow headed back towards his position, Willis came running from third man and persuaded him to swap places – a hint of precocious maturity. Willis, the Australian cricket writer R. S. Whitington wrote, seemed 'to worship Snow'. It was a grand choice of hero.

Willis emerged in the era in which, as it were, pace bowling became fast bowling, when abruptly it seemed that what every cricket country coveted was speed and spite. Australia set the scene with Lillee and Thomson. West Indies gathered Roberts, Holding, Garner and Croft. Pakistan located Imran Khan and Sarfraz Nawaz. If not for Willis, post-Snow England might well have fallen behind. For Mike Denness's beleaguered team in 1974–75, he took 17 wickets at 31; for Mike Brearley's triumphant team of 1977, he took 27 wickets at 19, at which point was dangled before him a contract to join Kerry Packer's World Series Cricket. Willis sided with the establishment with an ardour perhaps surprising in an otherwise questioning man, but it was perhaps more a reflection of how much he valued representing England.

On the second day of the Lord's Test in 1978, Willis managed the rather extraordinary double of attending drinks in the Long Room with the Queen and Prince Philip then attending a Bob Dylan concert at Earls Court, narrating it in his *Diary of a Cricket Season* (1979) as though it was his personal idea of heaven. Willis also wrote a perceptive primer, *Pace Bowling* (1978), having just been harshly criticized for bloodying Pakistani tailender Iqbal Qasim with a bouncer – Qasim had been hanging in for an hour having come in as nightwatchman the evening before. In a prescient digression, Willis prophesied that one day a bowler would kill a batsman with a bouncer, and find it hard to deal with the consequences. The passage came to mind recently on the fifth anniversary of the death of Phillip Hughes.

Willis led England in Australia in 1982–83, pluckily and unluckily, and was always more than a tourist here, taking a true traveller's delight in the wine and the Wagner. He swore by the ministrations of the Sydney hypnotherapist Arthur Jackson, whose relaxation tapes accompanied him most of his career. He relied on the Melbourne bootmaker Hope Sweeney, to whom he dragged Norman Cowans, Derek Pringle and Eddie Hemmings for custom-made bowling boots. And when he ceased bustling, he was as humorous and hospitable as he had been hostile.

# Derek Randall

## ONE OF A KIND (1994)[*]

The brief experience of being a spectator at the MCG again isn't an unfamiliar one. Like I said, this is my home town, and I'd be here even without my Uncle Rupert. Having been a Test match watcher at the MCG for two decades, I have salted away enough Test souvenirs for a small household shrine. One is the Centenary Test brochure from 1977. It's drab in appearance compared to the streamlined glossies you can buy today, but it's in tatters for the number of times I've read the Cardus portrait of Victor Trumper, Bill Bowes's Bradman study, and the contributions by Arlott, Benaud, A. A. Thomson, Ray Robinson, Lindsay Hassett, Frank Tyson et al. I can read again the perfunctory sketch of 'Randall, Derek William (26)'. It reported: 'Forcing right hand bat, who scored 1100 runs at 40 in 1976 and is a specialist cover fieldsman. No Tests.'

Can anyone have had a less prepossessing introduction to

---

[*] From *One Summer, Every Summer: An Ashes Journal* (1995).

the MCG? There can't be a subject in cricket's kingdom who doesn't recall Randall's 174 eighteen years ago. For youth brought up to see the shambling Pom as prey, it was an innings to challenge bonds of affiliation. When he wasn't batting like a mighty atom, Randall was a charged particle ricocheting round the covers. Nobody prowled like him: he started deeper and finished closer than any other of his ilk, executing every manoeuvre but a cartwheel. Which, of course, he did a few months later at Trent Bridge when he caught Rod Marsh off Mike Hendrick to win the Ashes for England.

It so happens that Randall's visiting Melbourne again, like many others, as a celeb cricket tour guide. And it's an act of pure wish-fulfilment when I decide that he might make an interesting interview subject. He answers his own phone and barely takes note of my name: 'Yeah, sure, coom round tonight and will go out for a feed. 'Bout seven in reception? Great.' That it is. Eighteen years after I stencilled his score into my Test souvenir, I'm having dinner with Derek Randall.

Actually I had met him before – I was captained by Randall in one of those 'play with a Test star' corporate days in England six years ago – though I'm hardly expecting him to remember that. Hoping he doesn't actually. 'Oh yeah, I remember!' he exclaims, just loud enough for the entire lobby of the Menzies Hotel to hear. 'You were the worst fielder I'd ever seen. You did take a catch, mind. I remember that.' Fact.

It was fielding, he explains, that eventually made him give the game away at the end of the 1993 county season. Ironically it was his old accomplice Hendrick – manager of Nottinghamshire – who told Randall that fielding the far side of forty was not a viable pastime. 'I didn't really have much choice in the end,' he says. 'Obviously you'd like to play for ever, but your legs can't stand it and I knew I'd passed my peak.' His first summer off the circuit was a little easier than he expected. 'There was a young feller at Notts, Graham Archer from Staffordshire, who's a good bat and a terrific fielder and he got his first full season because I wasn't there last year. And it was just as nice to see him out there performing so well for Notts as it was being out there myself.'

Randall's still all angles, elbows and coat hanger shoulders. We leave his hotel to look for a diner, and he admits to being homesick. He knows everything that's happening at home, and spends idle hours telephoning his wife Elizabeth in Nottingham: Randall's a print broker and runs a small dried flower shop after investing proceeds of a 1983 benefit and a 1993 testimonial in an investment property. 'I wasn't one of those players that really liked touring,' he says. 'I love English winters. It only takes a couple of weeks and I'm wishing I was home. 'Ere! this is your home town, isn't it? Do you know where we're going?'

I'm forced to admit that we're taking a scenic route, but it does allow Randall to talk about *his* home town a bit more. It's a sweet synchronicity that Randall was born in Retford on 24 February 1951 because, that night on the other side of the world at the MCG, his county's captain Reg Simpson enjoyed his finest Ashes moment: 156 in 280 to break England's thirteen-year drought of victories against Australia. Simpson became Randall's first cricket hero: 'I saw a lot of him, of course. Very courageous, very determined character, played well off the back foot, pulling and cutting, and great against fast bowling.'

When Randall came sneaking onto the Notts staff twenty-five years ago, there was another county star to revere, and the tyro made himself useful to Garry Sobers as an aide de turf: 'I was the quickest lad on the staff when I joined so I always used to be the one he sent to the bookies to place his bets.

When I got back, lads'd say: "Tell 'im 'e's lost or 'e'll get out so 'e can count 'is winnings.'" The twenty-two-year-old had his first serious bat with the West Indian at Edgbaston in June 1973, when Sobers joined Randall in the centre against Warwickshire. Randall recalls:

> We lost a wicket just before lunch and it was a great thrill when Sobers came out with me. First three balls from David Brown, he smashed 'em back past me at the bowler's end. Bloody marvellous, it was! It wasn't like batting with Ian Botham, because then it might go anywhere and you'd be watching your head. With Sobers it was all timing. I remember how he changed in this one particular corner at Trent Bridge, and he used to carry five or six light bats around with him and reach for the first one he found when he went in. It was just a shame for Notts that at the end of his career he bowled so many overs that his knees were boogered and he couldn't get around. He still had the ability. If the ball was anywhere near him, his reactions were still superb and his timing never left him.

For all his idols, Randall emerged as a Test cricketer three and a half years later never to be mistaken for anyone else. He trained to be the best. A friend of mine remembers him playing district cricket for Prahran a decade or so ago: every weekday, rain, hail or shine, Randall could be seen at the club ground circling and throwing at a single stump. There was accordingly no such thing as a standard Randall run out. He could hit from any angle. I remember him creeping up on non-striker Rick McCosker in the second innings at Headingley so stealthily that he could have virtually tapped the Australian on the shoulder before evicting him. I remember Randall materialising in mid pitch at Lord's as the 1979 World Cup final began and beating a backtracking Gordon Greenidge with a direct hit. He zipped in from mid-wicket to punish Sunil Gavaskar for a similar misjudgement in a Test on the same ground a few weeks later. What his arm and aim could not unsettle, Randall tried to undermine with a rambling patriotic monologue just within the batsman's earshot.

'England's shown how important fielding is on this tour,' Randall opines when we sit down. 'Not only your catches and the runs you might save, but the way it lifts your bowlers and your team. That Jonty Rhodes in England last year, he was brilliant at that, always encouraging the others.'

That 174, well it was one of those things you can do when you're young, wasn't it? 'That 'oondred and seventy was in a one-off game, and it's not the same as playing for that coveted pot,' Randall says. 'I think a few of the Aussies were out celebrating a bit early in that match because they didn't bowl so well.' And of his four Test man-of-the-match feats in Australia, the least characteristic is his favourite: one received for his gruelling ten-hour 150 at the SCG in equatorial heat, which effectively retained the Ashes for England in 1978–79.

Unlike me, Randall has no souvenirs. He gave the Centenary Test bat away, lost others, and passed on whatever gongs he earned during his career to his mother. 'I have something North Perth gave me after I played there three years,' Randall says. 'That means a lot to me, 'cause all the players signed it and I'd had a great time. But if me mom and me wife Liz hadn't taken care of the other stuff, I'd have given it away by now.' While Randall enjoys practising with his son, a seventeen-year-old dreadlocked club fast bowler, he feels passionately that English cricket has been scorched at the grass roots:

Cricket in England's died a helluva lot. You'll always find eleven good cricketers to play for the country, but consistently over the generations it's the enthusiasm for the game you generate that matters. It's the bloody love of it. We've lost that. I was in Cairns for four days recently, best of me bloody life, and somebody told me that every other boy in Cairns plays on a Saturday morning. That's incredible. We have nothing like that. I just hope John Major's Prime Minister for twenty years, 'cause he's a cricket nut and knows it's part of our heritage.

Randall looks meaningfully at my tape recorder. 'Reckon there's a knighthood in that for me? Coom on, y'must 'ave enough by now. Let's go get something to eat. Ah'm starvin'.' After dinner, I take Randall to an English boutique pub in Collins Street and see his eyes light up as he watches his pint being poured. 'That's the stuff,' he says. 'Just like 'ome. 'S been great bein' back 'ere actually, but three weeks is a bit long. Ah'm ready for 'ome now.' The world, Nottinghamshire County Cricket Club and Nottingham Forest are put to rights before Randall stumps off into the dark and I try to thank him. 'Aye,' he says, laughing. 'Ah could tell it were a great thrill for ya. 'Ere! Improve your fielding though.'

# Ian Botham and the Legend of 1981

## YEAR OF WONDERS (2016)

O ne worker in nine was unemployed. Inflation soared to sixteen per cent. There were convulsive riots in more than a score of cities and towns, and uproar everywhere, whether it was Irish paramilitaries detonating bombs and sinking ships, female peace protesters thronging Greenham Common or civil servants striking over public sector austerities; even the fairytale marriage of the Prince of Wales and Lady Diana Spencer would sour. Yet for cricket, the year 1981 retains a magical ring. Perhaps no series has so often been replayed, a guaranteed crowd pleaser thanks to its arc of adversity and deliverance, mysterious chemistry and spontaneous brilliance, England and Australia. Had the unavailable Greg Chappell toured rather than his younger brother Trevor, the balance may have been otherwise. As it was, two teams well matched man-for-man were separated by a single cricket phenomenon: Ian Botham.

Summer began with Botham at bay, his joyless year as captain of England a contrast to the three barnstorming all-round years before it, when he had averaged 40 with the bat,

18 with the ball. The patience of selectors had thinned. His commissions were being issued one at a time. His Australian counterpart, twenty-seven-year-old Kim Hughes, could take some confidence in the experience of star elders Dennis Lillee and Rod Marsh, and the promise of prodigies like Allan Border and Terry Alderman.

For Botham, the scenario soon deteriorated. Hughes sent England in at Trent Bridge where Lillee and Alderman shot them out for 185 and 125, and Border battled almost six hours to secure a five-wicket victory. Then, beneath the gaze of the game's governors at Lord's, Botham picked up an ignominious pair in a drawn match that left him without a win in a dozen Tests as captain. He felt, in his words, 'like a 200-year-old', and stepped down before he was pushed.

To go forward, England's selectors walked back, tapping Botham's predecessor Mike Brearley. Grizzled and cerebral, thirty-nine-year-old Brearley was Botham's opposite in almost every respect, including natural talent, his average from thirty-five previous Tests an unflattering 23.6. Yet for Botham he had always been a talisman: Brearley was 'someone I admire both as a person and a captain and whose judgement I respect'. For his own part, Brearley felt 'ready for the call'. He had been undergoing psychoanalysis since September 1979 as part of his training in that career; what he was to accomplish over the next four Tests demonstrated extraordinary capacities in empathy and insight.

For the first three and a half days of the Third Test at Headingley, any English improvement was difficult to discern. In conditions in which the home seamers should have excelled, Australia passed 400; England's batsmen then lasted barely fifty overs, and were forced to follow on. Their only source of satisfaction was Botham, who in nearly forty overs took six for 95, and from 54 balls made 50. But after the rest day, gloom continued descending: just after 3 p.m., with England seven for 135 in its second innings, still 92 runs in arrears, the new electronic scoreboard quoted odds on Australia of 1/4, on a draw of 5/2, and on England of 500/1. So outrageous were they for a two-horse race that Lillee and Marsh could not forbear a £15 flutter with Ladbroke's.

Botham was still at the wicket at tea, but had no plans to linger – he had been one of several England players to check out of their hotel that morning. Lillee and Alderman, who had so far carried all before them, were tiring. Botham took them on, in company with Graham Dilley, a tailender with free swinging pretensions; the field scattered; there were no-balls, overthrows, misses, mishits and confusion. Botham's first 50 took 57 balls, his second just 30, composed of eleven fours and a soaring straight six. Dilley's 56, slightly more sedate but often handsome, helped in the addition of 117 runs in eighty minutes.

England were still only 25 in credit when Dilley fell, but number ten Chris Old and number eleven Bob Willis kept Botham company while a further 104 were added in eighty-five minutes. Having been within a few tailend wickets of an innings victory, Australia found themselves twenty hours later commencing an awkward fourth-innings chase, and to Botham lost an early wicket. Still there was no logic to what followed. At one for 56, Australia needed 74 for victory with nine wickets left: the sun was out; neither time nor the pitch were a factor; lunch beckoned, and after that a 2–0 lead. When Bob Willis switched to the Kirkstall Lane End, he had not taken a wicket for more than forty overs, had been plagued by no-balls and ill-health. Suddenly, with the wind at his back, he struck thrice, the ball lifting vehemently. Suddenly, Brearley felt, England might even be favourites.

The momentum shift was complete. Australia's subsidence

continued after the break, until seven wickets had fallen for 19 runs in barely an hour's elapsed time, with Willis bowling almost in a disassociated state – he stood aloof from celebrations, stalked back and stormed in as if on a two-speed conveyor belt. With Australia 55 runs from victory, Lillee and Bright suddenly scored 35 in four overs, but a sharp catch and a pinpoint yorker quelled their brief uprising, rounded Willis's figures out at eight for 43, and made for an 18-run victory margin – Lillee and Marsh experienced perhaps sports betting's most rueful £7500 collect.

Restored to form and fortune, Botham would make the summer his own. The Fourth Test at Edgbaston teetered for three days without so much as a half-century, until Australia stood 46 from victory with six wickets remaining. But when a ball from John Emburey turned and bounced on the gritty Border, Brearley backed his intuition and turned to Botham, who took five for 1 in 28 deliveries, fast, straight and true. The Fifth Test at Old Trafford stood in a fine balance on its third day as England, after securing a 101-run first innings lead, found themselves in the doldrums of five for 104 in sixty-nine overs. Again Botham broke the game open, with 118 in 123 minutes and two moods: an initial reconnaissance of 28 in 53 balls, followed by a spectacular starburst of 90 in 49, largely at the expense of the second new ball. A record six sixes sailed into an ecstatic crowd. Of a partnership with Botham of 149, Chris Tavare eked out 28, part of Test cricket's third slowest Test half-century.

Having collapsed in their previous two fourth innings, Australia showed commendable pride: Graham Yallop made a fluent hundred, Border a stoic one, and England needed 136 overs to secure a 103-run victory and the Ashes. But what had started so promisingly would haunt the luckless Hughes thereafter. Lillee and Marsh fumed at his occasional naivety;

he was excoriated by the Australian press, as Botham had been by the English; there would for the Australian be no happy ending, his career ending just over three years later in tears of disillusionment. As for Botham, meanwhile, there was now no stopping him. His match figures in a drawn Sixth Test at The Oval, 91-22-253-10, were those of a man newly gluttonous for the game.

Half a dozen Tests gave the players of 1981 almost unprecedented scope: Botham's 399 runs at 36.3, 34 wickets at 20.5 and eleven catches stretched from horizon to horizon. There were other giant feats, too: Border's 533 runs at 59 including a period where he was not dismissed for eleven hours, while Alderman and Lillee claimed 81 wickets between them in 636.4 overs including 157 maidens. The averages, however, spoke only an approximation of the truth, for they showed Brearley as contributing only 151 runs for eight stays at the crease. Sometimes claims for captaincy can be fanciful, romantic, credulous. Without Brearley's faith and sang froid, there would almost certainly have been no English fightback, no Botham bounceback, and no legacy of 1981 to celebrate all the years since.

# Gooch, Gower, Gatting
## G-FORCE (2022)

Between the late 1970s and early 1990s, England had three batsmen of world-class: Graham Gooch, David Gower and Mike Gatting. It says something of the team's decade of disappointment that they managed to play only one entire series together. What an Ashes that was, when Gooch, Gower and Gatting piled up 1746 runs between them in 1985. How much better would England have been had the three Gs consolidated with the same alliterative tightness as the three Ws, Worrell, Walcott and Weekes, in the West Indian teams of the 1950s?

Maybe they were too disparate to prosper together. Gooch, the oldest, tallest and gravest, looked like the RSM in a tale by Kipling: swarthy, upright, unflinching, sometimes beaten but never defeated. The sun shone from Gower – however long he lasted, it never seemed long enough, such was the ease he radiated. Gatting was likened by Alan Ross to a minor Shakespearean character, a Pistol or a Bardolph, full of character and gusto. Their aggregate of 107,734 first-class runs included 21,540 in Test cricket. Gooch averaged 59 as a Test captain,

Gower and Gatting each 44. They were substantial figures, personifying different strains in English cricket: Gooch the consummate professional, Gower the lightsome amateur, Gatting the trusty yeoman. Why, we must ask, did so much fall into the cracks between them?

The short answer is selection, although also the political and the personal. Rebel tours cost Gooch and Gatting prime years of runmaking. Gatting was not chosen for Australia in 1982–83; Gooch stood out from Australia in 1986–87; Gower scorned to join the other two for the 1987 World Cup – had he and Ian Botham not chosen an English winter over the subcontinental sun then England might not have needed to wait another thirty-two years to wrest that trophy. That's even before we get to the vagaries of form, which neutralised Gooch and Gower in 1981, Gooch and Gatting in 1989.

But then, what splendour to the G-Force's success. Gower made five seemingly effortless hundreds in Australia, where his cross-bat shots bristled even as his touch was so delicate. Shane Warne used to greet Gooch as 'Mr Gooch' out of deference to his defiance and experience, and famously greeted Gatting with perhaps the single greatest delivery ever televised – itself a sort of tribute. Gower led England to the Ashes in 1985 that Gatting retained in 1986–87 that Gower lost in 1989 that Gooch strove valiantly but unavailingly to regain in 1990–91 and 1993. In and out they weaved of one another's careers, jointly but mostly severally, like characters in the teeming Dickens novel of English cricket in this era, with its hoity-toity administrative squirearchy and innocent young cricket orphans surrounded by furtive Fleet Streeters, unified every so often by the figure of Botham with his Micawberesque optimism that something would turn up (Brearley as Inspector Bucket and Tufnell as the Artful Dodger preluding Giles Clarke as Bounderby; the possibilities are endless). Of the three, Gatting's peak proficiency was briefest – basically the three years between 1985 and 1987 before his head fell, like Sydney Carton's, into a tabloid tumbril. But it was a far better thing he did than anything much done before when he joined Douglas Jardine, Ray Illingworth and Mike Brearley in leading England to victory in Australia. Only Andrew Strauss has joined them since.

Gooch and Gower go down as would Waugh and Warne, without the same degree of success, as contrary but defining figures. Remember the golden afternoon of their 351-run second-wicket partnership on the first day of the 1985 Oval Test, where they seemed set to bat 'til the crack of doom? None who watched it could forget. It was a consoling memory in those times when nothing seemed to go right, when English cricket felt, with some foundation, so much less than the sum of its parts.

# Allan Border

## THE BOULDER (2016)

No Australian cricketer has been appreciated in quite the same way as Allan Border, not so much the hero of a thousand fights, but the defender of its cricket honour for a challenging decade. Border scaled summits of triumph in that time – victory in the 1987 World Cup, conquest in the 1989 Ashes. Yet the abiding image of him is forming resistances, mounting rearguards, looking for a wall to put his back to, digging a last ditch to defend. His stocky, bustling, bristling figure was built for a crisis; even his left-handedness seemed a proclamation of defiance.

Greg Chappell thought Border the most negative cricketer he'd ever played with. What drove him, Border confessed, was the 'fear of failure'. Perhaps these characteristics were always there; they were certainly drawn out by his introduction to the game. Border was one of a number of young Australians whose advance to Test calculations was expedited by the absence of senior players with World Series Cricket in 1977–79. Of that group only he and Kim Hughes were to come out the other side of the Darwinian period in which the rival games were reassimilated, and Hughes only temporarily. Australia won on Border's Test debut, then only three times in his next twenty Tests. Border made five hundreds in that time, only one in a winning cause.

Early freeness and fluency in Border's game wore away. He formed himself into a kind of batting obstacle, best on the back foot, technically and metaphorically – junior baseball had left him with a powerful, retaliatory cut and pull. He was seen at his monumental best in England in 1981 when he went 313 runs between dismissals – although, again, Australia could not win. The winter of Australian cricket really set in after January 1984, when Greg Chappell, Dennis Lillee and Rod Marsh retired at once. Australia's subsequent mission to the all-powerful West Indies became an exercise in futility, save only for Border, whose undefeated 98 and 100 at St John's in a total of ten hours ensured a momentous stalemate.

Border became Australian captain, a position he never coveted and in some respects shied from, on the last man standing principle. When Hughes, deserted by luck, form and fashion, resigned in November 1984, Border found himself in charge of a demoralised side seemingly being stalked by the West Indies, even if he was able to take a consolation Test from them in Sydney at New Year on a crumbling, dusty surface. The burden Border bore for the next few years as skipper, number one player and number one wicket provided impetus for the creation of the post of a national coach in June 1986. Tough, leathery Bob Simpson had known Border many years at grade and state level; he would be at Border's side, sometimes even out front, for the rest of Border's near-decade as captain.

The turn around was slow. Australia's first tour with a captain and a coach, to India, included a stirring Test tie in

Madras, but at home Border led Australia to a second consecutive Ashes defeat. The team's first glimpse of the sunny
uplands was victory in the World Cup, Australia defeating
England in the final in Kolkata in September 1987. It was a
team in the image of its leadership, with Border's grit and
Simpson's work ethic, and players around whom a strong unit
could be built: Steve Waugh, David Boon, Geoff Marsh, Craig
McDermott, Dean Jones. The tributes paid focused on the
captain's long stoicism. 'No egotism mars Border's play,' said
the English cricket writer Scyld Berry. 'No more deserving
current Test cricketer could have taken hold of the fourth
World Cup . . .'

Another key contributor slotted in a year later, keeper Ian
Healy, although the tour on which *he* first went was a setback
to Australian progress and prestige – an acrimonious visit to
Pakistan, where a siege mentality set in after some home-town
umpiring decisions. Much promise was fulfilled at last in
England, where Border in 1989 led a bold team, harmonious
within, abrasive without. Border, now bearded, faded cap
tugged low, shrugged off a reputation as a gracious loser by
being an uncompromising victor, 4–0. Repeating the doses
in 1990–91 and 1993, Border bequeathed to his successors
both the Ashes and the term of 'mental disintegration' –
a phrase he thought of as expressing the business of defeating an opposition psychologically as well as skilfully, in
which big scores were complemented by body language in the
pursuit of demoralization.

There was one citadel Border never stormed, which was
the West Indies: he was not on the winning side in any of his
seven series against the world champion team. His epic of
resilience – born out in his playing in fifty Test wins, fifty-nine
draws and forty-six defeats – had to be in the nature of a down
payment. On his retirement in March 1994, Australia were

little more than a year away from retrieving the Frank Worrell Trophy, and turning excellence into dominance. The Ashes tide, however, had turned, and decisively.

# ASHES EYEWITNESS

*Since 1989, there have been eighteen Ashes series, twelve won by Australia and five by England with 2019 drawn. Notwithstanding the show stopper of 2005 and the gap bridger of 2010–11, the Australian ascendancy is marked still more clearly by the 53 to 22 margin in Test victories – England has not won a Test down under in more than twelve years. It's also been the period of my reporting life when I've been composing the first drafts of history, rather than the second and third, and this section opens with my very first dispatch from the Ashes, reporting a delivery from Terry Alderman at the Gabba in 1990 – a rehearsal, in a way, for that ball from Shane Warne at Old Trafford in 1993, now thirty years young.*

# A ball from Alderman

## SWING IS KING (1990)

Michael Atherton's rueful retreat after his second innings at Brisbane was one of those occasions when the expression of a confounded batsman says more than the collected Cardus. The Terry Alderman delivery that, having pitched on leg stump, veered treacherously round his rigidly straight bat to sting off stump, deserved nothing less than the pained half smile etched on Atherton's face.

Although it was greeted with cackles of long-distance omniscience by Tony Greig ('This is not a very good shot at all . . . I'm afraid that Atherton won't be very proud of that one'), it was a delivery almost too good to be true. So good, in fact, that one wonders whether it was wholly intentional.

'Yes, it was!' Alderman laughs. 'And it was exactly the same one as the one that picked up Robin Smith at Lord's in 1989.' Such is Alderman's skill that one is tempted to believe him. He has the control of sciences of swing and seam that other bowlers envy. Watching his former Kent colleague cutting Smith down at Lord's eighteen months ago, Graham Dilley felt as rueful as Atherton last week. 'It pitched middle and leg and hit the top of the off,' he wrote. 'You can only hope to get a little nick on ones like that. Robin had been batting four hours and even then it was unplayable.'

Having never aimed for express speed, Alderman has always been blessed with an ability to swing the ball away. Indeed, he was renowned in his first half a dozen seasons of domestic cricket for his 'repertoire of one'. It was not until he began trying to hit the seam – at the encouragement of Dennis Lillee while warming up at Edgbaston before his first international match in June 1981 – that he began extending his armoury with complementary skills off the wicket. Allied to his widening range of deliveries was a control of length that Mike Brearley remembered as metronomic enough to gouge a small patch of rough just short of length. It is a fuller length than most, giving the ball maximum air play before touching down.

Alderman has made England his spiritual bowling home. Five profitable northern seasons – two as an Australian tourist and three as an overseas professional with Kent and Gloucestershire – have brought him 370 wickets at just over 20, a third cheaper than his wickets elsewhere. Not surprisingly, Alderman is especially fond of the English cricket balls. 'Once the coating goes off the balls there,' he says, 'the quality of the leather is very good and you can work up a nice shine. The Kookaburras here, though, seem to get scuffed up once they lose their coating and are harder to keep shiny.'

Despite that, Alderman would now be reluctant to return to England as a county professional. He must guard against excessive wear and tear in the bowling shoulder reconstructed after his unhappy on-field stoush with an England supporter in Perth in 1982. This grows sore in cold weather, and Alderman says he has been forewarned of arthritic problems when his career is over. New restrictions on overseas players have also condemned foreign quicks to demanding workloads; he was further discouraged by a recent encounter with former Essex seamer John Lever, who passed on observations of the impact of smaller seams and hotter weather in the 1990 county season. 'I spoke to J. K. Lever in Darwin earlier this year,' says Alderman, 'and he was saying, "It's a good job you didn't come over last season; the ball was doing nothing." He said the summer had started dry and just got drier.'

There is something appropriate also in that the man Alderman displaced in the WA side sixteen years ago was the enigmatic Bob Massie, whose swing, so parabolic on his giant-killing debut at Lord's that he had to bowl round the wicket, had deserted him. That Perth schooling and postgraduate bowling study in county cricket has left him with the ability to produce jaffas that Michael Atherton and Robin Smith stumbled into eighteen months apart. The tourists might try to console themselves with the implication of the interval that Alderman can produce no more than one a series. Surely.

# A ball from Warne

## SPIN TO WIN (2022)

On the evening of 4 June 1993, the Carbine Club, a social club bonded by 'sport, fellowship and the community', gathered at the Melbourne Cricket Ground for its annual dinner. Its guest speaker was Terry Jenner, cricketer turned coach, recently identified with Shane Warne, rising Australian leg-spinner. As the evening flashed by, a television at the back of the room tuned to Channel 9 began screening the First Test of the new Ashes from Old Trafford; as the evening neared its end, it happened that a club member was standing beside Jenner as his protégé took the ball for the first time.

This part of the story we know: after first veering to leg, Warne's leg-spinner reversed course and cuffed off stump, leaving Mike Gatting between wind and water, and the world agog. The reaction at the MCG? 'You cunt!' swore Jenner. 'You fucking little cunt!' The club member, who recently told me this story, couldn't believe what he was hearing. 'But Terry,' he pointed out. 'That ball . . .'

Jenner's face broke into a smile. The day before, he

explained, he had had a long conversation with Warne about how to approach his initial overs against England. Nothing special, they agreed. Feel your way into the contest. Just be patient. Well, so much for that: Warne, he had decided, *was* the contest, and he would not wait. As he later transcribed his interior monologue: 'You gotta go. Come on, go, mate, pull the trigger, let's rip this.'

Thirty years on, Warne is gone, but his signature feat and its impact abide. One of the most remarkable features of the Ball of the Century is that nobody had imagined such a thing until it happened. We were ninety-three years into the twentieth century before it was proposed that a single delivery could so stand out from everything before it. Baseball had its Shot Heard Round the World. Football had its Hand of God. But cricket had never so isolated, analysed, celebrated and fetishized a single moment. Here was the mother of all highlights, ahead of a boom in the concept, expedited by a format, T20, geared to their mass manufacture.

Simultaneously leaning against that trend towards com-modification was also Warne, who never bowled a ball without expecting to appeal, who was always scorning the ordinary in quest of the extraordinary, who was always reminding us that we love cricket because we do not know what will happen rather than because we wish for an orderly procession of familiar events.

Nobody saw Warne coming; nobody has replaced him since he retired. He benefited, to be sure, by the Australian initiative of a cricket academy in Adelaide, which is where he first encountered Jenner. Yet Warne was there only because his preferred career as an Australian rules footballer in Melbourne had petered out, and he was rejected at first for his youthful wildness. 'Cricket found me,' he was wont to say, which was not quite accurate, but as an idea uplifting.

The balance of Warne's career, in some ways, had to contour itself to the template of that first ball he bowled in an Ashes Test. In the aftermath of his death, highlights reel after highlights reel was presented for our delectation, offering variations on the same theme. Warne's inimitable pause at the end of his run; Warne's seemingly artless approach; Warne's hugely powerful surge through the crease, where he was for an instant almost airborne; that little interlude of the ball's flight, beguiling but deceptive; then, at last, the springing of the trap, the baffling break, the bewildered response, the flying bails. Warne actually bowled only sixteen per cent of his victims. But disintegrating stumps, the bowler's vindication and the batter's abjection, are an entire story, accessible to everyone.

These reels hardly did his career justice. Warne bowled 51,347 balls in international cricket, which means that ninety-eight per cent of them did not take wickets. What really counted was the anticipation you experienced in watching him. You wouldn't be anywhere else. You daren't look away. He stretched our imaginations, and our credulity, even telling us so: 'Part of the art of bowling spin is to make the batsman think something special is happening when it isn't.' We were in the presence, then, of a master illusionist. To vary Arthur C. Clarke's line about technology, any sufficiently advanced leg-spin is indistinguishable from magic.

To reinforce this illusion, to practise what in magic is called 'misdirection', Warne brought a deliciously expressive repertoire of gestures: gasps, grins, moues, imprecations, scowls and stares. He could not even stand at first slip inconspicuously, given his unmistakable crossing of the legs between deliveries and his custom of favouring a broad-brimmed sun hat, thereby lightly disturbing the baggy green consensus. But it was when he ceremoniously surrendered this hat to the umpire that you took your seat to enjoy the show, starting with the trademark rub of the disturbed dirt in the crease and the casual saunter back.

The tennis writer Richard Evans once described the contrast between John McEnroe in repose and in action, how the spindly, puffy-haired, flat-footed figure at the baseline suddenly electrified when the ball was in flight. Warne accentuated this by first simply walking – walking! – to the crease. He might have been approaching the umpire to ask the time. Then, to borrow a recent movie title, everything everywhere all at once, the seamless delivery stride and follow through – the bowling action kept in trim by Jenner, altered over the journey only by age and attrition, and then but slightly.

Contrast, too, what was commonly believed about Warne's skill before 4 June 1993, and how he compelled us to adjust our understandings. For the decades before Warne, only Bhagwat Chandrasekhar, *sui generis*, and Abdul Qadir, *rara avis*, had nourished belief in leg-spin's match-winning properties. Leg-spin, we were advised, was an unpredictable faculty, an expensive luxury. It involved a great variety of deliveries. It lured batters to destruction by indiscretion. It needed congenial conditions, including dry, dusty or disintegrating pitches. It needed constant innovations to stay ahead of batters working one out, which precluded attention to the game's other departments. Captains might deploy leg-spin to afford their fast bowlers some respite. Otherwise it bordered on anachronism.

Apart from a fond regard he expressed for Qadir, Warne shows no signs of having watched any leg-spinner before him, or partaken of any of the skill's associated folk wisdom. By his own profession, his boyhood backyard heroes were Aussie pacemen, macho and theatrical, and batters, tough and leathery. That is completely understandable. When Warne

273

came to England that first time, it was fully thirty years since Australia had tackled an Ashes with a world-class purveyor of wrist-spin – it was a coincidence that that cricketer, Richie Benaud, was calling the Manchester Test when Warne came on to bowl to Gatting that first time and was there to pronounce, now and ever more: 'He's done it.'

By the time Warne had departed the Test stage, he had repudiated all those prior beliefs. Warne's cardinal virtue as a bowler was as much his accuracy as his degree of spin. He bowled with prodigious precision and relatively few variations; he hemmed batters in from all angles including round the wicket, and succeeded in all climes and countries. The discrepancy between his home and away bowling averages was less than two runs; his record was poorest, ironically, in India, previously held to be spin's great citadel. Nor did Warne revert to the mean: in the fourteen years after the Ball of the Century, his bowling average fluctuated by no more than 5 runs, while his most successful twelve-month periods were separated by twelve years (72 wickets at 23 in 1993, and 96 wickets at 22 in 2005).

Above all, Warne was never other than a frontline weapon. He saw bowling defensively as a contradiction in terms. He never sought protection or reinforcement. On the contrary, he rejoiced in being the sole spinner in the Australian line-ups of his era, and was notably less effective in partnership with another gifted leg-break bowler in Stuart MacGill. When MacGill supplanted him for a Test in Antigua in 1999, he never forgave his captain Steve Waugh.

His great confrère was instead Glenn McGrath, a pace bowler with similarly robust core skills, and a similar mix of patience and aggression. Warne enjoyed batting, was handy enough at number eight to allow Australia to do without a bona fide all-rounder, and excelled in the field, taking 205 international catches. No wonder Jenner was amusedly frustrated with Warne: he was leaving accumulated knowledge and established ideas in the dust.

Warne was also busily transcending our conception of a cricketer in the culture. It need hardly be said that he rewrote the book on fame. In Australia before him, Bradman had set the standard for deportment in greatness – a monument as much as a man, a faintly austere figure rather sealed off by his renown. Warne ascended no pedestal. By his colourful lifestyle he made privacy elusive, but by his personality he made public dealings easy. In the aftermath of his death, it seemed that almost everyone had their own Warnie story: he had a capacity for seeing others, for recognizing them, for making them feel a little special. There had been glamorous cricketers before Warne: Miller and Compton, Lillee and Imran. But nobody tackled fame so willingly, so hungrily, with an enthusiasm almost ingenuous.

Especially once introduced to social media, which allowed him to monitor and regulate his interaction with the outside world, he provided cheery relief from seriousness, and in a way that seemed breezily natural. 'If you're happy all the time,' he would say, 'good things will happen to you.' Notwithstanding that the latter also helps the former, he matured into a splendid advertisement for being famous, seeming to enjoy every minute of it.

But the celebrity perishes with him; it's as a cricketer Warne will endure. Warne unveiled his own statue at the MCG; now half the ground is named for him. When the Melbourne Cricket Club foreshadowed the Great Southern Stand in 1991 by explaining that the structure was 'too significant in every sense to be named after any one individual cricketer, footballer, administrator or public figure', and expressed the conviction that 'posterity will support the decision'. When the Victorian government decided within hours of Warne's death that the structure would be rebaptized the Shane Warne Stand, it seemed like the most natural thing in the world.

It's arguable that Warne has, quite inadvertently, proven a mixed blessing for those striving to following his example. It was expected he would inspire a generation to take up slow bowling, and perhaps he did, but he also set a standard that made it difficult for them to persist. Australia's men's team restlessly turned over a dozen spinners in the five years after his retirement before settling for the phlegmatic finger spin of Nathan Lyon. Warne's most successful imitators, unexpectedly, have been female: Australia's Alana King, Georgia Wareham and Amanda-Jane Wellington.

The only bowler Warne did not overawe, perhaps, was himself. After the day's play in that Old Trafford Test thirty years ago, Warne recalled in his autobiography, he and his colleagues sat around the dressing room watching a BBC wrap of the day, and replay upon replay of the delivery in question. 'Mate,' averred his keeper Ian Healy, 'that is as good a ball as you will ever bowl.' A daunting idea, one might think, at twenty-four. What to aim for now? What to do next? So it was that he started on the path to becoming as good a slow bowler as there will ever be.

# A declaration in Sydney

## HICK UP (1995)

Strokes are firm and consultations frequent when Atherton and Hick resume next morning, as England works towards the unfamiliar objective of a declaration, rather than deliverance. An Atherton cover-drive from Warne suggests that the rain has anaesthetized the surface, and Hick sweeps the leg-spinner with impunity. Though Taylor does his best to seek wickets, it's soon evident that it will take all his ingenuity to restrain England's scoring. Warne's frustration grows. May's trajectory flattens every over, and – dare one say it – Australia seems to have caught a case of English over-rate flu. England's captain has just hooked Fleming for four to begin his tenth hour of batting for the match when, seeking an avenue to third man, he edges to slip. It's not only the Barmy corner of the ground that is sorry to see him go. Atherton doesn't tackle the bowling frontally, but Australia appreciates solid sentries. Thorpe arrives and complicates Taylor's task by showing an interest in taking singles to make the left-right combination work. And Hick suddenly looks monumental, front foot like an ionic column. The only disturbance comes in the last over of the session when a rebound from May rubs against his stumps too shyly to remove a bail. Hick promptly restores his dignity by hitting the off-spinner over his head for consecutive boundaries.

Thorpe lends light feet and low slung strokes to England's effort after lunch. Hick greets McDermott's reintroduction with a square cut, like an executioner's swipe, then zips through the seventies with pull shots to the fence in front of square and into the crowd behind. It's looking at last like we're to get the procedural Test day we've been waiting for when Stewart appears with refreshments and representations from the rooms. The instructions, it will emerge later, include the advice that Atherton will close on the stroke of three. Hick is eight from a century, Thorpe seven from a half-century, England just shy of a 450 lead. It looks like it will all fit. Hick is nervous, but not unduly anxious in fending back the last three deliveries of Fleming's twenty-fourth over at 2.57 p.m. No force on earth appears able to deny him the two needed for his maiden Ashes hundred.

We should have known better. Atherton overrules himself and beckons the batsmen in. Hick approaches the gate, as if in a dream. He's deaf to congratulation and commiseration alike, and does not feel Thorpe's companionable hand on his shoulder. Atherton's priority is obtaining for his fast men a clear half hour at Australia's openers before tea. But Hick's carriage is not that of one whose first words at the dressing room door will be: 'Thank you, Captain, for sparing me the burden of scoring England's first hundred of the series.'

Side by side at slip, Hick and Thorpe spectate for the remainder of the day. Malcolm bounces a ball through Rhodes's gloves for four byes and causes Taylor to divert airily to third man, but otherwise simply hits the bat hard. Gough also commands little care and Fraser peers at the pitch suspicious that a substitution has occurred overnight. Fielding reverts to type and it is a fright to realize that Tufnell is England's fifth best patrolman. Gooch, Gatting, Fraser, Crawley and Malcolm do not so much field as retrieve. Australia is none for 41 at tea, which provides an opportunity to poll the press box on Atherton's declaration.

It's heresy, apparently, to suggest that Hick might have been allowed another over because 'the team is bigger than the individual.' But I suspect that this philosophy is less in evidence than that the team is bigger than *this* individual. Hick is not a journalist's favourite: rung-in from Zimbabwe, Zola Budd-style, after seasons of county cricketing plenty, but still short on media graces. Had it been Atherton declaring on Crawley, or Taylor declaring on Bevan, I'm not sure that consensus would have formed so swiftly. I also wonder how Gooch would have been received had he declared overnight on the third day of the last Ashes Test at the SCG with Atherton 94 at the time. In the first hour of the fourth day, as I recall it, a naturally tense young man added precisely one run. A week ago, the tourists craved a century, like a chain smoker caught between packets; now they've scorned one as though trying to give them up.*

---

\* From *One Summer, Every Summer: An Ashes Journal* (1995). The Test, finally, was drawn the following day, amid gloom unrelieved by floodlights.

# The 1997 Ashes
## THE BATTLE OF THE BOX

Winter 1997 in Australia offered two enticing competitions: one traditional, in the form of the Ashes; the other newer but growing more familiar, of Cricket versus the Rest of the World of Sport. Arriving at Heathrow in May, Mark Taylor's men were confident they had England's measure. But could they prevail in the battle for column inches and screen time against Australian rules football, two logger-headed rugby league competitions, the Bledisloe Cup in rugby union, soccer, Wimbledon, sundry Grand Prix and four golf majors? As it happened, the Ashes more than punched their weight, if in a fashion quite impossible to forecast. For not only did the campaign prove quite the most entertaining of the last decade, but dressing room dramas and commercial argy-bargy exerted a critical influence on the way events were seen. And not seen.

Preliminaries were inauspicious. After cutthroat series against West Indies and South Africa, few journalists were enthused by the prospect of watching Australia mete out six of the best to an English side incapable of matching Zimbabwe six months before. Correspondents of *The Australian*, in particular, left little doubt of their voting intentions at a future plebiscite on an Australian Republic. 'It is difficult to understand why England is still so widely regarded as a champagne series,' griped Malcolm Conn. 'Playing the beleaguered Poms is cheap and unfulfilling.' Columnist Mike Coward was even more damning: 'Apart from sentiment and tradition, England has nothing to do with cricket's real world at the end of the twentieth century.' Sentiment and tradition, of course, being things cricket should have no truck with. But perhaps they were merely echoing some of their own players. In the pre-tour *ABC Cricket Magazine*, Mark Waugh also implied a walkover in the offing: 'They [England] just haven't got the toughness you need to win Test cricket consistently. Man for man they are not that far behind us, but they lack hunger.'

One dissonant note as the tourists arrived was the captain's protracted spell in the batting dumps, which caused Ron Reed of the *Herald Sun* to liken the team to a Formula One racing car with a loose steering wheel. Among those urging Taylor to fall on his Stuart Surridge were an unlikely coalition of former coach Bob Simpson and the brothers Chappell. Greg of that ilk even turned amateur psychologist in the *Sunday Herald Sun*, contending that Taylor was a 'classic case of denial' and 'in no fit state to carry on'.

Taylor's redemptive 129 at Edgbaston a week later, consequently, became the greatest cricketing comeback since Graham Gooch's hair. 'Edge of Abyss to the Highest Peak', shrieked the *Herald Sun* front page, while beneath ran reams from a breathless Reed: 'Of all the many thousands of runs that have been scored in 120 years and 287 games of Test cricket between Australia and England, no more emotional shot has been played than the gentle push for a single that took Mark Taylor to his century at Edgbaston.'

The story of virtue triumphant came complete with several juicy subplots: it emerged that Olympic icon Kieren Perkins had spurred on Taylor with an inspirational fax; that Taylor's wife Judy had cleaned up by standing by her man at the betting tent. On the broadsheet editorial pages of *The Australian*, conservative columnist Frank Devine explored parallels between Taylor's innings and Gary Cooper in *High Noon*, with its 'eerily topical theme tune: "If I'm a man I must be brave and I must face the deadly killer or lay a coward, a craven coward, or lay a coward in my grave."'

Taylor's new lease on life – and England's – was by now competing for space. Kerry Packer's mighty Nine Network, which had gone to such lengths to get the cricket twenty years earlier, decided to leave its primetime schedules undisturbed and begin showing the cricket only after lunch. Full service was available only to pay TV viewers. Anyone in Melbourne turning on their sets to verify that Australia were really losing eight wickets before lunch on the first day of the series would instead have seen the celebrity panellists of *The Footy Show* cross examining a touring troupe of Sumo wrestlers.

Nine defended itself on ratings grounds, chief executive David Leckie telling the *Herald Sun*: 'You cannot disregard the viewers who choose to watch your regular programming week in, week out, and who would be appalled.' Many were appalled anyway. 'No wonder Michael Jordan is number one hero to our school children,' lamented Victorian sports minister Tom Reynolds in *The Age*. Nine could claim victory at the box office, where its evening ratings remained consistently strong. But, as a piece of public relations, it was a disaster. McGrath's opening salvos at Lord's and Jason Gillespie's lethal seven for 37 at Leeds, for instance, were supplanted by *Butterbox Babies*, *All-American Murder* and *Television: The Way We Were*. And of Steve Waugh's Manchester mastery, Nine viewers saw nothing at all: the Test had been dumped on the ABC to make way for the broadcast of rain from Wimbledon. The *pièce de résistance* was Nine's approach to the last day of the Fourth Test. It featured live coverage of one delivery, an apparent sign-off from anchorman Greg Ritchie, a ten-minute ad break and, unannounced, a replay of the first session. As 'You've Lost Us' of Barooga wrote to the *Herald Sun*: 'Great work with the cricket, Channel 9. Now can we look forward to seeing the last ten minutes of a movie before you show the beginning?'

Australia's eventual retention of the Ashes restored the cheery mood, *The Australian*'s Devine again leading the cheers for Taylor after seeing him *en famille* amid his Trent Bridge triumph: 'It is hard to think of a more resplendent demonstration of masculinity.' But in all the on- and off-field theatre, probably the tour's most significant story was overlooked. As the First Test unfolded, the *Sunday Age*'s shrewd Mark Ray reported that Australian Test cricketers had, under the auspices of their new Australian Cricketers' Association, recently discussed strike action as part of a fight for better pay and conditions with the Australian Cricket Board. Rather remarkably, no member of the travelling troupe in England elected to pursue the story. But, as the 1997–98 season dawned, the alert was sounded again. No cricketers, no cricket. That would at least allow Channel 9 to show *Butterbox Babies* in peace.*

---

* I watched the Ashes from home in 1997, when *Wisden*'s Matthew Engel asked me to write this report on the reporting. Our minds both boggled at *Butterbox Babies*, a telemovie I've still never seen about Nova Scotia's infamous Ideal Maternity Home. I've since read Bette Cahill's book, which I recommend.

# An English heist

## THE LONGEST DAY (1998)

Australia and England reversed roles on the last of the three extra-large days of Test cricket at Melbourne today, and there were telling lessons for both sides in this game's blockbuster finale. Like their guests on innumerable occasions, the hosts succumbed to the habit of waiting for someone else to do something, somebody else to pitch in. With the Ashes in safe keeping already, none of the Australian septet skewered in 79 deliveries for 32 runs appeared over-keen to recapture the initiative steadily oozing England's way. Even Steve Waugh, in exposing Stuart MacGill to Darren Gough during what proved the final over, trusted overmuch to fortune.

One should not make too much of Australia's supposed fourth-innings frailties, when they have in recent times chased targets at Port Elizabeth and Bangalore with composure and resolution. But here was a timely reminder that Test gauntlets thrown down must be accepted. England, in the meantime, displayed some qualities hitherto in this rubber associated almost entirely with Australia. There was an acknowledgment

284

at last that Test victories, while they sometimes hinge on freakish performances, are at least as often composed of subtle accretions.

Acclaim will be showered on the manful bowling of Dean Headley and Darren Gough, but two other factors should not pass unrecognized. Alan Mullally, the biggest bunny outside the kingdom of Hugh Hefner, had played above his station once on this tour already, his 23 not out at Townsville conjuring England's only previous first-class victory. The 23 he helped Gus Fraser raise for the last English wicket today proved as priceless as it was unlikely. Then there was Mark Ramprakash's gymnastic catch at square leg to upend Justin Langer at the very moment when all hope seemed gone, but which rejuvenated England's cause like a snort of snuff. In the areas of tailend batting and fielding, England have trailed Australia throughout this series; Mullally and Ramprakash narrowing this deficit today reinforced their importance.

In the context of the Ashes, England's victory is immaterial. It is even a little galling, demonstrating too late what the visitors are capable of, and might finally prove as meaningless as their similar consolation victory in Adelaide four years ago. But on all at the MCG it will leave an indelible trace: the one-day matches around the corner will seem especially banal by comparison.

They also serve in a Test match who only stand and wait, and three constituents of this game who helped make it such a rewarding spectacle should not be overlooked. First was the Melbourne Cricket Club, whose expensive but far-sighted decision in the early 1990s to underlay their ground with sand meant that only the first day of the match was lost after a deluge that might have robbed other grounds of several. Second were umpires Steve Bucknor and Daryl Harper, who officiated ably through three elongated and arduous days.

Last but far from least were the crowd, who bestowed favour with generous impartiality throughout. The Barmy Army, indefatigable from start to finish, deserved reward as much as their cricketers.*

* Australia duly won the 1998–99 Ashes by three matches to this one.

# An innings from Ponting (2001)

## COME IN NUMBER THREE

A n old but flavoursome Australian joke involves an Aussie being asked whether he can play the violin. 'I don't know,' he replies. 'I've never tried.' As well as imparting something about the national capacity for naive optimism, it reflects a long-standing Australian belief in innate talent.

Given time and luck, natural ability will out. Given time and luck, Ricky Ponting demonstrated his ample powers yesterday. The time in question was ten previous Test innings from which Ponting had garnered a mere 77 runs. The luck came with what appeared a low slip catch to Mark Ramprakash that contained sufficient slow-motion doubt to obtain Ponting the third umpire's mercy.

Ponting looked surprisingly composed as the video arbitration took place. He walked down the pitch, chatted to his partner, and continued without demur. He is an incurably confident character and, as his nickname 'Punter' implies, comfortable with the forces of chance. Perhaps he had seen the 4/1 odds on him to be Australia's highest scorer quoted by

William Hill before the match and sensed that his nineteen months without a Test hundred was about to end.

An incisive spell from Andrew Caddick gave all the batsmen a few alarms, but Ponting was soon into his stride. He has looked impatient this series, thrusting at the ball rather than waiting for it to come on. Yesterday, he was less eager, less hasty and found ample time for all his strokes. When Caddick dropped short in the first over after tea, Ponting was in position so early that he could have doffed his helmet and given his partner a wink before pulling it into the western terrace. He also showed discretion: later, when Nasser Hussain posted two boundary patrollers behind square leg, Ponting studied them intently and took care to pull along the ground. After all, he became Adam Gilchrist's vice-captain when Steve Waugh withdrew from this Test. Next time he plays a Test here it may be as captain.*

Australian Test cricketers have originated from some charmingly apposite places. The doughty left-hander Warren Bardsley, the first to make two centuries in a Test, came from the rural hamlet of Nevertire in New South Wales. Ponting's birthplace was Tasmania's Prospect, as he quickly became and in some respects remains. At four, Ponting's grandmother clothed him in a T-shirt featuring the legend: 'Inside this shirt is an Australian Test cricketer'. He had his first equipment deal with Kookaburra at the age of twelve, played for his state at seventeen and his country at twenty. His maiden Test hundred on this ground four years ago suggested not so much a coming man as an arriving and disembarking one.

Since then, Ponting's career has been of the coming-and-going kind; more coming than going, as a Test average of

---

* Ponting did indeed return to England as captain in 2005, then 2009.

better than 40 suggests, but he has been a noticeable under-achiever against England. Since a breakthrough hundred here four years ago, he had until yesterday scored 220 runs in thirteen subsequent innings at an average just shy of 17, a curious exception to the Australian rule that runs against England are to be hoarded against possible tougher times ahead. In India a few months ago, too, Ponting was unsettled by Harbhajan Singh's vicious bounce; suspicion lingers that he has a weakness against off-spin, though the likelier truth is that he merely has a weakness against great bowlers. Luckily, none were in evidence yesterday.

Nasser Hussain's determined pre-match words notwith-standing, England seemed merely to rue their past luck rather than genuinely seek an even break. Rather like his absent skipper, Ponting never hinted at offering it. It was Mark Waugh rather than Steve who kept Ponting company for most of yesterday, though this was in its way appropriate. The senior player in the Australian side since his brother's injury – and who yesterday passed 2000 runs against England – Mark Waugh is no stranger to the breath of selectors on his collar. Indeed, it has often been in the crucial extra innings granted him that fortune has smiled. If Ponting needed confirmation yesterday that ability does out, he had merely to look down the other end.

# A declaration from Gilchrist

## EXCITEMENT CONTAINED (2001)

'Dead cat bounce' is an expression in foreign exchange markets to describe the behaviour of sharply discounted currencies that suddenly seem to recover. It is a warning not to be misled: dropped off a tall enough building, the deadest cat will bounce just a little.

Does that describe yesterday's English revival at Leeds? It would be as easy to tear down as it would to build up: a victory in a dead Test, abetted by a sporting declaration, in conditions as suited to batting as the previous day's had been suited to boating. Although it may lead to a television documentary some twenty years hence entitled *100 Per Cent Butchery*, it probably means as little about the English game's long-term health as it proved did Headingley '81.*

---

* The reference is to *100 Per Cent Beefy*, a BBC documentary about Botham's great match at Headingley in 1981, screened nostalgically during the Test. In hindsight, I'm surprised how downbeat I was about this day. Perhaps I imagined the Australian riposte, which duly followed at The Oval, led by twin hundreds from the Waughs.

Yet the day was not entirely out of keeping with a series in which an excellent cricket team from Australia has beaten a good cricket team from England. Part of the Australian achievement in retaining the Ashes has been to prevent England sustaining its potential rather than merely brushing against it at intervals. A subtle release of Australian pressure and urgency – for there is no doubt that its bowling and outcricket were below par yesterday – and a state closer to equilibrium prevails. As Adam Gilchrist observed succinctly afterwards, in a tone suggesting some unfamiliarity with the words: 'It felt like Test cricket.'

It would be wisdom after the event to criticize Gilchrist's declaration. There is a story told of England's famous Test win at Port-of-Spain in March 1968 following a charitable closure; when Garry Sobers arrived at customs in Georgetown for the next Test and was asked if he had anything to declare, he allegedly replied: 'Not again.' One hopes that Gilchrist will not feel the same way. One could no more have planned for Mark Butcher's innings than make contingency for a Lara or a Laxman. Certainly Gilchrist was altogether more nobly motivated than the last captain to issue such a challenge to a team led by Nasser Hussain, who it turned out had picked up a leather jacket and a fistful of rand for his trouble.

Still, Gilchrist might have helped himself a little more. His use of Glenn McGrath for only eight overs after lunch and faith in Brett Lee seemed hard to follow, while his failure to patrol the point and third man regions was costly. He also gave his untidiest display behind the stumps since Edgbaston. In the looming discussion about the successor to Steve Waugh, questions remain about what would be his triple burden as captain, keeper and key batsman. It would be like appointing as chief executive of Qantas someone already piloting the planes and passing out the peanuts.

Hussain, by contrast, was a figure of increasing authority yesterday. While Butcher's innings was a freak of nature, his skipper's influence was at the outset not less significant. As he did for Essex against the Australians at the end of June, he pulled Gillespie for an early six. The ball took an eternity to retrieve, as either an English supporter rubbed it on the concrete or an Australian smothered it in the juice of a Murray Mint, which seemed to underscore the blow's authority. Hussain's body language was similarly positive. Some batsmen wander to square leg between deliveries, some prod away at a length; Hussain seldom deserts his post and steps punctually into line.

More positive body language was visible at intervals during this match behind the Rugby Stand. Under the supervision of Australia's physiotherapist Errol Alcott, Steve Waugh could be seen jogging back and forth; he also led Australian slip-catching practices and batted a number of times in the nets. This series has produced one astounding comeback; Waugh's could be the second.

# Steve Waugh

## BURIED TREASURE (2009)

Steve Waugh is an Australian Living Treasure. That is not the airing of an opinion, but a statement of a fact: he is one of a list of about a hundred nominated and elected by this country's National Trust. It's an eccentric and obviously subjective list. Erstwhile prime minister's wife Hazel Hawke is there; the erstwhile husband who left her for a younger woman, Bob Hawke, is not. Hugely popular, widely admired and softly spoken indigenous athlete Cathy Freeman is there; hugely popular, widely admired and extremely noisy indigenous athlete Anthony Mundine is not. In other words, this is no place for controversialists. It is a pantheon in which Steve Waugh fits snugly.

Nobody has played more Tests than Steve Waugh. No Australian has played more one-day internationals. It's a record as uncompromising as the man himself, and the team he led to success upon success. It was built, moreover, in a relentless forward march. 'What about the next game, Steve?' asked a journalist after one night game in January 2000. 'Who are we playing?' Waugh responded, adding amid chuckles:

'We just get on a plane and go somewhere and find out who we're playing.'

At the time, he was one of three to-die-for wickets in international cricket, while having nothing in common with the other two: the classically correct Sachin Tendulkar, the free-spirited Brian Lara. Waugh was neither a straightforwardly orthodox, nor even a particularly gainly batsman – crouching, jumping, cutting all sorts of capers as he refrained from hooking. But all the while he would be accumulating, like compound interest, occasionally essaying a signature slog-sweep to reinforce his ownership of the crease. He was a batsman of his era: at home in all conditions, never daunted, always ready, seldom satisfied.

Yet for a figure whose cricket was so embedded in the modern, the terms in which Waugh is usually understood are deeply traditional. No sooner had he appeared on the scene in the mid-1980s than Bill O'Reilly was describing him as Stan McCabe reincarnate; he became known for his friendships with past masters Stork Hendry and Bill Brown. When he made his first real impact as a Test batsman in England in 1989, the praise was for his model technique, of a purity no local batsman could emulate. When he came to the Test captaincy in 1999, he was lauded for his regular appeals to the past, and an almost demagogic espousal of the cult of the baggy green. Even in articulating the doctrine of 'mental disintegration', Waugh was seen as following time-honoured Australian mores: he was the old-fashioned indefatigable Aussie who did not give up a chip of a bail, while expecting what happened on the field to stay there.

His career knew torrid times. There was the claimed catch of Lara at Kensington Oval in April 1995, for which, as he put it, he was 'carved up' by the likes of Michael Holding and Viv Richards. There was the manipulation of the points system in the World Cup in 1999, in an attempt to progress the West Indies at New Zealand's expense, after which Waugh famously explained: 'We're not here to win friends, mate.' Nor did he shore up relations with the media when he muttered, pithily, that his press conference inquisitors were a 'bunch of cockheads'.

Yet this was a rare dropping of the guard: for a cricketer who played so ruthlessly, and whose team was wont to push the line of acceptable aggression, his career had few personal black marks. He never transgressed the ICC Code of Conduct himself, and was once even its beneficiary, Ian Healy's suspension in South Africa in March 1997 smoothing his path to the vice-captaincy. A stroll through the index of his magnum opus, *Out of My Comfort Zone* (2005), underlines how seldom he became part of public disputes. One lights hopefully on 'moped incident, Bermuda', only to find it refers to minor hijinks at the end of the 1991 Caribbean tour rather than being Australian cricket's secret Pedalogate.

Off the field, Waugh maintained an almost sunken profile. In person a shy and self-effacing man, he was instrumental in welcoming wives into the Australian team's fold as a kind of civilizing influence, receiving the phone call that offered him the Australian captaincy while watching *Sesame Street* with his daughter. When Shane Warne publicly dissed Adam Gilchrist's leadership aspirations by philosophizing that a captain should be more like the Fonz than Richie Cunningham, it was possible to cast Steve Waugh in the scene as a kind of Howard Cunningham, all rumpled integrity and paternal wisdom.

Speaking of Howards, the period of Waugh's ascendancy in Australia was encompassed by the prime ministership of John of that ilk, self-styled 'cricket tragic' who cheerfully acknowledged himself the most conservative leader his conservative party had ever had. Waugh was not an exact fit with this period. He welcomed the compulsive innovator John Buchanan into his team's inner circle; he sought, with a touch of the New Age guru, to 'get to know the guys as human beings and not just cricketers'. As his fame grew, and he was compelled to become a public figure, he became as famous for exchanging words with Mother Teresa and Nelson Mandela as he did with Curtly Ambrose, putting his reputation to use in a variety of philanthropic works on the subcontinent.

Yet in an age of compulsive extraversion, Waugh cut a self-contained figure on the field, lean, dour and unsmiling, to complaints about which he retorted: 'If you're in your office trying to work, do you smile all the time?' Instead of flamboyance, the keynote of Waugh's captaincy was continuity. He existed, even in an age of abundance, as a reminder of leaner times in Australian cricket, the last of his generation to have an Ashes defeat on his conscience. He pressed also to create 'new' traditions, having a special cap minted for the first Test of the 2000s modelled on the cap worn in the first Test of the 1900s, involving himself in the manufactured memorabilia industry as a shareholder in the firm Blazed in Glory.

Nor was it just the surname that lent his leadership a martial air. His Tests were frontal assaults, carefully plotted, relentlessly executed. No captain to lead their country in more than ten Tests has a higher proportion of wins or a lower proportion of draws. He believed in rank, in *esprit de corps*, even in the power of a uniform, embodied in his storied cap, so distinctive in an era of helmets and sunhats. His nationalism was of the same unselfconscious, celebratory if sometimes defensive character that flourished during the eleven years of Howard's premiership. 'I'd like to see Australian people own more of Australia and not sell it all off to overseas companies and corporations,' he told an interviewer fifteen years ago. 'It seems to me that the Japanese own half of Queensland – that's one thing I'd like to see changed.' But if all the John Williamson songs and odes to the Southern Cross sometimes seemed contrived, nor were they easily imitable. Waugh initiated the numbering of players' headgear and attire, inviting eminent past players to hand new caps over to Test debutants, beginning with Bill Brown's welcome to Adam Gilchrist ten years ago. England have tried something similar, but watching Nasser Hussain hand Jonathan Trott his new lid at the Oval a few months ago still seemed perfunctory. Taking his teammates to Gallipoli sat more naturally with Waugh than with any other leader; when England dropped in on Flanders earlier this year, it looked phoney even before Andrew Flintoff elected to drink for his country.

Quite why Waugh reinforced his captaincy with so many props and symbols is an intriguing psychological question. Some saw it as self-promotion; even now, Waugh has a quiet caucus of detractors in Australian cricket, who see him as out primarily for number one. Waugh himself has answered to the charge: 'Life as a full-time professional teaches you to be selfish in many ways.' Yet a personal suspicion is that Waugh coveted the captaincy before quite grasping what it entailed. The activities and artefacts with which he invested his leadership helped distribute the burden; he could thereby make himself less an individual, more the representative of a lineage.

Waugh was famous for his diaries and his photographs. Both can act as means of ordering and controlling experiences, putting a comforting distance between the act and the observer. Sport, of course, is replete with ego, and Waugh could not have competed without a sizeable one. But his wife Lynette, who writes as perceptively of her husband as anyone, has noted: 'Stephen has never – even as a baby, I'm told –

liked a lot of attention.' And it's telling, I think, how swiftly and completely Waugh has receded in public consciousness since that final, rather fevered farewell season five years ago; not for him the love of and comfort in the limelight of his most eminent contemporary, Shane Warne. 'Treasure', of course, is something proverbial tucked away, not necessarily recognized as such, even when in plain sight. In this sense, the National Trust truly knew its man.

# A Test at Edgbaston

## NOTHING BETTER (2005)

It did not take long after it finished for the Edgbaston Test to feel slightly unreal, even ridiculous. A game containing more than 700 runs in boundaries won and lost by two runs? Test cricket has no business with results so close. Tight finishes are meant to be the prerogative of one-day and T20 cricket. It's the nature of Test matches that they multiply possibilities and magnify differences. But not, gloriously, over this contest's ten taut sessions in which England made the running but Australia somehow kept tapping them on the shoulder.

Nor were the ten sessions all there was. *The Man Who Wasn't There* is now not only a Coen Brothers movie; the title befitted Glenn McGrath, whose absence at Birmingham proved as influential as his presence at Lord's. At 9.15 a.m., during Australia's tough rugby warm-up, McGrath groped for a pass from Brad Haddin and trod on a cricket ball ready for a fielding routine. Word of the Grade 2 ligament strain travelled around England like the good news from Ghent to Aix. Michael Kasprowicz, who had arrived expecting to wait the drinks, was routed to a date with destiny.

There was also *The Pitch That Never Was*. At the time of McGrath's laming, Ricky Ponting was scrutinizing Steve Rouse's surface, the subject over the preceding week of all manner of horticultural speculations; the tornado that had cleaved a path through Birmingham on 28 July had interfered with Rouse's preparatory work, and he had been busily broadcasting pre-emptive excuses. Ponting had resolved to bowl first, did not change his strategy on learning of McGrath's injury, and walked into his own tornado: sent in, England were one for 132 at lunch. Trescothick and Strauss cannot have compiled a more crucial century partnership for the first wicket than this, their sixth. Strauss was dropped by Warne at slip off Lee, Trescothick caught at backward point off a Gillespie no-ball; otherwise they took advantage of bowling that tended to the short, the wide and the delectable and, beyond emergent scuffing at the Ryder Stand end, the pitch offered bowlers little. Even after Warne bowled Strauss by using that rough from round the wicket, England continued attacking, Vaughan ended his cameo with a mishook, Trescothick with a faraway waft. Flintoff and Pietersen, having never previously clicked, suddenly double-clicked, ransacking 103 from 105 balls. Pietersen, who hit ten fours and a six, looked every inch an accomplished Test batsman; Flintoff, who cudgelled five sixes and six fours amid lots of sightless groping at Warne, embodied the gifted village slogger; Ponting paid a heavy price for merely awaiting their self-destruction. Nor did England's tail dither: 114 runs in 133 balls, including the ninth and tenth sixes of the innings from Harmison and Jones. There was a suspicion that England should have made more than 407, but their 5.13 runs per over was tell-tale. No-one had scored so many runs at such speed in a Test against Australia since Ashes primordial.

After Hayden's early departure, Australia's reply was almost as sprightly, Ponting striking ten fours, and Martyn getting smoothly underway. On the stroke of lunch, however, Martyn dawdled between wickets and was narrowly thrown out by Vaughan at the non-striker's end. Although Clarke played a poised hand in partnership with the adhesive Langer, England now had the scent of wickets. The reverse swing of Flintoff and Jones came to the fore as the tail crumbled round Gilchrist. In the last hour of the day's play, the ground announcer was heard to request the attention of 'Mr Ivan Milat'. Ah, those jolly Australian japesters; at least it made a change from the evergreen Mr Hugh Jarse. But England, leading Australia for the first time on first innings since the corresponding Test in 1997, were now hot on the trail of cricket's most wanted serial killer.

Warne stole the second day show when he landed a ball in the footmarks to bowl Strauss behind his legs, registering 35.8 degrees of turn on the Channel Four protract-o-meter: his 100th wicket in England, unexampled among visiting bowlers. England subsided to four for 31, but Pietersen and Bell parried Australia's thrust with a partnership of 41 off 69 balls before getting on the wrong ends of Rudi Koertzen, and Flintoff rallied the tail, Jones in particular standing fast as 51 were added for the last wicket in forty minutes. Flintoff countered Warne more coolly now as he collared the others, dishing out four more sixes to go with six fours in his 86-ball 73, before being bowled by the spinner backing away – not their last duel of the match.

Langer and Hayden started patiently on Australia's chase – less a chase than a stretch really, considering that the match's allotted time was barely half over. At an early stage, however, the ball started reversing, and a stampeding Flintoff trampled Langer and Ponting in his first over, going from round the wicket to the left-hander to over the wicket to the right-hander in the flicker of a dial, amid Barmy Army chanting more reminiscent of an FA Cup final. He seemed preceded up the pitch by a wave of aggression, and followed by a gale of goodwill. When Jones's swing confounded Hayden, the noise was likewise deafening. The Barmy Army has its detractors, but in this match marched in lock-step with their team, filling Edgbaston with a cacophony of hope.

Warne's rough was now the province of Giles, and he used it well. Neither Martyn nor Gilchrist had the patience to fight back, although the precocious Clarke did. With Warne, he almost guided Australia through the extra half hour that England took to try wrapping the match up. Then, with the sanctuary of stumps close enough to touch, Harmison held back a yorker over which the young man stumbled. Australia began the last day needing 107 runs to win from its last two wickets.

Warne and Lee set out, as they later put it, to 'have some fun', which was very little fun for the vast majority of the crowd, who would have been content with a day lasting two deliveries. They played their shots, missed what they had to, bunted into space and soaked the pressure from the decidedly hostile Harmison and Flintoff. Warne gave himself his usual room to slash and loft; Lee wore what he could not work; as they added 45 in 59 balls, Vaughan appeared at a loss to contain them. Finally, Warne's groping back foot knocked his off stump awry, but the audience's ordeal was not over yet. Lee and Kasprowicz combined robustly, lofting Giles, parrying Flintoff, geeing each other up in mid-pitch. When Kasprowicz survived an lbw appeal from Harmison and guided a ball to third man in and out of Jones's clammy hands, the unthinkable lurched into likelihood.

It felt perilously like history in the making, at least in its first draft. Devotees of Ashes history will know of the famous team sheet of the original 1882 Oval Test match which features the names of the England XI in a scorer's hand apparently growing more fragmentary with the tension; the last name, Peate, is written so shakily that it looks like 'Geese'. My own scribblings attained an unintelligibility almost doctor-like. As the bowler came on with the Lee–Kasprowicz partnership worth 59 in 76 balls, 'Harmison – Pavilion End' might as well have read 'take two after meals' or 'beware drowsiness'.

Harmison's third ball was a last desperate bouncer. Number eleven leaned away, leaving his bat and gloves in danger, and Geraint Jones, who had batted ineffectually and kept untidily, interposed a glove between the ball and the ground. Bowden's crooked finger was a cue for the ground to erupt and England's players to fall on one another in a disbelieving huddle, with the exception of Flintoff who stooped chivalrously over Lee, down on his haunches, to congratulate him on a fight well fought. The Man Who Wasn't There remained out of sight, although Flintoff and Harmison shook Rouse's hand in token of appreciation from his Pitch That Never Was.

Some barrack-room lawyers – perhaps in cricket it should be dressing room lawyers – afterwards discerned a chink of light between Kasprowicz's glove and bat handle while poring over the final replay and began muttering 'benefit of the doubt' as solemnly as if they were discussing habeas corpus. Doubt is inherently personal and subjective: in any case, only Bowden's counted. And if you could not relish this result, opening the Ashes out as not in decades, you were surely watching the wrong game. This was a classic – and yes, it really happened.*

--------

* Edgbaston 2005 is still the best Test match I have ever seen, though Headingley 2019 has since run it close.

# A spell from Warne

## MARATHON MAN (2005)

When Australian film makers churn out their monthly documentary about Sir Donald Bradman, they often make up for the general shortage of archival footage by dwelling on a famous newspaper poster bearing the headline 'Bradman v England'. Shane Warne has by now more than deserved the same.

The Australians bounded from the Bedser Stand like a team on a mission yesterday – as well they might have. The captain seems to want substitutes to present their passports and driver's licences at the gate. Their coach could not be under more scrutiny had he started checking into hotels as Mr Eric Jones.*

Warne has very little to prove – on the cricket field anyway. He could pass away tomorrow, leaving his spinning finger to

---

* 'Mr Eric Jones', for those who have forgotten, was the alias used by England football manager Sven-Göran Eriksson when he checked into hotels for his assignations.

Lord's and his texting thumb to science, and remain a cricket immortal. Still, the occasion made his competitive sap rise: once he came on after an hour, only dull convention prevented his bowling from both ends. Warne struck first in his third over, continuing his toxicity to Marcus Trescothick in Tests: unusually for an opener, he has fallen more often to only Makhaya Ntini.

Michael Vaughan then struck a blow against the Kansas Board of Education. It was twenty minutes to lunch when England's captain tried tugging a short leg-break against the spin, hit it in the air as is his regrettably casual habit, and was caught at mid-wicket: no evidence of intelligent design behind that shot.

When Warne bowled to Ian Bell, there was barely time to remember that the batsman's Test average coming into the Lord's Test was 297, before it had been further reduced to 46.8. It took Warne eleven deliveries to trap his young opponent with a straight one at Lord's; here it took two. Merlyn the leg-spin machine's manufacturers will not be turning to Bell for an endorsement.

Three for 11 in 22 deliveries: Warne never looks bored on a cricket field but now he was snatching off his hat as each preceding over ended and he headed for the umpire. He polished the ball as though it was a family heirloom. He posed and pursed his lips as if he had taken some lessons from Graham Norton on Monday night. There is simply no more spellbinding bowler. Warne has, we are often reminded, two deliveries – one that turns, one that does not. But he no more needs additional variation than The Ramones needed a third chord. Yesterday he came at the batsman from every angle, over and round the wicket, close to the stumps and wide of the crease, with the arm high and low, slower and faster, higher and flatter. He even bowled a string of googlies, including one which turned as slowly as an old watch and elicited a laconic smile from Strauss.

Warne's *jeu d'esprit* was reserved for Kevin Pietersen. Warne greeted his old mucker with two mid-wickets, one-third and two-thirds of the way to the boundary. The first, Simon Katich, soon became short leg; the second, Michael Clarke, remained in place. The slog-sweep, which Pietersen has played so profitably, thus remained an option, but a risk if mishit. On top of this pressure Warne fastened the seal of precision. His first over to Pietersen was a maiden – a gauntlet thrown down. Pietersen did not score from the first dozen deliveries, then in resisting the impulse to hit over the top botched a turn to leg.

Warne's thinking was not, perhaps, exceptional; his delivery was not, ultimately, a candidate for ball of the twenty-first century. But if you seek a reason for Warne's 616 wickets, it is the ability to lay a snare like this in the decisive Test of an Ashes series, when others' hands are trembling. Warne might have run amok but for Andrew Strauss, who repented earlier days on the back foot to leg-spin with a constant forward press, pad closely escorting the bat when it was not leading the way. If this testifies to Merlyn's influence, the machine deserves at least a level two coaching certificate. Andrew Flintoff, who used to confront slow bowling as though he had just consumed a crate of Red Bull, also proved to have learned a trick or two.

Some cricketers fill you with awe; Flintoff makes it look as though you could have a bit of a go at this Test lark yourself. Three consecutive boundaries from Warne were followed by an almost parodic defensive shot and a genial smile, as if to share a joke between them. When a quicker ball took a thick inside edge to fine leg, he again smiled at Warne, acknowledging that the joke had almost been on him.

As Strauss and Flintoff survived the afternoon, Warne's

yakka grew harder. On several occasions, he went past the bat and began to jump about like a child on a bouncy castle. When Strauss finally exposed his bat while pushing forward, Warne had taken more wickets in a five-Test Ashes series in England than any Australian.

*Wisden* does not mention all the occasions on which a leg-spinner has taken three wickets before lunch on the first day of a Test. Warne makes you think of stats nobody records, because they are so extraordinary it never occurred to anyone to keep them. Three more wickets and Warne will have dismissed more Englishmen than any other bowler. He will get them. The other newspaper poster on which the documentary makers lovingly dwell is 'Bradman Bats and Bats and Bats and Bats'. By the time he's finished here, Warne will have deserved the bowling equivalent.

# A draw at The Oval (2005)

## GOOD FOR CRICKET

In the Australian vernacular, if an event is classified 'good for cricket', it usually means that the national team has lost, and is almost invariably said through gritted teeth. In light of the first occurrence, there will be a lot of 'good for cricket'-ing across Australia as you read these words. There is, however, little need for the grudging tone.

It was hard to watch England retrieve the Ashes yesterday, but only because the fingers of one's hand tended to obscure the view, as the teams presented another gift of a game that just kept on giving. It was a drama, thriller and comedy rolled into one, though not a tragedy. Nothing much is genuinely tragic in sport, least of all an end of sixteen years' one-way traffic. For the duration of Australia's dominance, Ashes cricket has been like the Giant's Causeway: worth seeing but seldom worth going to see. This series would have justified taking out a second mortgage to witness, and its last instalment merited pawning the family silver.

No one arrived at The Oval entirely happy yesterday morning. With ninety-eight overs to play, even signs of confidence seemed grotesquely misplaced. *The Sun*'s 'Ashes Coming Home' bus has been the ghost at the feast these past five days, its banner potentially as collectible as the newspapers that announced Dewey had beaten Truman in the 1948 presidential election.

Perhaps it will now be decreed that it was *The Sun* Wot Won It, but after forty minutes that bus looked like it bore the destination Hubris. Glenn McGrath and his elbow, far from fit in this game, took time to warm to their tasks, but then found that traditional nagging length. Vaughan followed one that went away to send a tremor through his team, and Bell responded to his first delivery as though he had been passed the Black Spot. By that time, after two exploratory overs from Brett Lee, Warne was in harness. In the inaugural Ashes Test at The Oval in 1882, it was Fred Spofforth who assured his colleagues that 'this thing can be done' before going out and doing it; it was tempting to ascribe similar sentiments to Warne.

Like the volatile, mephistophelian Spofforth, Warne wears his heart on his sleeve and his cricket on his face. He has at least as many guises as he has deliveries, from pent-up fury to barely suppressed hilarity. Though he leaves the crossing to Matthew Hayden, there is even pious Warne. During the pre-lunch session, he regularly returned to his mark with eyes upturned, muttering to the individual he calls 'the man upstairs' – a phrase ambiguous when he was on Kerry Packer's payroll, but now more obviously aimed heavenwards.

Marcus Trescothick, meanwhile, resembled a London bobby trying to quell a riot, somehow retrieving his equilibrium each time a breach of his defensive line was threatened. It is no discredit to him that it never looked an equal contest. Could Warne's unearthly chaos ever have been contained by the forces of law and order? From round the wicket at the extremity of the crease, with his arm at the same elevation as Clarrie Grimmett's, Warne turned one delivery out of the footmarks so far that it was almost a breach of the spirit of cricket – by the standard unit of measurement, it spun a Double Gatt and would have rolled to backward square leg had the batsman's pads not been struck, a micron or two outside off stump. From this point, Trescothick's fall was almost foretold: another Double Gatt, and umpire Koertzen almost did not need to be asked. The wicket was Warne's 168th against England; no one has taken more, and it will be a long time before anyone does.

Warne had no more left-handers to bowl to, but did have Kevin Pietersen, whom he had devoured in the first innings like Hannibal Lecter. Pietersen again looked like a juicy morsel. But for a touch of Adam Gilchrist's gauntlet, his under edge would almost certainly have been swallowed whole by Hayden at slip. The eyes that closed all over The Oval when he played his first slog sweep may have included Pietersen's own.

Warne's chief impact on Pietersen's innings, however, was to prolong it. Pietersen was a skittish 15 when he edged to slip face-high to his Hampshire captain, almost infallible in the position this season but not yesterday. The roles had been reversed at Old Trafford, Pietersen dropping Warne in the gloaming; Pietersen could not have asked for cricket to be the great leveller at a more telling juncture.

Warne flashed predatory eyes on Pietersen for the rest of the day, twice removing the bails at the bowler's end when he went wandering down the pitch in mid-over, perhaps only half-jokingly. As he stood rather forlornly at third man after tea, stretching his sore and weary fingers, he was, as ever, the toast and the bait of the crowd, whose choruses alternated between 'There's only one Shane Warne' and 'Warnie dropped the Ashes'. The first is beyond contradiction, a tribute to the bowler and a haunting thought for Australians. The second is unsupportable: with 40 wickets at 19.93 and 249 runs at 28, it is arguable he made them. 'We wish you were English' sounded much more like it.

The contest between Lee and Pietersen was the day's leading indicator. At first, Lee treated him as a punch bag, pounding his body from short of a length. Especially after gloving one short ball over the catching cordon, Pietersen looked grateful for the asylum of the non-striker's end. His retaliation was, in its own way, still harder to watch: a face-to-the-wall rather than a backs-to-the-wall effort. He hooked thrillingly, crazily, just millimetres each time from having his head turned into a turnip by the tabloids. Paul Collingwood's involvement in their 60-run partnership was so minimal that he might have been tempted to a chorus of 'Eng-ger-land Eng-ger-land Eng-ger-land' just to feel more part of the action.

In the end, Lee had one of those days where he mistakes shortness of length for hostility of intent. On the Test's driest day, he had the ball reversing at 95mph when he pitched it up. The opportunity to turn England's best weapon against them was lost in the backwash of testosterone. With Shaun Tait too callow for lifting this heavy, too much labour was left for the unflagging Warne and the unfit McGrath. With Ashley Giles a loyal sentry, Pietersen stood guard over England's series lead until it was impassable. A fifth bowler might have been handy, although perhaps only if his name had been Lillee or O'Reilly.

In any event, there will be time for inquests later. For the moment, an Australian gives thanks. For years, my fellow countrymen have publicly pined for a 'competitive Ashes series', without perhaps something so competitive in mind. But sporting rivalry is only a rivalry if there is the danger of defeat: England have not only won the Ashes but reflated the whole currency of Anglo-Australian cricket. That is, unambiguously, good for the game.

# An innings from Gilchrist

## ROCKET MAN (2006)

In years to come, people will probably wonder about the
dot ball that commenced Monty Panesar's thirty-fourth
over at Perth yesterday. A dot? What happened? For the
record, Adam Gilchrist leaned coyly forward and defended on
the off side. Gilchrist doesn't play many defensive shots, and
in Test cricket's second fastest hundred yesterday, even fewer
than usual. So there: now you know.

People will wonder because, in all likelihood, they'll be
aware what happened next: it already has the stuff of endless
replay about it, like David Hookes's fours in the Centenary
Test, or Garry Sobers's sixes at Swansea. After two through
cover to reach his fifty in 40 balls, 6, 6, 4 and 6 pealed from his
bat in ecstatic succession over mid-wicket. Each blow was a
little different: the four was not quite middled, but the sixes
travelled increasing distances, carried by a stiff breeze that
Panesar should probably not have been bowling into in the
first place.

None of them was a wild or reckless shot by any means.
The eye never left the ball and the follow through of each

312

stopped abruptly, as though every hit had been aimed at one spectator in particular. Before the last delivery, a fourth man was sent to patrol the leg-side boundary. He might as well have been sent to buy ice creams.

Bishan Bedi believed in applauding sixes off his own bowling; his fellow Sikh did not go so far, but was brave enough to smile and game enough to want to continue bowling. His captain relieved him. No one could relieve the captain. Andrew Flintoff has, in all probability, one more night as custodian of the Ashes. The recollection of his supremacy over Gilchrist last year must seem like a childhood memory.

Flintoff actually started the bowling against Gilchrist yesterday, and elicited his only false shot: the Australian's stroke to get off the mark was an ungainly shovel backward of point. Last year it would probably have been out; this year it wended its way wide of Bell in the gully for four. The next stroke, a superlative back-foot drive to the extra cover perimeter, started the trend, in which fielders were reduced mainly to a retrieving role. At one stage, eight men were stationed on the fence, with Flintoff alone at point – perhaps for the view, because he never looked likely to stop anything.

Viv Richards's twenty-year-old, 56-ball Test hundred record, also in front of his home crowd, seemed at one stage bound to fall. With his last six, from Hoggard, in the direction of the Gatorade van that delivers the players' refreshments, Gilchrist seemed to be making his shot selection according to the priorities of product placement. A bit of width and bounce slowed him down. The fastest Ashes hundred had to suffice.

England had hung in well throughout the first session under a pitiless sun. After lunch, however, affairs went Colin Cowdrey-shaped, Hussey and Clarke taking advantage of England's vanishing vim, and heady from a healthy whiff of the Ashes. Hussey's Test average, which yesterday brushed 90, must by now be causing some concern to John Howard: special legislation to ring fence Bradman's iconic average of 99.94 may be in the works. Ironically, this was Hussey's least secure innings of the summer; he admitted later that he was troubled by the heat, found his concentration wavering, and urged himself on with the thought: 'If it's hot for me, it's twice as hot for them.'

The day's smoothest and calmest batting was from Michael Clarke, who in a way has been even more of a surprise than Hussey, given that he began the summer outside Australia's first-choice XIII. The headstrong colt who squandered a century at Lord's last year has become the most patient and practical of accumulators, and he played Panesar superbly, driving him for six and four down the ground in his twentieth over, then profiting from errors of length later. His overhead smash from Flintoff to extend Australia's lead to 400 was the shot of the day until . . . well, you know what happened next.

# An Australian win in Adelaide

## WARNE OUT (2006)

England's cricketers shook their Australian opponents' hands at the end of this Test yesterday. Very sporting. Then they shook one another's. What on earth for? Adelaide '06 deserves to haunt this generation of English cricketers as Headingley '81 once haunted Australians. Having waited fifteen years to recapture the Ashes, they donated them back in an hour, treating Australia like a charity to rank with Make Poverty History.

Australia, ineffectual for long periods of the Test, had been intent for four days mainly on preserving their series lead. 'Turning a Test around like this,' admitted Ricky Ponting afterwards, 'well, it just doesn't happen.' But England, who after declaring their first innings might well have had Australia following on had Ashley Giles held Ricky Ponting at backward square leg when he was 35 on Saturday, turned up on the last morning apparently daydreaming of the next match in Perth. 'It's a bit of a shock,' conceded Andrew Flintoff amid his usual platitudes.

The shock treatment was administered, as ever, by Shane

Warne. When he dished out a few verbals on the fourth day of the Second Test, they were nothing very special, even the much-publicized allusion to the Shermanator in the context of Ian Bell. *American Pie* buffs will know that the Shermanator winds up with comely Nadia: it is not as though Warne likened Bell to Boris Johnson.

Warne's sledging, moreover, is seldom about his likes or dislikes among opponents; it is almost always about motivating himself, stimulating a little conflict, then feeding off the adrenalin. He wouldn't have intimidated any of his English opponents on Monday, but he probably got a few personal juices flowing – the competitive ones at any rate.

Those opponents approached their concluding task in what can only be described as a state of firm equivocation, expecting to bat on a plumb pitch that had so far yielded 1123 runs for 17 wickets, but with no obvious plan. Draws used to be a dime a dozen in cricket, and no country excelled England in the art of slow batting: forty years ago, Geoff Boycott and Ken Barrington were dropped for being so damn good at it. Now draws are infrequent and regarded with a sneaking contempt. England, then, were in a situation they wouldn't have feared but wouldn't have relished. And no bowler unpicks conglomerated thoughts like Warne.

Australia's sole objective at the beginning of the day was to keep it tight. To their surprise, England helped. In his first few overs, Warne's exhalations were beginning to sound a bit like Homer Simpson's 'D'oh!': his trademark response to error. In fact, it was others' misjudgements about to bring him joy. First in a catalogue was by umpire Steve Bucknor giving his first really poor decision of the summer against Strauss. The rest were England's.

Collingwood fanned wearily at his second ball. Had he touched it, the cat would have been among the pigeons. On the other hand, Collingwood would not then have been involved in the run out squandering Bell's wicket, setting the cat among a whole pet shop full of plump, defenceless, flightless, feathered snacks. Bell was guilty of ball watching, Collingwood of overlooking that Michael Clarke in moving left was running on to his throwing side, perhaps both of disrespect for Australian fielding. The Australians hadn't run an English batsman out since January 2003, and almost didn't this time. The dismissal wasn't Warne's, but he deserved at least a share of it, for moving quickly to cover a wide return while always keeping the stumps in his peripheral vision.

Two needless wickets were followed by three errors of what is now referred to as 'shot selection', as though batting is an affair of push buttons and exact duplications. Kevin Pietersen played the only stroke that could get him out to a ball of no special merit, an act as premeditated as OJ's, although it will be Warne who writes the book about it. Were Flintoff and Jones to be submitted to the Ludovico technique, meanwhile, replays of their second-innings dismissals would do the trick. You wouldn't even play such strokes in the nets.

Australia's progress had been so leisurely on Monday that they found themselves with an awkward chase. Again, England overlooked opportunities to make it harder – failing, for instance, to post a third man, to which a quarter of Australia's runs accrued, and sticking with a mid-on, who barely touched the ball. Flintoff dickered endlessly with the field: when two deliveries turned to take outside edges in Giles's first over, each going for two, slip was immediately removed. He also made ten bowling changes while allocating only four overs to his best bowler, Matthew Hoggard.

Ponting benefited from the indecision, Hussey prospered amid it. England's outcricket was as slipshod as their batting, and the pair advanced without ever taking undue risks, or even due ones. There was laughter at mid-pitch conferences between them, and bigger guffaws when the winning runs were registered. Warne likened the victory to his first at Test level, when Sri Lanka lost eight wickets for 37 runs to forfeit a Test in Colombo fourteen years ago by 16 runs.

For their part, England have found a way of cancelling out their chief good recent memory of Ashes cricket. They will always have Edgbaston '05, but they will now also always have Adelaide '06.

# A record from Warne (2006)

## SEVEN HUNDRED MEMORIES

Shane Warne and his admirers awoke on Boxing Day in a frame of mind similar to that of children the day before: bursting with expectation, aching with the effort of their own patience. As it was for children, the wait for Warne's 700th Test wicket seemed to take ages, but was really no time at all.

Talking to Channel 9 before play, Warne even remarked that the occasion would be enough to 'turn me on' – the sort of sentiment he used to impart so liberally by text message, but with which he is now more circumspect. Melburnians responded: the turnstiles stopped clicking at close on 90,000 despite traditional local weather, with all four seasons being experienced before the first ball.

Warne did nothing but stand at slip for the first forty overs, carrying the close-in fielder's helmet from one end to the other, as the overhead conditions kept the fast bowlers stimulated and the lush outfield preserved the shine on the ball. All the same, Warne still seemed to be everywhere. In commercial breaks, he could be seen spruiking a hair regrowth treatment, proving that no bare patch is beyond his exploitation; he was interviewed at length in the luncheon adjournment on television; one half expected a pilot for his own sitcom at tea.

Those at the ground had eyes for only one man. As Warne, polishing the ball, swapped ends after the thirty-ninth over, Langer smirkingly pinched the hat off his head: the crowd, believing the moment was nigh, roared its approval. Warne acknowledged minimally – yeah, good one, JL: but, y'know, leave the jokes to me.

Soon the familiar routine began, Warne pacing out his approach at the Southern Stand End, placing his mark where they will probably eventually place a commemorative plaque, and moving his fielders in cahoots with Ricky Ponting. Paul Collingwood failed to dispose of the exploratory full-toss, cuffed a quicker one over mid-wicket for four, then was beaten outside off stump as Warne warmed to his task: the game was afoot.

'Whoever writes my scripts is doing an unbelievable job,' said Warne afterwards. Quite so: they are guaranteed only nine further days of work, for their scenarios now tax credulity too greatly. Andrew Strauss had been batting intelligently, without getting ahead of himself. He advanced on Warne's twentieth delivery – not recklessly, not over-ambitiously, simply searching for an on-side gap. Next he knew, he was repentantly studying his disarranged stumps. 'I'm still not sure how I missed it,' he admitted later: he could have been speaking for any of the previous 699 victims.

The celebration was heady, then heartfelt. After the spontaneous lap of the infield, the shaking of hands and the highing of fives, Warne emerged from the celebratory huddle and held up the ball to each quarter of the ground. His expression was almost rheumy-eyed. It was his fiftieth Test wicket at the Melbourne Cricket Ground in the arena's 100th Test as well as his 700th, and his home-crowd fans love saluting milestones as much as Warne likes providing them.

These had again not looked like conditions in which Warne would necessarily prosper. With floodlights on, sawdust down and fielders in pullovers, the prelunch session was a far cry from the fierce heat and bright light of Brisbane, Adelaide and Perth. Australia acclimatized immediately, and Glenn McGrath gave a predatory, almost crocodilian, smile when his first ball bit into the turf and arrowed towards first slip. Warne, nonetheless, holds to the view that 'if it seams, it will spin', the grassy thatch also providing purchase for slower bowlers, the stitches retaining their hardness and prominence. Part of his thirty-seventh bag of five – Chris Read, Monty Panesar and Steve Harmison – now have to agree.

Gilchrist might have stumped Kevin Pietersen when Warne's old mucker was on four and a tram ride from home. But Pietersen was later successfully isolated, before being tempted again into misadventure. He has tried a variety of approaches to batting with the tail from number five and none has worked. His batting there is no longer a luxury; it is a waste.

Warne finished his spell with another impression of a child at Christmas when Koertzen denied him an lbw verdict against Panesar: the bowler looked like he would hold his breath till he burst. Still, as he led his comrades off, Warne's beatific expression suggested satisfaction with his booty. The cricket season, after all, has one big advantage over the festive one: Christmas has no second innings.

# Warne and McGrath

## SO MANY GOODBYES (2006)

One was bouncy, beamish, a prankster, a prestidigitator; the other was tall, taut, dependable, a natural foil. Shane Warne and Glenn McGrath: it was hard to imagine one without the other. And now, it would seem, we will not have to.

Steve Waugh was great. Ricky Ponting is great. But no two cricketers so separated Australia from the rest of the cricket pack in the last decade or so as Warne and McGrath: the best slow bowler of all, and the best seam bowler of his era. It is extraordinary that they should have ended up playing more than a hundred Tests together. To call them a combination, implying planning and foresight, is not quite right. They were more, as Palmerston described his coalition with Disraeli, an 'accidental and fortuitous concurrence of atoms'.

When they departed The Oval together at the end of last year's Fifth Test, their smiles masked a brooding determination. Australia had lost the Ashes. That would never do. The physical expense of going on was outweighed by the potential psychological toll of stopping. Their last two years have been full of personal upheaval: McGrath took time off to be with his wife; Warne, rather more publicly, took time off from his wife. But target 2006–07 became their objective, and is now to be their swansong.

Warne seems to have been around for ever, and not long at all, so vivid is the memory of him in England in 1993 as a twenty-three-year-old blond blur with turn to burn. But the man who bowled the ball of the last century has kept serving up candidates for the ball of this, even if they haven't been as rippingly obvious. For all the talk about his flipper and his zooter, his woofer and his tweeter, it was his subtly but scientifically varied leg-break that remained the eternal mystery ball. As Graham Thorpe observed last year in comparing the Australian with his statistical shadow Muttiah Muralitharan: 'Warne was always varying the degree he spun the ball, while Murali generally just tried to spin the ball as much as he could.'

In his private life, of course, Warne has marched to a different drum, listening for his personal bongo while others in this Australian XI have kept in step with the martial snare. That has involved one of his most amazing feats, persuading Australians to cut him the slack he always thought was his due. Today he is like the eternally mischievous kid brother, incorrigible to an endearing degree.

The 1993 Ashes series where Warne made his name was watched at the Australian Institute of Sport Cricket Academy by McGrath, also twenty-three, who got by on four hours' sleep a night so he could follow the feats of Allan Border's all-conquering team. He witnessed the vacancy open that he would fill. Craig McDermott was injured; Merv Hughes was injuring himself; McGrath was picked for the first home Test of the southern summer as a kind of research and development project. His breakthrough tour was eighteen months later in the West Indies, when he met the challenge of Curtly Ambrose and Courtney Walsh with his own brand of homespun hostility.

McGrath's bowling career began on a dirt track on a poultry farm with an upturned water trough for a wicket. It retained that unadorned, unrefined, self-sufficient practicality. 'Keep everything simple,' was his golden rule. 'Don't complicate things for the sake of it.' He brought to fast bowling Henry Ford's philosophy of the Model T, mass producing deliveries just short of a length, just wide of off stump, just doing enough, just about unimprovably.

Warne and McGrath both epitomized Australian excellence and embodied Australian aggression. Warne was a tease, a flirt, a provocateur, tripping up even the nimble feet of Mark Ramprakash. 'Come on, Ramps, you know you want to,' he taunted the young batsman in a famous spell at Trent Bridge in July 2001. 'That's the way, Ramps, keep coming down the wicket.' So Ramps did – too far, and another English Ashes challenge stumbled and staggered to a halt.

McGrath was trash talker extraordinaire. In *The Wicked-Keeper* (2002), New Zealand's Adam Parore took the trouble to transcribe a standard McGrath monologue: 'You guys are shit. We can't wait to get rid of you so we don't have to play you. Get the South Africans over here so we can have a real game of cricket. We can't be bothered playing you guys. You're second raters.' Rubbish, of course – but annoying rubbish, the kind to ruminate on, as did Parore.

Above all, the Australian pair have been winners, each a talisman for the other. McGrath has been on the winning side in eighty-two out of his 122 Tests (67.2 per cent), Warne in ninety of his 143 (62.9 per cent). No bowler with more than 200 Test wickets has played in a greater proportion of victories;

no bowler can have contributed so consistently to victories so often.

The farewells of Warne and McGrath will elicit tributes aplenty. What they mean for Ponting's Australians is less clear. Cricket in this country has nursed a dread of a sudden glut of retirements since the Sydney Test of January 1984, which first Greg Chappell, then Dennis Lillee and finally Rod Marsh chose for their final curtain call. They left in charge Kim Hughes, who proved unequal to the burden, and Border, who took a while to feel comfortable with it, and the Australia XI for three years marked time when not retreating.

McGrath now has a near body double in Stuart Clark, probably the most consistent component of Australia's attack this summer. But while Warne has an effective understudy in Stuart MacGill, the wrist spin ranks thin drastically thereafter. Warne made leg-spin look easy – much easier than it was, in fact, as numberless imitators have discovered. No new Warne looms, any more than does a new Bradman.

That is something, however, Australian cricket will have to deal with on its own. McGrath's wife is sick. Warne's is sick of him. Age is only one factor in their decisions. As important as their pasts are their personal futures. These are not simply retirements about where Warne and McGrath have been; they concern where the pair want to end up.

# Justin Langer

## THE BATTLER (2007)

Justin Langer, one of nature's second fiddles, will finish his career as third fiddle at the Sydney Cricket Ground this week, announcing yesterday that, like Shane Warne and Glenn McGrath, this will be his last Test.

At the instigation of Australian cricket's telco sponsors, ground staff had already painted on the grass at each end at the SCG an SMS farewell: 'Thx Shane' and 'Thx Glenn'. Yesterday afternoon, they set to work on a third dedication on the Members' Stand side of the ground: 'Thx Justin'. Summer's first retirement, Damien Martyn, did himself out of so much as a smiley face with a spur-of-the-moment decision: the Australian retirement machine is now landing it in exactly the right areas.

At his SCG press conference, thirty-six-year-old Langer confessed that it had not been a straightforward decision: 'There hasn't been a waking moment for the last twenty years where I haven't thought about playing Test cricket and wearing the baggy green cap, so this is a tough moment.' Langer, too, has previously come close to a C U L8ER M8 moment. On Australia's 2001 Ashes tour, he was made redundant at number three by his captain-to-be Ricky Ponting, and wandered round looking like a man after a harrowing family bereavement – which, as a cricketer of screwed-up, tight-wound intensity, he probably felt like.

In truth, Langer was not batting well. His Test average had slipped below 40 and he could not buy a run on tour. After failing again – against Sussex – he ended up pouring his heart out at Brighton's Grand Hotel to Australia's coach, John Buchanan, to whom he had grown close at Middlesex. In parting, Buchanan gave him a fatherly hug. A week later, Langer received something only slightly less rare and still more valuable: another chance at Test cricket, at the expense of Michael Slater. His 63 subsequent Tests have been worth 5073 runs at 49.25 with sixteen hundreds; his partnerships with friend and familiar Matthew Hayden have aggregated 5575 runs at 51.62.

Stories about Langer tend to be studded with numbers, perhaps because he can be a hard batsman to get worked up about dramatically or aesthetically, with his strong bottom hand and penchant for nudges and nurdles. Commentator Tim Lane adeptly paralleled him with John Howard, the Australian prime minister, who is the butt of satirists and his country's intelligentsia yet is now the office's second-longest occupant. Langer is the quintessential 'battler' – one of those psephological phrases ritually applied to Howard's core, lower-middle-class constituency. He showed from his Test debut at the Adelaide Oval, in a gruelling Australia Day Test against West Indies in 1993, an almost compulsive gameness. Asked by Allan Border if he would be prepared to bat at number three, he replied: 'No worries, AB, I would love to.'

'Love' was not then a word associated with facing Curtly Ambrose and Courtney Walsh – least of all in the last home series that Australia lost – and it proved to be a pretty tough love. When Mark Taylor was out to the first ball of the innings, Langer had only one pad on. When the third ball hit his helmet, making his head ring like the bells of St Clement's, his partner David Boon counselled: 'JL, there are no heroes in Test cricket. I suggest you retire hurt.' Langer declined, was hit five times on the body in seven overs, but saw the Australian cause through to stumps and batted almost six hours in the match.

Devastated to be overlooked for the 1993 Ashes tour, Langer hung a sign in his shower bearing the advice: 'The pain of discipline is nothing like the pain of disappointment.' He became Australian cricket's chief Stakhanovite, constantly out-training, out-toiling, out-running and out-philosophizing his peers. The bottled-up brooding, he revealed in his autobiography, could drag him to uncomfortable depths. Langer describes his personal nadir as a drunken evening in Karachi's Australian Club in August 1998. Having blown another Test recall by falling lbw first ball, he stood before a mirror telling himself out loud that he was good enough for Test cricket.

In the next Test, at Peshawar, Shoaib Akhtar hit him in front first ball – so hard that his knee buckled beneath him. But Steve Bucknor spared him, and Langer clawed his way to the first of his twenty-three Test centuries. Although it was the occasion of Taylor's 334 not out, Langer's inconspicuous innings was probably of greater long-term significance to Australian cricket. Yesterday was more typical Langer, extolling the virtues of his comrades: 'It's been a privilege with Shane and Glenn and Adam Gilchrist, the greatest wicketkeeper of all time, and Matthew Hayden and Ricky Ponting, who is the greatest batsman this country has produced after Bradman.' Great names indeed: by the time this Australian team has moved on, ground staff will have given the country's grass a veritable pounding.

# Matthew Hayden

## THE BULLY (2008)

The retirement of Matthew Hayden almost calls for one of E. J. Thribb's mock heroic valedictions. 'So/Farewell then/Matthew Hayden/"Mental disintegration"/That was your catchphrase/Keith's mum pointed out that you have a higher Test average than either Viv Richards or Denis Compton/But I found you as interesting as your nickname/Frankly/Haydos.'

The International Cricket Council found a form of farewell perfectly reflecting popular ambivalence, first announcing confidently that Hayden was 'in the top ten Test batsmen and top twenty ODI batsmen of all-time' according to that unimpeachable acid test of batsmanship 'the Reliance Mobile ICC Player Rankings', then clarifying in response to protests that the rankings did 'not necessarily mean he is the tenth-best Test batsman or eighteenth-best ODI batsman in the history of the game'. Well, obvs.

Like Keith's Mum, Ricky Ponting stuck to the tried-and-true benchmark of averages. 'Look through the history books of the game and try and see if there has ever been a better opening batsman,' he demanded, with a confidence that could only come from having not read any of those history books, with their references to such obscure old lags as Hobbs, Hutton, Gavaskar, Greenidge, Morris and Mitchell. Veterans of life under the Caribbean cosh, meanwhile, suggested some qualitative difference between ducking Roberts, Holding, Garner, Croft, Marshall, Ambrose and Patterson and sauntering down the wicket to Andy Blignaut and Trevor Gripper.

All of which is vaguely unfair. Sportsmen don't have the discretion to choose their eras. There were other challenges for Hayden, too. In an age of incessant international competition, he had to be fit, and was so constantly until the last year. In an era of sporting ego, he kept his effortlessly hale, while shrewdly manipulating those of others.

Few *mano a mano* duels in cricket in the last decade have rivalled the one involving Hayden and Shoaib Akhtar during Australia's Test in Sharjah in October 2002. Hayden scored 119 in more than seven hours, winding Shoaib up until the fast bowler was roused to fury – fury that, because of the fifty-degree heat, quickly depleted him. Six months later, in the World Cup final, Hayden stared down a wild-eyed Zaheer Khan, belting a flurry of boundaries, then baiting him with equally sweet timing. 'Smell that, Z?' he smirked. 'That's your house in India burning down.'

Between times, that Ashes Test at the Gabba where he carved 300 runs (197 and 103) out of 380 deliveries with 170 in boundaries, and Bill Brown tentatively mentioned him in the same breath as Bradman. This was truly Gulliver among the Lilliputians, even if not even the Lilliputians had sent Gulliver in, as Nasser Hussain did on that first, fateful morning.

Nonetheless, Hayden's rude average and talismanic, Tarzan-like presence obscure some instructive wrinkles in his record. He was, for example, considerably more effective in

Tests at home (average 58) than away (average 41), benefiting from trends of convergence in Australian groundsmanship. Few players with such an extensive career, furthermore, can have scored such a great proportion of their runs under a single captain. In the four years of Steve Waugh's leadership, Hayden averaged 67; in the rest of his career, 41. This seems more than coincidence – that Waugh's all-out aggression emancipated his burly colleague, as other more circumspect approaches did not. Under Mark Taylor, with whom Waugh the captain is often unflatteringly compared, Hayden averaged just 24. Was this linked to Taylor's own travails as a batsman for part of that time, to Hayden's drafting in place of the popular and successful Michael Slater, to a general sense of time borrowed?

More than most players, I suspect, Hayden benefited from continuity, not just of his own selection but of others. During his peak of proficiency, he paired up with Justin Langer; they became as familiar and inseparable as a pirate and his parrot, Obelix and Asterix. Selectors take note: a player is not just a sum of his abilities, but also his relationships with comrades. And no cricketer is so dependent on another as an opening batsman on his partner.

In his recent book *Seeing the Sunrise* (2007), which quotes almost everyone bar E. J. Thribb, Langer put Hayden's form lapse a few years ago down to distraction: 'He was saying how busy his calendar was for the next year and how he was worried about fitting everything in . . . Matty Hayden, like all true champions, learned his lesson and came out better and stronger than ever.' Maybe; maybe not: in the middle of his recent run of outs, Hayden was talking optimistically about jetting off to play for the Chennai Super Kings in the Champions League, and the further-off goal of a fourth Ashes tour. The comeback was always being deferred – at last, indefinitely.

Rating Hayden exactly is more difficult than either 'the Reliance Mobile ICC Rankings' or 'the history books' make it appear. Hayden was very much a cricketer of his time: a time of big bats and shrinking boundaries favouring his strength-through-joy methods; of sharply improving rewards that made it worth his while to keep playing to the age of thirty-seven; of non-stop competition maximizing his opportunities to perform while also taking the edge off opponents who might have subdued him. For professionalization and global-ization have not bestowed their benefits equally. Where a Matthew Hayden can undertake the drill of hitting a thousand balls in the nets before a Test innings, it is physically impossible for Brett Lee to bowl a thousand deliveries the same way. Batting is an easier art in which to groove oneself; bowlers are more susceptible to the vagaries of the day, fluctuations of confidence, ration of luck. Thus may Hayden have punched above his true Test weight, while Lee has perhaps never quite sustained the lofty heights and searing velocities expected of him a decade ago.

By the same token, I remember a remark of Michael Holding's many years ago, that he preferred bowling to Greg Chappell than Ian: Greg had the silken skills, he explained, but Ian had the power 'to embarrass you'. Hayden had similar capacities. A great many international bowlers will breathe more easily at word of Hayden's retirement – a tribute reserved for few.

# Adam Gilchrist

## THE X FACTOR (2014)

In his autobiography, Mike Atherton recalls sitting in England's dressing room during the Oval Test of 2001 and looking across at the clipboard of coach Duncan Fletcher with its tactical summaries of how to bowl to Australia's batsmen. Next to the name of Adam Gilchrist was simply a question mark. Oppositions would try this, that, the other thing, and all the foregoing in reverse order during Gilchrist's near-decade at the top, and never find a solution of any reliability: he was a first-rate wicketkeeper with an elastic physique, but will be remembered primarily as one of the freest strikers of a cricket ball ever seen, in all classes, conditions and scenarios of cricket.

His career had a wholesome gilding. Aged fifteen, the youngest of four children growing up in Lismore, Gilchrist slipped into a diary a piece of paper stating his ambition to play cricket for Australia. Five years later he was granted a scholarship to the AIS Cricket Academy. The only major challenge he experienced was, as a wicketkeeper, securing one of the six state vacancies on offer: he relocated to

Western Australia, forebearing some initial parochial hostility, although it was not long before his athleticism and aggression endeared him to locals. In his second season, he averaged more than 50 to go with 62 dismissals, including an undefeated 189 from 187 balls in the Sheffield Shield final.

Australia's incumbent wicketkeeper Ian Healy forced him to bide his time, but Gilchrist seized opportunities to understudy him in India, South Africa and England. What advanced his cause was Australia's defeat in the 1996 World Cup, where pacesetters Sri Lanka were propelled by a combustible opening partnership, Sanath Jayasuriya and wicketkeeper Romesh Kaluwitharana. Australia's one-day cricket looked rather staid in comparison. When selectors laid off Healy and Test captain Mark Taylor for limited-overs matches, Gilchrist had a mandate not just to play his natural game but to expand it. New captain Steve Waugh indulged a whim in the C&U Series finals of 1998 by promoting Gilchrist to open. Alongside Mark Waugh then Matthew Hayden, Gilchrist became to Australian one-day cricket what the wing-tipped keel had been to *Australia II* during the Americas Cup: a new way, a unique edge.

In Test cricket, his feats of escapology reached Colditz proportions. Australia's top six through the 2000s were as gifted and garlanded as any in the country's history, yet it was generally acknowledged that the line-up's most dangerous member came in at number seven, and could yank the game from your grasp in an hour. Gilchrist held the bat high, as high as Victor Trumper in cricket's most famous photograph, and swung it with similar abandon. His pull and sweep had a 360-degree swing, like Saladin's scimitar. Yet his chief gift as a striker was his spontaneity. He played the same way regardless: a half-volley was a half-volley at five for 50 or five for 500, whether he was on a king pair or had scored 150; he would hit an Australian record one hundred Test sixes.

There was no particular bravado about this. Indeed, Gilchrist professed to being a man of fragile confidence, a 'conformist deep down', a 'big public crier': he was deeply stirred when the Australian team visited Gallipolli in 2001. It was just that adrenalin clarified and channelled the game for him. His highest Test score, 204 against South Africa in February 2002, was made 'in pure anger' and 'almost in tears', as a result of a scurrilous rumour published on a cricket website, shortly after the birth of his first son. It was the fastest Test double-century to that time, 213 balls; it did not seem even that long.

Gilchrist's batwork and glovework were complexly related. He was tall for a keeper, with a huge reach, which allowed first slips to stand slightly wider, and hair-trigger reflexes, shown to advantage accepting rebounds. Most importantly, he liked keeping. It was a job that made him comfortable within any side, released the pressure from his batting, allowed him to play with the freedom he favoured. Sometimes it was thought he might prolong his career by surrendering the gloves; it was, to Gilchrist, never an option. In 2004 he added a third role, captaincy, leading Australia, as locum for an injured Ricky Ponting, to its only series win in India since 1969.

To all Australia's three consecutive World Cup victories was Gilchrist indispensable, his finals treble reading out as 54 from 36 balls, 57 from 48 balls and 149 from 104 balls. Yet perhaps his chief contribution to the event's folklore was his dismissal, in the 2003 semi-final in Port Elizabeth. Given not out by umpire Rudi Koertzen, Gilchrist fessed up to an inside edge, and walked. It was an unpremeditated decision, and a quickly worrying one when other wickets fell: 'I felt more lonely than I had ever felt among a cricket team.' Yet he also felt he had 'done the right thing', and professed a bemusement that 'a simple act of honesty made such headlines.' What stood out like a good deed in a naughty world was also, of course, a gesture of faith in his ability. Asked if he would walk if he nicked a ball with Australia needing two runs to win the Ashes with one wicket in hand, Gilchrist replied coolly: 'I wouldn't nick it.'

Gilchrist did nick some. His temporary eclipse in 2005 was fundamental to England's compelling Ashes victory, although Andrew Flintoff conceded that the success of his round-the-wicket angle was mainly a fluke: 'I high-fived my teammates and talked them through my carefully orchestrated plan – they believed me, happy days!' Redress was at hand. In the Test in which Australia regained the Ashes fourteen months later, Flintoff as captain looked on as Gilchrist ransacked the second fastest Test hundred to that time in 57 deliveries. Ironically, his international retirement coincided with the advent of T20, a game his batting might almost have foretold: he was a welcome addition to the Indian Premier League, where he led the Deccan Chargers to victory in the second season. By then the question mark had tailed off into a series of exclamation marks.

# A draw at Cardiff

## NEUTRAL TERRITORY (2009)

Try explaining this to an American. For much of this First Test at Sophia Gardens, England were a shambles, virtually finishing fourth behind Australia, Wales and then some daylight. Yet thanks to their last pair, James Anderson and Monty Panesar, who warded Australia off for 69 deliveries, they go to Lord's with the series still 0–0.

Cue the cod psychology. Is it as good as a win for England? Is it a form of defeat for Australia? Ricky Ponting admitted last night that the visitors' dressing room was 'quiet' at the close, with the qualifier that this would only be for an hour or two. Andrew Strauss spoke of feeling 'pride', but mainly 'relief', with the concession it had been 'horrible to watch'.

Both sides have certainly learned a lot; in England's case, this has been at best salutary. The Australians – captain, players and press – were feeling hard done by at the end, sensing perfidious Albion behind late on-field, time-wasting sorties by England's physiotherapist and twelfth man. Perhaps the series needed just such a result: drama 2009 style, rather than a warming over of 2005. For this was a day's play full of dramas and intrigues, a fine advertisement for what, in the spirit of Twenty20, will probably soon be called Four-Hundred-and-Fifty450.

Before play, Cardiff was enough to make any Melburnian homesick. Rain was pouring one moment, sunshine gleaming the next, with the best cricket weather probably at 6 a.m. Play began beneath cloud cover, but by noon the arena was flooded with sunlight, surprisingly warm, and full of fans trying to make the most of a day which few could see going past tea.

Pietersen apparently exchanged words with the tourists during the morning's warm-ups, when a ball he struck interfered with an Australian routine. It was his last effective stroke. Indeed, he went as close as one can to playing a shot without actually playing one: it was like smoking without inhaling. Two overs earlier, he had allowed Hilfenhaus to hit his back pad while letting a ball go that came back slightly; this time, he held his bat high as a ball zeroed in on middle. At the last split second, the bat began descending, but posthumously; the delivery held its line, collecting the top of off.

Pietersen might have been leaving on length, banking on the bounce to save him; Pietersen might have been leaving on principle, to show, after his first-innings indiscretion, exactly how responsible he can be. Who can say? The contents of Pietersen's head enthrall English cricket fans, as the contents of Michael Jackson's spellbind the tabloids. Whatever the case, his technique at the moment is a train wreck, balance amiss, front foot barely budging. This was a dismissal with a touch about it of Michael Vaughan, a high-class batsman who could nonetheless make a nondescript delivery look like the proverbial sostenutor.*

With Pietersen's dismissal, odds on an English victory were officially listed at 501/1. Longer than Headingley '81! Time for a plunge, surely! On the other hand, a pound's a pound. Five of them and you almost have enough for a cup of coffee in London. When Andrew Strauss was then caught at the wicket in Nathan Hauritz's first over, the odds shot out to 601/1. Here was a lost cause in which not even Dennis Lillee or Rod Marsh would have invested.

The Test would have been over by lunch had Katich been perched a couple of feet closer at bat-pad when Collingwood (11) got a glove on Hauritz. Next ball, too, rolled to within a nanometer of the stumps, until Collingwood's groping back foot interposed. These alarms apart, he batted with commendable coolness. No England player looks quite so grim on the field; none stretches his talents so far. Nor did he make the same mistake as at Adelaide Oval two and a half years ago, when the strokelessness of his defiance (22 not out in 198 minutes) cost runs that might have extended Australia's victory chase.

Awkward slip catches made to look simple accounted for Flintoff and Prior, and Broad completed a poor match lbw to Hauritz, having the nerve to shake his head afterwards when any umpire other than Billy Doctrove would have given him out first ball hit on the boot by Johnson. The chirpy Swann provided Collingwood with the most productive support and also the most protracted, spinning the seventieth over out to ten minutes by twice calling for cold spray after he was hit on the arm and finger. He might have requested it a

---

* An arcane cricket word overdue revival, devised by Tom Emmett (1841–1904) to describe the ball that pitched leg and hit off. 'What else would you call it?' he asked.

third time for his ears after some gratuitous advice from bowler Peter Siddle.

The second new ball finally did for Swann, lbw in what proved the mysteriously underbowled Hilfenhaus's twelfth and final over for the day. And at this pass, as the match came to its climax, Ponting seemed to miss a trick, depending on a swift Siddle but a wayward Johnson, then, anxious to squeeze in the maximum number of overs, Hauritz and Marcus North.

Siddle had Collingwood caught at backward point, and the Australians rejoiced again; Collingwood, devastated, could be seen in the dressing room window for the rest of the innings, still wearing his pads. But Johnson bowled three wides in a sloppy six overs and, apart from some speculative running, Anderson and Panesar looked unexpectedly untroubled, the pace bowlers operating without a short leg, the spinners failing to extract the turn they had earlier. England went into the lead with 45 deliveries to go, an Anderson thick edge flying for four to third man, followed with another to point. From the ecstatic crowd, one half expected a chorus of 'Land of My Fathers'.

After North had bowled the 102nd over, England's substitute fielder Bilal Shafayat came on with fresh gloves, and physio Steve McCabe with an urgent consignment of Juicy Fruit – or something. The message imparted was that the match was being played to time rather than overs, so it was essential to reach 6.40 p.m. – ten minutes before the scheduled finish, but the effective end because of the time required for change of innings.

Ponting was decidedly unimpressed, and let the interlopers know it. To his credit, Anderson was hardly more impressed, turned away, and looked faintly embarrassed: it could just as easily have worked Australia's way by disturbing the batsmen's concentration. Strauss later called it a 'misunderstanding', a convenient euphemism. But in the end, the 105th and last over beginning at 6.39 p.m., it probably did not entail any net loss of bowling time. Anderson met each ball from Hauritz with the deadest of bats, until the last, from which a bye was scurried. Actually, never mind an American. Try to explain this match, and the sheer fun and excitement of the final hour, with defensive shots being cheered to the echo, attacking strokes sending a chill up the collective spine, to Lalit Modi.

# An English win at the Oval

## SWANN'S WAY (2009)

T he Ashes, for a generation almost thought of as an Australian birthright, will have to become used to shared custody. When Mike Hussey's long, largely lone hand, 121 in five and a half hours, ended to a bat-pad chance at 5.48 p.m., Australia lost the Fifth Test at The Oval by 197 runs, the series 1–2, and possession of the trophy they recaptured only thirty months ago.

Never all that great in Ashes cricket, the difference between what is and what might have been has this summer been measurable in millimetres: a dropped catch here, a no-ball there, and at The Oval a coin toss, which delivered England an advantage they never quite ceded. The gap was widened today by the infinitesimal distances involved in two run outs, costing Australia their captain and their vice-captain at crucial stages.

After batting so skilfully on Saturday evening, Australia's openers struggled to regather themselves this morning, Stuart Broad bowling a testing wicket-to-wicket line and Graeme Swann extracting considerable turn, although it was a ball from the latter going on with the arm to which Katich padded up in the fourth over that gave England their first breakthrough. For the fourth time in five innings, Watson then fell lbw to a straight ball, chest on, head outside the line – not the position one expects an opener to get into, really, as, indeed, Watson still isn't quite.

Two scoreless batsmen could hardly have been a more propitious beginning for England. Ponting was determined to neutralize Broad. Hussey faced Swann surrounded by two slips, a silly point, a short cover and a short leg, taking thirteen tense deliveries to escape his pair with a jab into the off side. But for almost forty overs, both offered an object lesson in batting on this pitch, which required immense care, great concentration, and a sense of humour, accepting that one would periodically be beaten, learning to think past it. The smile that crossed Ponting's face when he played and missed at Broad after lunch was probably the broadest of the tour.

There is pressure on bowlers under such circumstances, too. As at Edgbaston, Swann sometimes tried too hard, Ponting driving him through cover from consecutive deliveries off back then front foot, Hussey pulling successive boundaries to raise the hundred stand. While Harmison hit the deck hard, extracting as much lift as anyone during the game, the conditions offered few incentives to Anderson or Flintoff. With Australia two for 217, the last nine wickets in the match had fallen in the span of 551 runs, making the popular licensed-to-kill pitch story of the last few days that bit more difficult to sustain.

Then Hussey chipped to mid-on, called promptly, set off, and Ponting was guilty of ball watching, much as at Trent Bridge four years earlier when fate and Gary Pratt interposed. He was still transfixed as the ball reached Andrew Flintoff at mid-on, and fully underway only from half-way through the run, so that the all-rounder's clean gather and powerful side-arm throw beat him by a distance. Flintoff contributed little to this his farewell Test, but here was some wonderfully intuitive cricket: an overarm throw would almost certainly have gone over the stumps after bouncing on the hard pitch square.

This brought to the crease Michael Clarke, seemingly in the pink of form, although discomfited by three sharply turning balls from Swann. The fourth offered a glimpse of relief, a ball he could clip to leg and get off strike. All summer, Alastair Cook had stood beneath the lid at short leg to no obvious purpose, as ornamental as a bird-bath. Now he extended his left leg, and the ball deflected from his ankle to Strauss at leg slip as Clarke turned to regain his ground. Strauss's throw was swift, underarm and accurate, dislodging a single bail as the bat reached but did not quite cross the line.

All this happened in a fraction of the time it will have taken you to read that paragraph – so swift it almost eluded umpire Billy Bowden, who seemed a little loath to call for the third umpire, finally as he walked in to repair the stumps making the appropriate signal, which in Bowden's case is rather like the barrel girl on a quiz show making the shape of a microwave oven. A roar announced that Australia's best two batsmen had fallen for three runs in six deliveries.

When Prior stumped North smartly, the batsman's ambitious sweep a stretch-too-far, only the margin of victory seemed in dispute. But England is still short of making the excellent habitual. Collingwood grassed a regulation outside edge offered by Hussey (55) from Swann, and Onions dropped Haddin (14) at short mid-wicket off Anderson. Hussey now looked utterly rehabilitated, moving into the nineties with a perfect pull shot from Anderson's predictable loosener with the second new ball, through them with a cover drive from his salad days, and to his first hundred in twenty-eight innings with a like stroke. Then a lucky break. Having celebrated his escape with two demob-happy shovels over cover, Haddin perished to a wretched shot, trying to clear the two fielders back on the leg side on a turning pitch – a shot that, at last, savoured of defeat.

Australia's last five ended up coming quietly, for 21 runs in 46 deliveries, Cook actually taking two catches, and Graeme Swann finishing the match with eight for 158, although Stuart Broad's first-innings five for 37 earned him the individual award. The celebrations were noisy but, compared to 2005, relatively brief. Perhaps the spectators grasped that it had been a close-run thing; perhaps they also concluded this was something they might even get used to.

# An innings from Pietersen

## KP OR NOT KP (2010)

In all the pre-Ashes soundings among former Australian greats, even those involving a pro-forma prediction of five to zero, there was one common denominator. Whenever an opinion was sought about the identity of England's key player of the coming summer, the answer came back the same: the KP was KP.

Part of this was probably general ignorance. Australians are used to letting English cricket look after itself. Some pommy bloke making runs? Some promising new bowler? Yeah, well wait till they get out here. But Kevin Pietersen? Hard to forget him getting the better of Australia at The Oval in 2005; hard to forget Australia getting the better of him at Adelaide in 2006. A bit of a show pony, but Warnie likes him – that's gotta count for something.

It's arguable that Australians in underestimating England overestimate Pietersen: he forms part of a more consistent and uniformly competent visiting unit than that which he joined. But, especially after today, you will never convince those grudging Australian admirers otherwise. His undefeated 213 was Pietersen in total command of himself. That meant it was not quite the Pietersen that Australians first saw, circa 2005. He offended no orthodoxies. He cut no capers. He met Xavier Doherty with a defensive bat so doornail dead and plumb-line straight that it bordered on parody, although this was meaningful deliberation. At last. He'd worked it out at last. To think, after all his travails against it, that left arm spin was *this* easy to play.

When Pietersen then went after Doherty – indeed, took 57 from his 58 deliveries, including nine fours and a six – it was hard to avoid the sensation that the hapless Tasmanian was paying for Pietersen's previous indignities at the hands of other members of the genre. That Ponting entrusted North with eighteen overs to Doherty's twenty-four suggests that Australia's ninth post-Warne spinner is about to go from being a Test cricketer to part of the answer to a trivia question.

All the same, Australians saw again the qualities in Pietersen that first caused them discomfiture. A Pietersen playing soberly is still like a conventional batsman spontaneously brain-storming. Thanks to wrists that rotate like gimbals, he scores in more areas of the field than perhaps any other contemporary batsman. Most wagon wheels tell you not much. Batsmen score in different directions: who knew? But Pietersen's formed almost a complete asterisk. He does not have one sweep, for instance, but many. He swung Doherty as fine as forty degrees to square leg, then North as much as thirty degrees in front, all along the ground.

This latter shot, played in the over before lunch and taking England's lead to 200, was followed by a similarly con-founding boundary that split Bollinger and Hussey, meant to be protecting the leg-side boundary, but each aborting approaching the ball out of consideration for the other – commendable from an occupational health and safety point of view. Such is the confusion and dismay an in-form Pietersen can spread.

When Doherty resumed to Pietersen after lunch, it was with six men deep: Siddle at deep mid-on, Watson deep mid-off, North deep mid-wicket, Bollinger deep backward square, Harris deep point, and Ponting deep trouble. They were brought in as Pietersen's double-hundred loomed, but he was not to be denied, dropping to his knee as he completed the climactic single as though about to receive the Order of the Garter on the spot.

Pietersen foregrounded his boldness and ingenuity when he advanced on both Bollinger and Siddle to pick them off through the leg side from off and middle. But a subtler feature was Pietersen's strength straight: more than thirty per cent of his runs were acquired in the 'V' demarcated by mid-off and mid-on, often by no more than leaning on the ball and harnessing the transference of his weight.

One is never permitted to speak solely of Pietersen the batsman. No member of the current England team is the subject of more cod psychology. Twenty-eight innings without a Test hundred had left plentiful opportunities for sentiments like 'he needs to feel loved', as though this is a breakthrough insight about Pietersen rather than an embarrassing channelling of Oprah. It's true that Pietersen has caused England teammates to sigh with exasperation almost as often as to gasp in astonishment. Just over three years ago, for example, he promised that his team would humiliate Australia in the World Twenty, only for the promise to boomerang as England subsided to heavy defeat. 'Kevin's obviously Kevin,' was Paul Collingwood's Gertrude Stein-esque explanation, amid sage nodding. Born to tweet, he has, of course, tested the limits of the ECB's social media policies in Adelaide.

Yet Pietersen's analysts sometimes seem to reveal as much

about themselves as the analysand. John Buchanan and Shane Warne both addressed themselves to his status in the England line-up before the series, Buchanan opining that Pietersen was potentially a 'major problem' where England's 'strength and unity' were involved, Warne that Pietersen was being treated as 'a bit of an outcast': 'KP might be The Walking Ego with the way he struts around, and sometimes he is unpopular with his own teammates, and he can rub people up the wrong way. But he has to be made to feel important and like he is the man. If he feels like that, he will give you everything.' It was the bureaucrat ruminating about the presence of the occasionally disruptive virtuoso, the occasionally disruptive virtuoso raging against bureaucracy. It sounded like Buchanan talking about Warne, and Warne talking about, well, Warne.

Does any of this matter? There is a cast of mind that every cricket team must harmonize like the Mormon Tabernacle Choir, that all traits of individuality must be effaced for the sake of a uniform whole. Cricket – and team sports in general – are more complicated. In any event, what today attests is that Pietersen's most significant psychological impact this summer will not be on his own team but on the Australians. They saw today coming perhaps more clearly than the English.

# An innings from Cook

## LONG PLAYING RECORD (2011)

**B**efore Australia's second innings in Melbourne, Shane Watson was asked what would be his approach to his team's huge first innings arrears. Without a second thought, Watson revealed his 'plan': he would bat for two and a half days. Never mind that his limit in this series has been about two and a half hours. Later that afternoon, another start was duly wasted.

Nobody has asked Alastair Cook for his 'plan' this summer. He says 'obviously' a lot in press conferences, but so does everybody else, and in his case it's almost apologetic. The way he plays, batting is obvious, containing no obscurities or hidden subtleties. He is like a skilled expositor with a gift for making complicated ideas sound simple. 'I don't really know what else to say,' he confessed to a television questioner at day's end. His batting this summer has already spoken volumes.

Of today's 189, it suffices to comment that it broke Australia's spirit, glimpses of which Michael Clarke's team had shown on the second day. It felt like a part of the single continuous innings Cook has played all summer, during which he has batted as though involved in the painting of the Sydney Harbour Bridge, no sooner finishing at one end than starting at the other.

The SCG in the morning was an uncommonly cheerful sight, awash in pink in aid of the McGrath Foundation and its good works. Even the statue of Steve Waugh unveiled before play was adorned in a fuchsia neckerchief, so that Australia's great champion resembled a Mardi Gras cowboy. For a moment it appeared that Cook would be expected to recommence batting in a pink helmet. In fact, Cook even eschewed the popular pink grip, settling instead for being in the pink of form – and if you were hitting the ball like Cook at the moment, you'd be careful about altering what you had for breakfast every morning lest somehow it interfere with your luck.

Four years ago on this ground, Cook recalled that comment of Douglas Jardine's about batting against Bill O'Reilly: 'I cut out every shot that got me out and found that I didn't have a shot left.' It was hard to see how he would ever score a run, and precious few of them did he obtain. Now his leaving the ball is part of a bigger, wider, more complete game. 'Knowing where your off stump is' is one of those cricket expressions that sounds perennially mysterious to the uninitiated. After all, doesn't it just sit there alongside the other two? Cook the expositor reveals its meaning: by letting balls go that compel no stroke, he draws bowlers into his pads, coaxes them to pitch the ball further up for driving, and generally tires them, little by little, minute by minute. He makes the non-stroke into a kind of stroke, silence into a sort of statement.

Cook has also turned the press box into a fastness of anorakism. All day could be heard whispered exchanges: 'most runs since'; 'most by a left-hander since'; 'between Sutcliffe and Hammond'; 'just like Gavaskar'; 'level with Lara'. Behind every hard-bitten cricket hack is a boy with a pencil, a scorebook and a *Wisden* or two. The most flavoursome record of all was the one concerning the length of time that Cook has batted this summer. Read it and reel: with potentially an innings still to go, he has been at the crease for thirty-six hours and eleven minutes, breaking a record of delicious obscurity set in the Ashes of 1970–71 by John Edrich.

Tennis has its records for epic five setters, but only cricket keeps such close tabs on durations, because in order to score one must first survive. In its way, Cook's batting harkens to the origins of cricket, when the roughness of pitches first compelled batsmen to work out ways to defend themselves, and its place in nature, when the format was dictated by the passage of the day.

In recent times, T20 has chewed away at that essence of batting, utterly skewing the dynamics of risk and reward. The abbreviated game marches to the drum beat of the strike rate, which makes a celebrity of Kieron Pollard, and a slowcoach of Michael Clarke. But while the strike rate sounds somehow more scientific, it's a reductive precision, for pretending that batsmen are only active when actually facing the bowling. But you don't cease to be part of the game at the non-striker's end; you aren't absolved from responsibility, excused from concentration or invulnerable to dismissal. In addition to the 242 scoreless deliveries of Cook's innings, he was a faithful back-up through 351 as a partner. On the measure of a strike rate, these did not exist. Minutes, by contrast, are immediately suggestive. On the rule of thumb that there are 360 in a day's play, you can tell at a glance that Cook has been at the crease for roughly six entire days in this series – almost a third of the total play. In his own self-effacing way, he has utterly hogged the centre.

# AN INNINGS FROM COOK

Fifteen years ago, *The Times*'s chief cricket correspondent saved a Test match for England against South Africa. Mike Atherton faced 492 balls, although what did this imply other than a lot? Far more evocative is to recall that he endured for 643 minutes. The image of Atherton's innings that most people recall is not of any shot or even milestone, but the one of him looking up from his haunches and giving his partner Jack Russell a smile – weary, wary but game. Cook, then, has done still more than be the fulcrum of England's exertions in this Ashes series. He has given us a little commentary on cricket – by his deeds, of course, rather than his words.

# A Test at Durham

## BROAD ACRES (2013)

Thanks to Stuart Broad's impenitence at Trent Bridge and Usman Khawaja's misfortune at Lord's, umpiring had been a talking point throughout the first three Tests of the 2013 Ashes; in the Fourth, the talking did not even wait for the match to begin. Its preliminaries were overshadowed by reactions to a Channel 9 news story about the reliability of Hot Spot being compromised by silicone tape on the edges of bats, with attention drawn to the conspicuously spotless edge of Kevin Pietersen's bat when he was adjudged caught behind in the second innings at Old Trafford. Imputations, denials, tweets, statements: it kept the cogs turning for a few days anyway. Perhaps the most surprising aspect of this story was that it was not called Batgate, given the low bar set for —gate suffixes by Homeworkgate, and being about what was and was not recorded by tape – after all, as Matthew Parris recently observed, Watergate would these days be called Watergategate. All we were reminded of was the absurdity of vesting authority for decision-making in a technology never designed for that purpose. In the event, this was the Test least shaped by adjudication. There were some bizarre moments, notably Tony Hill giving an lbw with the players already off the field, Ryan Harris having repented his referral: the umpire as wallflower. But Aleem Dar had an excellent game. You didn't notice? Just so.

Riverside also offered perhaps the best pitch of summer, or at least the most interesting, with quick bowlers able to nibble it about throughout and slow bowlers gaining some assistance. The bounce was consistent, too, and on the last day scary indeed, as Stuart Broad bore down from the Lumley End, turning a bum-nipping Aussie run chase into a high-fiving English rampage, bettering Anderson's ten for 158 at Trent Bridge and Swann's nine for 122 at Lord's with eleven for 121. Clocked by the radar at up to 93mph, he should really have been measured on the Beaufort Scale.

England was first to find batting a precarious occupation, their innings a listless, sometimes strokeless affair. Jonathan Trott was the only batsman to achieve any sort of shotmaking ease, looking good, as for most of the summer, until he got out, bat-padding a nondescript ball from Lyon to short leg. Pietersen went into his shell too quickly, Bell tried to burst from his too soon, and Cook simply never left his, labouring almost four hours over 51, until he perished, padding up to Jackson Bird. Two normally enterprising batsmen in Jonny Bairstow and Matt Prior took 116 balls to eke out a partnership of 34, only to succumb within three overs of one another. It was fine 'dry' bowling from Australia, if rather arid batting from England, that certainly did not achieve its objective of taking control of the game. It took England's pace bowlers to retrieve them a share, reducing Australia to four for 76 shortly after lunch on the second day.

Throughout this faltering progress, Chris Rogers held firm, taking strike as if armed for urban warfare with what looked like a square of carpet underlay on his arm and a phone book down his shirt. Deep in his crease, striving to resist as he was tugged round and drawn into playing outside his safe zone, he somehow kept accruing runs – cuts, glides, nudges, nurdles, thick edges, inside edges. Content to be beaten in return for remaining active, he avoided becoming simply a stationary target. Pressure eased when Watson, after an anxious first half-hour, slotted in to his new nook at number six, and began loosing some retaliatory strokes, forcing England onto the defensive. By tea, the colony of Fanatics in the temporary terraces had been restored to cheerful voice and beersnake-lengthening humour.

After the break, the game tightened, as Australia glimpsed a lead, England probed for a breakthrough, and light towers switched on to counteract the gloom somehow intensified the contest – it was like a suspect getting the third degree. For much of the series, thirty-five-year-old Rogers had played as you'd expect of a batsman with sixty first-class centuries; Swann's quizzical spell reminded you that there remained the business of Rogers's maiden Test hundred to see to. Gifted a full-toss, he disposed of it gratefully to go to 96, but remained there for the next half hour. He didn't quite nail a cut, and picked out point; he played a couple down in front and let a couple go; he tried finding space on the on side and turned the face too early; then he did it again; at length, he and Watson almost had a moment between wickets. Deep breaths all round.

An appeal: Watson out, nicking unluckily down the leg side. By now, Rogers seemed to be ageing by the ball: when he played and missed at a cut, he bent his head for a few penitent seconds. He was almost still reliving it when he swept the next ball for four to reach his milestone, and celebrated as soberly as his balcony did noisily – no exultation; just relief.

Finishing at five for 222, just 16 in arrears with five wickets remaining, Australia could take some quiet satisfaction from their day as well.

At last, England got a little busy. Some bolshie blows from Harris apart, Australia's tail contributed little. And while England lost three in erasing their arrears, they were clearly exhibiting more purpose, and Pietersen and Bell embarked on setting Australia's target with an impressive sure-footedness. Pietersen caught the eye, as he cannot help, with his long limbs, tiptoe walk, and seemingly delicate grip of a shiny bat; Bell, nonetheless, cast a shadow at least as long. From Pietersen it is hard to avert your eye: with every ball there is a sense of imminent possibility. From Bell it is actually easy to look away: he is predictably efficient, imaginably controlled; you feel like you could pop out to the shops, or the pub, come back in a hour or two, and still find him doing much the same, playing similar strokes, forming the same physical shapes. Next man in when they are at the wicket together must be an alternately churning and lulling experience. Bairstow did not do quite enough again when called on, but Bell batted serenely into the evening, his progress interrupted only when Harris came round the wicket for a final short-pitched burst, lifting him off his feet, and on one occasion sitting him on his backside. Otherwise his third century of the series had an easefully recumbent character, Bell as relaxed as a man warming at his fireside. And although Harris burst through him, Prior and Broad first thing on the fourth morning, Australia struck another line of resistance in Bresnan and Swann, who laid cheerfully about them as England's last two wickets added 55. To deepen the visitors' frustrations, Bresnan (12) let a straight ball from Bird hit him on the knee roll and was somehow reprieved both downstairs then upstairs, and Swann (17) shovelled Lyon down long-on's throat only for

Smith to gag. Little things they were at the time; like overlooked clues in a whodunnit, their importance emerged later.

For having survived four awkward pre-lunch overs, then sat through an hour of rain which would push the game into the twilight, Australia's openers looked their 299-run target right in the eye, the powerful left hook of Warner and the counterpunching left jab of Rogers a potent combination. Warner used timing to cut and drive Anderson and Broad, strength to plonk Swann into the crowd beyond mid-off; Rogers was, again, all nous and nerve, watching an edge go to ground, seeing off one referral, deploying another, soft bottom hand one ball, hard bottom hand next. England's appealing had a tone of imprecation, and the openers a brisk solidity as they shook hands on raising their three-figure stand amid the twenty-seventh over. At last, after building through three consecutive maidens, Swann tempted Rogers to push out, and Trott accepted the chance at slip. Australia moved on smoothly after tea, one wicket down nearly halfway home as Warner took toll of a flat spell from Anderson, but there was a sense from here on that the game might be won and lost in a short time.

Although Broad would be responsible for the demolition, it was Swann and Bresnan who created the initial breach, the former trapping a motionless Khawaja, the latter startling Warner with bounce. At once the game was afoot; English chins and chests stuck out; English chatter made stump mics blush. Enjoined to 'spice it up', Broad passed Clarke's groping bat with the first ball after drinks and poleaxed off stump, and Australia suddenly looked like an undermanned riot squad trying to kettle a seething crowd, with pressure points all over. Smith gloved a bouncer onto his stumps, Watson and Haddin both reviewed lbws to no avail, leaving Harris with no recourse had he sought it. To all intents a county ground, Riverside rocked for half an hour like a Test match colosseum, reading Broad's velocities off the video screen with audible relish. Dar and Hill consulted their light meters when Broad dropped short at Lyon, but stumps went everywhere next ball anyway, and the bowler took a breather after a spell of 9-2-21-5. Cook coolly turned to spin from each end for six overs while the sun was cloudbound to ensure play continued, then recalled his quicks as it re-emerged, Broad delivering the *coup de grâce* when Siddle spooned a drive to mid-off. The margin of victory, 74 runs, looked the healthier for those morning runs, even if the morning itself now seemed like days ago. Certainly, nobody was talking about Batgate, which is one of temporary controversy's appeals: it is only ever filler material, for which the need disappears in the event of anything resembling good cricket.

# A Test at Adelaide
## MITCH'S MOUSTACHE (2013)

England's 218-run defeat in the Second Test at Adelaide Oval flattered them. It was all that did. Perhaps no team holding the Ashes has ever been written off as completely after a loss, such was their melting in Brisbane in the face of Mitchell Johnson's white-hot speed. They had a share of early exchanges at Adelaide, but it took only a day for spirit and ambition to overhaul and overwhelm professional proficiency and preparation. After the match, Michael Clarke was low-key, but you could sense his excitement; Alastair Cook was dignified, but you could detect his horror. More than four years after regaining the Ashes, England appeared within days of giving them up.

Before the match, Australia cheerfully reselected the same XI, while England seemed to be trying to finesse a XV, seeing the need for more spin, more speed and more batting. At last they went with Monty Panesar's left-arm slows rather than Chris Tremlett's right-arm talls, and replaced the departed Jonathan Trott with the coming all-rounder Ben Stokes – something of a surprise when Tim Bresnan was available to them again and reverse swing was predicted on the ground's new drop-in pitch.

Also on debut, effectively, was the new stadium – for that's what Adelaide Oval now is rather than a cricket ground, albeit conceived on lines less brutal than the Gabba and less monumental than the MCG. The home of South Australian cricket has gained tens of thousands of seats in return for losing some of its connection with the city, now invisible from within, and accessibility, its picturesque gates having been replaced by cavernous vaults of ingress; the Cathedral End has become so in name only, St Peter's now being completely obscured, while the long, straight boundaries that were a distinguishing characteristic of the playing surface have been truncated. What they say isn't true, by the way: you *can* stand in the way of progress. What you can't stand in the way of is football.

Australia again won the right to first innings, and again did not make the best of the first day, which dawned dimly and remained so until lunch, there being three rain inter-ruptions in the opening session. After David Warner had flared briefly, Chris Rogers and Shane Watson dealt with the fluctuations, Rogers at one stage pulling away just as a cloud passed to flood the ground with sunlight, only to be running off minutes later as the players sought shelter from a downpour. It was hard going, with both Swann and Panesar obtaining surprising turn. At times, Rogers had three fielders close in on the leg-side, close enough to be sharing a table with him in a café.

There was a sense of imminent major happenings that didn't quite. Rogers (27) should by rights have been lbw to Panesar, but the DRS, as it is inclined to out of a false politeness, upheld a poor decision by Dharmasena. In the next two overs Rogers cover drove Swann and cut Panesar for four, his first assertive shots; on other occasions, wandering world-wearily to leg between deliveries, he almost looked sick of his own struggles. Watson, meanwhile, played soberly if not sombrely in the 'V', in search of his timing, and his entitlement to the number three berth. For all their application, the Test was nicely balanced when Australia lost three for 19 in 39 balls just before tea. Advantage only tilted in their direction after the break, when George Bailey took the initiative against the spinners, using his feet and hitting down the ground towards a newly inviting perimeter, while Michael Clarke settled in, already with an eye for the morrow. Clarke contributed barely a third of their 87-run partnership, but it was only a deposit on his planned purchase. And if they had but known it, England was also in the process of losing the match. Panesar muffed a caught-and-bowled chance when Bailey was 10, Root missed a mid-wicket clip when Clarke was 18, and Carberry a loose cut when Haddin was 5, after England had broken through with the second new ball: acceptance of that last chance would have reduced Australia to six for 265, with their tail exposed. As it was, England returned for the second day with a faint sense of dread – it proved well-founded.

To the first delivery of day two, Michael Clarke came down the wicket to Panesar, did not quite get to the pitch of the ball, and miscued just over extra cover's head. It wasn't quite the Ashes, but it was one of those moments when fate considers its options. Having come down against Australia on a semi-regular basis in England, fate nodded Clarke's way, and he, perhaps sensing the same, continued to attack, the ball being at its hardest and the pitch at its flattest after a rolling. Australia would dictate or be damned; Cook reacted unpredictably with some novel fields, including a short cover, a leg gully and two men back for the hook. The problem with the last was that one of the men was Panesar, who never looked likely to get under a top edge from Haddin (30) off Anderson. Anderson bowled his best spell of the series so far, obscuring his bowling hand as he sought reverse swing, but Australia was now surging. England had one last opportunity to retard them, when Stokes, zippy if generally too short, drew Haddin (51) into a drive and celebrated what should have been his first Test wicket. Third umpire Tony Hill, however, detected a no-ball that Ray Erasmus had somehow missed, prolonging the partnership into the afternoon. Fate had clearly decided it was payback time.

By now, Clarke was in superb touch, turning length into a thing for the batsman not the bowler, with twinkling feet and brimming confidence. The short stuff that had troubled him at Brisbane was here hardly an option, and Broad and Anderson barely tried it; in fact, Cook used his fastest bowler for only eleven overs in the day, seemingly resigned to containing the damage for England rather than inflicting further on Australia. Clarke (91) gave another chance, straight into and straight out of Bell's hands at short leg, before reaching his twenty-sixth Test century, and his sixth at the venue. He must feel like rolling the pitch up and taking it with him. Now it is a drop-in, he probably can.

Captain and vice-captain had added 200 in 304 balls by the time they were separated, and the ball could not have been deeper in Australia's court had the game been taking place next door at Memorial Drive. Haddin donned the baggy green that seems perfectly contoured for his head and swept three sixes off Swann, who ran exasperated fingers through his own newly short-cropped hair. Australia's vice-captain then made short work of the nineties with a drive through mid-on, a nick through a vacant slip and a pull shot off Stokes, celebrating with another swept six from Panesar. At last, Harris, with a full body swing but a minimal backlift, hit a hearty half-century, sweeping Swann for consecutive sixes to raise Australia's 500 and expedite a declaration.

Twenty-one overs of the second day remained, and Mitchell Johnson was given the first of them. Straight outta Brisbane, he proceeded to bowl the seven fastest balls of the match. They were also some of the fullest, the Australians having observed the pitch's muted bounce and the tendency of the odd delivery to stay down. The effect was electrifying. Cook's defence yielded like a flimsy door under a pounding; Carberry and Root held on, nervously strokeless. Harris and Siddle steamed in as well, before Johnson resumed for a final thrust, hitting Root resoundingly in the chest. When Root soon after sought a single to get off strike, Carberry responded with a seeming reluctance that almost cost him his wicket. One for 35 at the close, England were lucky it was no worse – although that was not far away.

It was Lyon who achieved the breakthrough for Australia early on the third morning, when Root swept imprudently at a ball that bounced more than he expected. A fretful Pietersen then picked out the finer of two mid-wicket catchers as he came impetuously down the wicket at Siddle – the kind of shot to silence a dressing room that would already have been subdued. At length a phase of five maidens got under Carberry's skin, and he wasted a commendable half-century, his first in Tests, by pulling to the left of Warner in the ring, who took a brilliant catch in an outstretched left hand. There was no longer much point in talking about England's arrears in terms of runs – it was measurable in parsecs.

The afternoon became The Johnson Show, with a bill of passing guests, all pausing briefly, none looking comfortable, and a general air of chaos. Stokes was thought to have nicked a delivery into his pads and awarded four for overthrows, then given out lbw on referral; Prior nicked the first ball in his half;

Broad and Anderson were bowled by the first balls they received. Broad prolonged the agony nearly seven minutes by asking that shining bolts on the sightscreen be obscured – as Robertson-Glasgow once said of a batsman holding up Larwood, 'seized with that last love of life which must have urged victims of old to address some trivial and delaying remark to the executioner'. Worst of all, perhaps, was Swann throwing his bat at a near-wide, making a mockery of Bell's efforts to keep the innings alive at his end. Panesar put the conditions in perspective with an hour's blocking while Bell played some superb strokes, including a six over cover from Harris, and some lofted drives from the spinners that dissuaded Clarke from enforcing the follow-on. But that was England's only accomplishment. Johnson's seven for 40 was virile fast bowling meeting impotent batting, with the stumps, demolished four times, bearing the brunt.

Though Anderson briefly checked Australia by removing Rogers and Watson cheaply, and Panesar bowled Clarke with a lovely delivery, Warner's free-flowing strokes maintained the home team's momentum towards victory. In the evening press conferences, Johnson predicted more of the same, although his captain sprang a surprise the following morning by declaring at the overnight score. It transpired that Clarke merely had an eye on the weather, but at the time it seemed marvellously Machiavellian, for it left Cook with barely fifteen minutes to compose himself before taking up arms against Johnson again, and the bowler found the perfect response to a batsman anxious about the fuller ball: a hissing bouncer along the left-armer's alleyway of anxiety, inducing a top-edged pull. Hovering on the newly-near fence, Harris had time to make ground and take a tumbling catch.

With two days to bat, and their best long-distance batsman gone, England had never looked more forlorn. When Carberry got a bigger piece of his pull shot but picked out Lyon at backward square leg, another four-day Test was in prospect. In the event, Root took root and Pietersen took note as they had not the day before. For an hour either side of lunch, the pair toiled honourably against hostile bowling and fielding. If it wasn't too little, however, it was too late. Pietersen's staid half-century was ended by a skimmer from Siddle, who thereby claimed the wicket of England's number four for the ninth time – not quite McGrath v Atherton, but on the way. After giving up some inviting dross earlier, Steve Smith then conned Bell into shovelling a low full-toss to mid-on – a third Smith win over England's best player, forming a third of his Test wickets.

Root carried on studiously and Stokes hung in roughly, the former looking as much like a batsman of Test quality as the latter did not. Calm-browed, smooth-chinned, Root made a fine impression, justifying his succession to Trott with a visible relish for the contest, and falling unluckily when Haddin interposed between a falling edge and the ground. If not quite in his class as a batsman, Stokes did look in his league as an opponent, absorbing and turning back some Australian aggression. A brush of shoulders with Johnson as they passed in mid-wicket briefly detained umpires Dharmasena and Erasmus who reported both, perhaps to give them something to do – otherwise, with their recourse to video for virtually everything, including a check on the front line after each wicket, they seemed almost completely redundant. ICC referee Jeff Crowe dismissed the reports anyway.

Prior's first half-century in nine Tests, which began diffidently before opening out, extended the Test into the final day, but not for long or with much conviction. He and Broad became the third and fourth batsmen to succumb to pull shots; Swann and Panesar fell wildly and timidly, so that even if the rain that ended up skirting the ground had fallen it would have been irrelevant. The flattery was now all for the Australians.

# A day at Edgbaston
## RUNAWAY TEST (2015)

Australian cricket didn't have an altogether bad day on Thursday. A young opening batsman built an impressive hundred, helping to establish a big lead over highly rated opponents in challenging conditions.

Unfortunately this day was in Chennai, the team was Australia A against India A, and the opener was twenty-two-year-old West Australian Cam Bancroft – one for the future, perhaps.* In Birmingham, the present was busy smacking Michael Clarke's team around the chops.

This is a series that hasn't so much fluctuated as oscillated. In Australia's case, one of the reasons has been their acute dependence on the formula of Mitchell Johnson times Steve Smith. At Lord's their fast bowling and acquisitive batting expanded exponentially as they won by 405 runs; here it has retreated arithmetically.

---

* Little did I know what the long-term future held for Cameron Bancroft, now forever associated with Sandpapergate. The near-term future for Australia was defeat the next day by eight wickets.

Johnson started yesterday by striking sparks off a still helpful surface, twice in three deliveries. But Australia was already a long way behind, their batsmen having deliquesced in the dankness of the previous day. Johnson hurled himself into the fray as long as he could before his replacement brought respite. He retreated to the outfield, and the sideshow of the Hollies Stand.

When Australia then batted again, Smith fretted and strutted twenty-six deliveries before top-edging a pull shot. It was hard to recall him having been dismissed in similar manner; it didn't seem to reflect an abiding weakness or technical glitch; it could be thought of as the shot of a batting generation tutored to respond aggressively to every match situation. But there was also a touch of ennui – that having led one fightback in this series, Smith simply could not summon the wherewithal for another.

The significance of Smith's wicket these days is a reflection of the dwindling of his captain. A couple of years ago, Clarke seemed threatened only by the internal enemy of his fitness; age was creeping up on him all the while, and this there was no arresting. He has not imposed himself on a Test for eighteen months; all the coaching, counsel and encouragement not-withstanding, he has here struggled simply to cling on. And within half an hour of his fall, the batting order had become a casualty list.

Australia remained in the fight thanks only to David Warner, who had one of those days when bowlers taking him on must feel like tamers entering a lion's cage. He streaked to a half-century in 35 balls without ever seeming in haste, clumping drives off both feet, landing cuts of martial fury. There was one brilliant pull off Finn, a whisk with a horizontal bat – a humblebrag of a stroke. But with precious little activity at the other end, Alastair Cook could afford to defend in order to attack, securing the perimeters, and thereby sealing the exits. Deprived of the strike, Warner tried to repeat his earlier pull shot, and simply repeated the top edge of a kind seen in the World Cup semi-final and the Roseau Test.

Australia's task should not have proven so difficult. Batting was easier than the first day, at times almost a bit of a romp, especially when Moeen Ali and Stuart Broad teamed up at an inflection point in the game, when England's lead was only 54 with numbers ten and jack to come. During the last instalment of the Ashes, the tails of the respective teams were a leading indicator of their fortunes. Australia's kept coiling until it was round Cook's throat; England's was docked as easily as a lamb's. But neither tail had detained their opponents overlong in this series until yesterday, and Moeen, not for the first time, recalled David Gower, in the lissom ease of his driving, and his laconic acceptance of defeat outside off stump. Basking in the afternoon sun, he scattered seven boundaries in a span of 16 deliveries. Broad's fight for a semblance of batting form has been a story within the story of these Ashes. Since having his face rearranged by Varun Aaron at Old Trafford a year ago, he has been cowering at square leg like Julian Assange in the Ecuadorean embassy. But over the last three Tests, he has tentatively re-emerged, and actually made more runs than Michael Clarke in fewer innings. Yesterday, tall and upright, he was briefly reminiscent of his father.

Nothing became the match's highest partnership so little as the manner of its ending, the partners holing out to Josh Hazlewood in consecutive overs as though there was a declaration in the offing – a cavalier sacrifice considering the value of runs in this game. Bell and Root having earlier surrendered their wickets in haste, you wondered at such abandon – on this surface and in a series of such tendencies, fate is best not tempted.

The headlong trend also seemed in keeping with the runaway nature of this very modern Test match, which has hurtled along at four runs an over, with a wicket every six overs. The morrow, under such circumstances, always seems far away. But the morrow always comes. And when the alternatives to your current XI include thirty-seven-year-old Brad Haddin, thirty-four-year-old Shane Watson, thirty-three-year-old Fawad Ahmed, thirty-two-year-old Shaun Marsh and thirty-year-old Peter Siddle, then maybe the future is what you have to start focusing on.

# A day at Trent Bridge

## DISASTER AREA (2015)

With twenty minutes to go before lunch at Trent Bridge on Thursday, Darren Lehmann walked purposefully towards the middle, bat in his gloved hands. He strode the length of the pitch on which his Australian team had just been bowled out for 60, scanning it intently. He stood at the crease and looked towards the pavilion, then played a lugubrious shadow block, a rueful shadow leave.

As he then wended his way off, it was tempting to eavesdrop on his thoughts. Was he about to make a comeback? After all, apparently form is temporary, class is permanent. But perhaps he waxed more philosophical – here was one of those days that dramatizes the coach's plight.

For games of international cricket nowadays, players have never been better prepared. They are fitter, stronger, train harder, eat better, know more about their oppositions, conditions and challenges generally. Yet it is still the case that at 11 a.m. each morning, they go out on their own. For the game does not hinge on how diligently players have worked or how assiduously they have war-gamed; it is determined by their capacity to reproduce skills under pressure. And seldom can an Australian team have experienced such a collective skills seizure as on Thursday at Trent Bridge.

Every batsman would have known what to do. Chris Rogers has made thirty-eight centuries in England. This is Steve Smith's fourth visit to this country in six years. This was Adam Voges's twentieth first-class match on this very ground. Shaun Marsh was coming off consecutive hundreds, and Michael Clarke has been, by his own account, working like Alexei Stakhanov.

Conditions overhead and underfoot were conducive to seam movement. For batsmen that entails lots of discretion around off stump, playing from alongside the ball so as best to afford it free passage, rather than trapped behind it. Yet within half an hour, all these technical commandments had been violated – not once, but serially. Batsmen turned chest-on rather than side-on. Batsmen chased what they needn't have. Instead of hard heads and soft hands, there were hard hands and soft heads. It was 'batting with intent' in the same sense that Jonestown was Kool-Aid drinking with intent.

Clarke's shot was most abject and culpable of all – a wild drive at an all-day sucker of a delivery for a batsman desperate to feel the kiss of willow on leather. Australia's captain had almost been bowled by his second ball and caught from his ninth. Remember when we used to talk of Australia's 'aura'? Clarke's is collapsing, vortex-like. His wicket is ceasing to be a scalp, becoming a souvenir.

Was it the pitch? It looked before play to be drumming on minds. The respective camps presented a study. Cook gave the surface only a perfunctory nod on his way back from the nets. England enjoyed their kickabout and adjourned. Clarke looked pensive, careworn, brooding perhaps on the similarity to conditions when he won the toss and batted at Edgbaston, perhaps trying to remember those old meteorological nostrums ('Grey sky at morning, captain's warning'; 'Rain before seven, choose another eleven').

Long-headed Brad Haddin joined him. Smith, Nathan Lyon and Shane Watson looked in. Adam Voges imparted local knowledge as captain of Nottinghamshire. Clarke conversed longest with chairman of selectors Rod Marsh . . . then proceeded to lose the toss. The Australians looked up now and saw Stuart Broad – not James Anderson, their nemesis two years ago, but Broad, their nuisance. Broad galls the visitors. He throws down markers, picks up gauntlets. He chats freely about the Aussie batsmen's weaknesses, about the peculiarities of English cricket balls. He features in an advertising campaign for an Australian wine company sponsoring the England team, playing up to his reputation. It is pretty funny; more than that, it is on Broad's part a gesture of cheeky confidence.

Eighteen months ago, Brisbane's *Courier-Mail* famously refused to use Broad's name in their match descriptions, referring to him instead as an 'England medium-pacer'. Their front page tomorrow will need to be an entirely blank sheet, which may not be wholly inappropriate – a spell of eight for 15 needs as little elaboration as the Gettysburg Address. Yet it did need help, and got it, from six slips – not four slips and two gullys but six proper slips, like a chevron of razor wire which nothing escaped. Ben Stokes made one miraculous snare. Otherwise it was made to look as natural as a practice drill.

Perhaps this was a reflection of the efficacy of good coaching. On England's jolly to Spain at the end of June, new coach Trevor Bayliss made slip catching his solitary focus. Although his charges paid for a drop at Lord's, since then they have missed precious little. When England batted, Cook's edge bisected Clarke and Smith, as painful to them both as a poke in the eye.

Lehmann by now was looking on from his team's balcony – subdued and serious, weighing up plans and plots, while knowing full well that 60 is not so much a total to defend as to apologize for. Batting, bowling, fielding and conditional coaches, management and administrative staff came and went. Shane Warne, Glenn McGrath, Ian Healy and Michael Slater were in the commentary boxes; Allan Border was in the crowd. What names, what talents, what legends. And nothing to be done about what was happening on the field by any of them.

# James Anderson
## KEEP WALKING (2018)

ustralians have never warmed to James Anderson. The feeling may be mutual. In his autobiography, he recalls his first Test tour as uniquely unpleasant, in a social as well as a sporting sense: 'Australia is home to some of the most poisonous creatures on earth, and most of them seemed to dwell on the streets of Sydney and Melbourne.'

Some time in the next few days, thirty-five-year-old Anderson will take perhaps his last new ball for England in an Australian Test match, with few regrets – he'll hardly be sought out for a testimonial by Kookaburra. Yet few cricketers of his time have been more stealthily remarkable.

So many records did Alastair Cook and Steve Smith leave in their respective wakes in Melbourne that another passed unnoticed. By playing his 133rd Test, Anderson became Test cricket's most capped pace bowler, overtaking Courtney Walsh. The only bowler to have played more Tests is Shane Warne; the rest of those ahead of Anderson on the list, Jacques Kallis and Mark Boucher apart, are specialist batsmen.

Anderson has endured in his uniqueness, too. At 188cm,

he stands just taller than his boyish captain Joe Root. At 76 kg, he weighs the same as his bantamweight antagonist David Warner. He should hardly bowl 100 kmh, let alone 135 kmh. These Ashes are an advertisement for fast bowling as an occupation for giants: both attacks are composed of towering men, while Australia is breeding monsters like Billy Stanlake and Peter George. Anderson belongs to a more ancient lineage, of smaller figures, compact and rhythmic, like Ray Lindwall (178 cm) and Harold Larwood (173 cm), although he is more lightly built than either, while no cricket or conditioning coach would recommend the way he rotates his back and completes his action by looking at the ground.

Yet there is no evidence of his performances attenuating – on the contrary. Since turning thirty, in an era of flat pitches, fat bats and machine-stitched balls, Anderson has taken 254 Test wickets at 24.15. In 2017 alone, he claimed 55 victims at 17: almost twice as many wickets at less than half the cost of his old confrère Stuart Broad, four years his junior. The skill he has polished to a remarkable lustre has been bowling at left-handers, and from over the wicket, departing the round-the-wicket angle that for a long time was a default mode among faster bowlers.

For a pace bowler, Anderson wastes nothing: his run is economical, his follow through abbreviated, his walk-back brisk; he gets through overs in almost one continuous motion, as though to leave the batsman, like Rosencrantz and Guildenstern, no shriving time. The problem for England this summer is that Anderson has been unable to bowl all the time, although he has done his best, delivering more overs (189.3) more economically (2.2 an over) than anyone on either side. England had similar problems here four years ago. It is a damning comment on their cricket that while Australia has remade its attack almost entirely in the interim, English bowling still consists of Anderson, Broad, TBA, A. N. Other and Subject to the Crown Prosecution Service.

So why the Australian reluctance to extend admiration? Anderson is partly penalized for his excellence at home. Using his own pitches, overhead conditions and cricket balls he has taken 335 wickets at 24.29; his record away is 187 wickets at 32.8, leading to his derogation as an 'English bully'. Yet Mitchell Johnson paid 25 for his wickets at home and 32 away, and nobody here considers him an 'Australian bully'. Nor, save in his career's earliest stages, has the gap between Anderson's best and worst ever been as pronounced as Johnson's.

There is also that Anderson is a notoriously ornery opponent – proud, perfectionist, prickly. It does not seem personal. Anyone in range with a bat becomes a target. The first time they were formally introduced as English players, having previously only been county opponents, Alastair Cook noted: 'The last time we met you called me a cunt.' It's not obvious whether his verbals have ever actually intimidated anyone: Brad Haddin said he found that Anderson's northern accent rendered his sledging unintelligible. If anything they may have stimulated the competitive juices of others. In his autobiography, Chris Rogers noted that England's verbal hostility in the 2013 Ashes inculcated a sense that 'these guys need to be put in their place' in 2013–14.

In Anderson's case, the on-field abrasiveness has been cultivated with the help of psychologist Mark Bawden to compensate for an off-field reticence. The objective has been to distinguish the warrior persona 'Jimmy' from the shy homebody 'James', whose friends of longest standing are those made at the outset of his career at Burnley CC, his 185-year-old Lancashire League club.

This means, I suspect, that Anderson has never quite been

able to negotiate dealing with opponents as anything other than that. There's no deficiency in this – in some ways it is a form of sincerity, and it is an issue that each cricketer must solve according to their own lights. But it may have hindered appreciation of an unusually diverse and thoughtful athlete.

This summer Anderson is contributing to an engaging BBC Radio 5 Live podcast, 'Tailenders', with his friend Felix White, founder of the indie pop group the Maccabees. He's relaxed, drily humorous, steadily loyal, sometimes very insightful. Anderson's passion for music extends to his being a long-time supporter of the music therapy charity, Nordoff Robbins. He was also executive producer of an excellent documentary, *Warriors* (2015), about Kenya's soul-stirring Maasai Warriors cricket team.

At this film's launch in London, I was struck by Anderson's presence. He was clearly conscious that his involvement had drawn a sizeable proportion of the audience, yet equally abashed about it, and anxious not to distract from the work of the film's director Barney Douglas. In such glimpses can be the measure of a man. I wondered also why the subject had appealed to Anderson. Perhaps it's that, in his own way, he is also a tribal man, loyal and wary. It will be interesting to see how one who has expressed so much of his personality through cricket comes to terms with life beyond it; in the meantime, take the opportunity these next five days to study one of the game's finest craftsmen.*

---

* I love that I dashed this off under the apprehension that Jimmy Anderson was playing his last Test in Australia. Five and a bit years on, he's still going, and I like him all the more.

# A duel at Lord's

## SMITH v ARCHER (2019)

Not often does the promotion of a cricket match, and a Test match at that, condense to the clash of two cricketers. Very seldom indeed does that competition then fulfil the expectation. But for an hour at Lord's today, Australia and England had second billing, and the Ashes were left to gather dust on the mantelpiece. The duel, amply promised for the preceding week, was afoot: Steve Smith versus Jofra Archer.

At lunch, the records still seemed to be forming an orderly queue for Smith's delectation. He had become the first man to accumulate seven consecutive Ashes fifties; he was within sight of the rare feat of registering three consecutive Ashes centuries. Australia had lost a solitary wicket in the first session, and the sun was out on a day where the light otherwise fluctuated like an expiring neon tube.

Then came Archer, his international career just two months old, three days into his first Test, from the Pavilion End. Though he famously scorned to wear a helmet on grounds that it involved acknowledgement that a bowler was fast, Viv

Richards would allow that a certain bowler was 'serious'. Archer is serious. It's fortunate that the consequences of his spell after lunch were not more so.

The speeds the scoreboard flashed were more reminiscent of a sports car than an English pace bowler: sixteen consecutives were clocked, in cricket's defiantly imperial way, at in excess of 90mph. The fastest, at 96.1mph, was 155kmh in the new money. Jack Leach's contrastingly gentle arcs were measured at half that speed. But you did not need radar to sense the rapidity. Archer's tightness to the stumps and the gradient of the ground added a serration to his sharp edge: he jagged a ball back that rendered Tim Paine helpless, then released a bouncer that did the same to Jonny Bairstow.

Before the match Australia's coach had cast doubt on his stamina, his capacity to sustain velocities amid the hard grind of Test cricket. 'I think Justin Langer has another think coming,' Archer had retorted, and now added deed to word.

Above all, for the first time this series, Smith's jerks and jives seemed to have more external than internal influences. Archer had Smith playing and missing; Archer had Smith fending; Archer had Smith hooking in the air. At length, he hit Smith's arm, raising an angry haematoma that required an X-ray. At last, he hit Smith's neck, laying him out face down.

The innocent days when batsmen shrugged off blows with a shake of the head and the replacement of a helmet are long ago. Nothing has seemed the same since Phillip Hughes was laid to rest, not least for the four occupants of Australia's dressing room present that fateful day. Nowadays – quite rightly – there is immediate concern. As Smith crumpled, medical staff hurried from both benches. A photograph captured him with his eyes closed. An overhead camera showed him laid out like a flattened fighter in a ring. For a moment the World Test Championship bore a more than passing resemblance to the World Heavyweight Championship.

'Retired hurt' is one of cricket's more genteel expressions – it sounds like a polite withdrawal following a mild indisposition, for a cup of tea and maybe an ice pack. As Smith was escorted off for the now mandatory concussion tests, something more like 'urgent triage' seemed necessary.

Is this the chink in Smith's game for which England has been searching? Let's just say that the 'serious' causes every batsman discomfiture, even on a surface as relatively slow as this. Nobody likes it, runs the proverb: it's just that some show it more than others. But the Australian's back-and-across step does add a degree of difficulty to evasion, and without the standard rear-facing protection and arm guard he did seem a tad underdressed. Three years ago Smith sustained a similar blow from Neil Wagner in Christchurch, and was lucky the ball expended itself against his helmet; two weeks ago in Birmingham he was left groggy by Ben Stokes. Smith certainly looked a little peaky three-quarters of an hour later when he resumed his 80 not out, although this is just as likely to have been from the pain in the arm as any bells in his head.

Smith had a drive, a hoick and a hack, padded up to a straight ball and walked, his request for a review more like an adieu. The only anomaly was that the bowler was Woakes. Archer's earlier spell of 8-2-31-1 reads like a good day's work in a one-day match; his final analysis of 29-11-59-2 sounds in the nature of a containing effort on a shirtfront wicket. But you can no more believe everything you read in the scorebook than you can in the newspaper.

After tea, the Ashes resumed, and excitingly. When we talk of the way luck pervades cricket, we usually have the players in mind, but it applies to spectators, too. All those with first day tickets in this Test match got was a refund; those with third day tickets had the afternoon for conversation and conjecture. On fourth days a Test match often idles, gearing up for the denouement. Instead, they went home having enjoyed a contest chock-full of incident containing ninety overs, ten wickets and 266 runs.

All four English second innings wickets fell from the same end as Archer bowled from, sauce for the gander. Nathan Lyon probed away from the Nursery End, extracting turn, kicking up dust. On the ground where their virile strokeplay inspired England in the World Cup final just over a month ago, Stokes and Jos Buttler dead-batted through the last hour to insure against an Australian countercoup, and took eagerly for the pavilion when rain dropped in one final time. Tomorrow's events will bear heavily on the course of these Ashes. They will also pit Steve Smith against Jofra Archer again. After a lot of waiting, a compelling Test match is coming, literally, to a head.*

---

* In fact, of course, Smith was subbed from the game overnight and replaced by Marnus Labuschagne, whose fine batting helped Australia eke out a draw.

# A coup at Headingley

## STOKED (2019)

Every modern Test match is a quiet referendum on the format's future, and referendums, ahem, don't always turn out as you expect or hope. Yet here was a referendum that, just for a change, had no loser. Nobody who played, watched, described or officiated in this Third Test could feel anything other than honoured to have been part of it.

On Thursday, Ben Stokes bowled nine expensive overs. On Friday, he was caught from a ball he could hardly reach. Yet Test match cricket offers the cumulative drama of second chances – during his twin centuries at Birmingham, Steve Smith had linked his second chance with his first.

Stokes's influence on this match began with Australia nearly 200 runs ahead and three wickets down, when he seized the ball from the Rugby Stand End. Twenty-four overs he bowled off the reel but for four deliveries from Jofra Archer, keeping England in touch with a game, and an Ashes series, that had been accelerating off into the distance. And yesterday . . . well, perhaps you've heard.

There has been some worthwhile and watchable Ashes

cricket in this last decade and a bit. But what the premium Test match brand has wanted for is a genuinely close result, the nipper of Trent Bridge 2013, where England won by 14 runs, being the solitary exception. It's not too early to call this series a classic. Cricketers are, almost always, also cricket lovers. You could hear the lingering excitement in Tim Paine's voice afterwards as he saluted an 'amazing' game of cricket, a 'bloody exciting' advertisement of the long format, and a rival player who 'plays the way you would like to play'.

It's not stretching things to say that England enjoyed most of fortune's favours in this match. The visitors were deprived of their best batsman, forced to bat and to bowl in the tougher conditions. Sixty-seven all out in bright sunlight on an unmarked surface? Of the hosts it remains an indictment. But the last day was utterly, cruelly, wonderfully fair, with times when the Ashes must have seemed close enough for Paine to sniff. David Warner's sixth catch in the match, left hand bandaged around the bruising for the earlier five, was seemingly the most important; with Joe Root's wicket, one end was open through which Australia might pour.

To that stage, England had carried on their painstaking care of the previous evening, having added four from five overs. Half an hour in, Stokes had scored three from seventy-three deliveries, had the stem guard knocked from his helmet by Josh Hazlewood, replaced his gloves and had a drink.

With the advent of the second new ball and the industry that Bairstow at his best lends an innings, Stokes opened out. The pair added a run a ball for ten overs without appreciable risk. When Lyon resumed, looking to repeat his last day coup at Birmingham of six for 49, he quietly removed the bails on the non-striker's stumps and swapped them. Umpire Joel Wilson looked on understandingly at the twitch of superstition, but there was no further joy for Australia before lunch, by which time England had winnowed their target away to 121.

The stakes thereafter rose with every over. When Bairstow reviewed a caught behind decision against him, he brandished his bat and arm like a missionary a crucifix; when he edged to Marnus Labuschagne at slip, he tipped his bat upside down in ceremonial surrender. There ensued many breaks, for drinks, gloves, injuries, a replacement bat, which for once added to the scene, as one peered down on individuals: the frustration of James Pattinson as his rhythm faltered from the Kirkstall Lane End; the insouciance of Jofra Archer in wearing his chunky chronometer while batting; the cheek of Marcus Harris sitting on the fence chatting to the crowd when Australia needed a wicket to win. We know the players so little; perhaps, by these vignettes, we get an impression of them. That's Test cricket also.

Stokes allowed very little to intrude. He has few mannerisms, just a profound oaken strength. He hardly acknowledged his fifty; he would offer only a belated wave for his hundred. Complicit in the misunderstanding that cost Jos Buttler his wicket, he nervelessly cut two boundaries off Lyon. There was a roar as England's target shrank to double figures. With each run, spectators on the Western Terrace rose and fell like organ stops. Stokes exuded no superfluous effort. Everything was harnessed to his batting.

As the Australians commenced to lop off England's tail, Stokes's energy surged. Hits started soaring over fielders who could be scattered no further and who could leap no higher. With Jack Leach myopically inert but stoically scoreless, Stokes unfurled strokes of skill and subtlety, down the ground and over square leg with a straight bat, over point and fine leg with a reversed bat. The pace bowlers who had cut England to pieces forty-eight hours earlier were treated with disdain.

Hazlewood had given away 2.3 an over on Friday; now his last over went for 19.

Paine turned at last to Lyon. The spinner had earlier in the day passed Dennis Lillee's Australian wicket-taking tally. Now he looked small, vulnerable, the sun shining off his pate, his chiaroscuro features tight. He bowled a respectable over. The ball spun out of the rough to slip, defeated two attempted reverse sweeps. But in Lyon's next, with eight to win, Stokes hit a straight six – mishit, actually, but no matter, for the batsman's conviction carried the ball well into what Richie Benaud called the 'confectionery stand'.

In years to come, Australians will cast back on the run out they then missed, and the review they did not have – maybe Englishmen will, too. But I'm not sure they should worry long. Even in this age, obsessed with precision and quantity, the rational and logical, there remains in cricket an abiding belief in the rub of the green, which Stokes had by then mightily earned. What a cricketer. And what a Test match.

# An ambush at the Gabba

## ONE PERFECT DAY (2021)

B efore 'super shot that' and 'tew for tew hundred and twenty-tew', the sayings of Richie Benaud included a famous line about captaincy being ninety per cent luck and ten per cent skill, but never to try it without the latter.

Viz Pat Cummins, nineteen Australian skippers on from His Richieness, at the Gabba yesterday. That he had the ten per cent sorted was confirmed by his first Ashes five-for – a ruthless display, befitting the world's top ranked bowler. But he was lucky, too – in his well-drilled men, in his undercooked opponents, and in even the unfavourable fall of the coin.

Cummins said, frankly, he would have batted. But no batting display could have been so emphatic as the way Australia's bowlers broke, becalmed then battered the unit of his counterpart Joe Root, leaving them the only people in Queensland sorry that quarantine does not last a full month.

In his wonderful pageant of Australia's Test captains, *On Top Down Under*, Ray Robinson described watching Benaud leading Australia in his first Test at the Gabba in 1958, and opportunistically bringing in a short leg after a single delivery: 'A field change before a ball touched a bat!'

Australia yesterday had a wicket before the ball touched a bat, and a captain similarly busy and involved, whether posting a short cover to Jos Buttler, a short mid-wicket to Chris Woakes or a leg gully to Ollie Robinson, replacing Cameron Green after a one-over spell that included his first Test wicket, and most portentously relieving Mitchell Starc after two overs in order that he, Cummins, might bowl at Root.

Hoodoos are almost always over-estimated: batters must get out to someone. But Cummins's ascendancy over Root is now so marked he seems able to exercise it without actually bowling to him; no sooner had Cummins delivered a maiden to Haseeb Hameed than England's captain nicked off to Josh Hazlewood.

So much for the impossible burdens of the bowling captain, how Steve Smith would have to act as an additional hemisphere of Cummins's brain. There were a few semaphores from Smith at slip yesterday, but no mistaking Cummins's signals, or the exactitude of the bowlers' lengths, as full as they were short the last time Australia bowled at the Gabba, sparing the bouncer, endangering both edges. Cummins even had the presence of mind to allow Nathan Lyon a chance at number eleven as the spinner searches for his 400th Test wicket. No junior coach could have fulfilled his brief to encourage participation more closely.

As much as this was a classic Aussie Gabba ambush, England also arguably ambushed themselves, with a little too much thinking and not quite enough cricket. James Anderson and Stuart Broad did loom this summer as an either/or package; neither was a tad too subtle and a bit too cute. Root winning the toss on a sultry morning on a mat of grass then seemed to cry out for a rerun of Broad v Warner in 2019, to which even Australians, invested in their inalienable right to chant 'Broad is a wanker', would have looked forward.

Root's choice, of course, was shadowed by the lore of the coin at the Gabba, specifically the fateful decisions by Len Hutton in 1954 and Nasser Hussain in 2002 to send Australia in. But from these stories are tactfully excluded such decisions as Graham Yallop's to bat in 1978, after which Australia subsided to seven for 53, and Greg Chappell's and Allan Border's successful insertions of England in 1982 and 1990. And for a team like England whose preparation has been so scant, bowling would surely have been the more forgiving choice.

Certainly the precision and decisiveness that comes from recent competitive cricket was altogether lacking from England's top order. Burns missed one he should have hit and Malan played one he should have left, leaving Root to face the innings's twenty-first delivery and fall to the thirty-fifth. Had England's innings been on Netflix, you'd have been tempted to 'skip intro'. After an hour, it'll be all right on the night had become nightmare on Vulture Street.

Stokes stepped into the line of a ball at his armpit, bequeathing the innings to the juniors, Hameed and Ollie Pope, hemmed in on all sides. Pope clattered Lyon's one drag down into Labuschagne's shin pad. When the sun emerged briefly, England's tail wagged a little – maybe spasmed is a more accurate description. But Cummins's day wound down with another final flourish of luck: battleship-grey clouds united over the Gabba and finally burst, sparing Warner and Marcus Harris an initiation in the gloom. One wonders whether Cummins will develop the reputation that settled on Benaud, famously summed up by Dusty Rhodes: 'Richie, if you stuck your head in a bucket of shit, you'd come up with a mouthful of diamonds.' So far, so good.

# Joe Root

## HOME ALONE (2021)

S hortly after tea at the Gabba on Friday, Joe Root played back to Nathan Lyon, in that way he has of going very deep in the crease, and playing very late, right under his eyes. Fielders around the bat tensed. Lyon threw his arms in the air. Then down came the bat, descending like a cat flap. The ball dropped dead at his feet.

Root looked up towards the video screen, as though running through a checklist: footwork, stumps; head, hands; turn, bounce. Not, one presumes, score – that was still, from England's point of view, a little dismaying. But he did not look away until he was quite satisfied, and until the onlooker was aware of the oddity of watching Root watching himself being watched by others.

Everyone is looking to Root on this Ashes tour. There are his colleagues, seven of whom in this Test are appearing in Australia for the first time. There are his team's followers, especially those courageous enough to have braved Covid-crazed Australia. There are Australian fans, who would like a contest worthy of the Ashes name, and for whom he almost *is* England.

His Australian opponents, meanwhile, will have dedicated hours and resources to plans for Root's extraction. Every time he goes to the crease this summer, he will be viewed as the key block in the jenga tower of England's batting. It seems an unfair burden for a man to bear.

Yet as he went about his task yesterday, this could be seen from a different, happier perspective. The crease is, to use the therapeutic argot, Root's happy place. The possibilities are bounded. The ego is secure. In the middle, nobody can quiz him about James Anderson and Stuart Broad; nobody need be updating him on Ben Stokes's knee or Brisbane's weather; he will not be required to provide statements about Azeem Rafiq or trauma counselling to Jack Leach. Nor does anyone come this far in professional sport without getting comfortable with scrutiny, and even learning to enjoy it, at least a little.

This is Root's thirteenth Test of the year. That is a staggering amount of time to be on show, on parade, flying the flag. His team has been struggling, but a tide has come in the affairs of his batting: at stumps last night, he had 1541 runs at 67 in the calendar year. That first-day duck felt like an aberration rather than a prophecy.

Yesterday, at least, England's first two wickets afforded Root twenty-one overs' grace, and he enjoyed solid support from Dawid Malan, upright and minimal, like a Grenadier Guardsman in his sentry box. Malan has returned to England's colours this year as a kind of human shield or personal bodyguard for Root, filling the number three slot that England has really failed to fill since Jonathan Trott's departure. So wonderfully precise in the minuet of his footwork, so refreshingly positive in his strokeplay, exhausting every possibility of a productive shot before he settled for playing defensively, Root hardly seemed to need such an escort. Early drives in the 'V' announced him. Flicks to leg kept his score ticking. A cover drive off Mitchell Starc was what West Indians call a 'not a man move' stroke, defying your eye to follow. At tea, Root walked off chatting amiably to his former Prospect CC colleague Nathan Lyon. Either side of the break, he made Lyon's life hard indeed, with an array of sweep shots, orthodox and reverse. Having backhanded to third man, he looked down and marked his guard, so clear from the quality of the contact and his mind map of the field that the stroke was four.

Lyon was whirling through his overs in pursuit of that 400th Test wicket, which like Sachin Tendulkar's hundredth international hundred has been scheduled by Tantalus. The left-handed Malan should have presented an inviting target. In truth, Australia's premier slow bowler never really looked like breaking through, on what was, after all, a third-day pitch. As Australia struggled to penetrate, it was Root's counterpart who appeared to be scratching round for answers. The ball had stopped swinging, not started reversing, was not spinning. Cummins and Hazlewood could not be bowling all the time; Starc's length fluctuated; the part-timers did not do the trick. That Australia's two best bowlers got through only twenty-two of their seventy overs was the first check in his pageant of success. Australia clamouring; England hanging on; it might be the story of these Ashes.

# Future Ashes

## 2023: AN ASHES ODYSSEY

About concentrating on the Ashes, there is always a slightly false pretence, in that you are ignoring the periods between. Ten Tests off the reel is not unknown (1901–02, 1974–75, 2013–14), but there is usually some intervening hiatus, and a team between times can be radically reshaped by the addition or subtraction of a name or two. Consider, for example, the impact of absences, from Dennis Lillee's in 1977 and Greg Chappell's in 1981 to Ben Stokes's in 2017–18 and Jofra Archer's in 2021–22. We are dealing with human *matériel*. Nothing is ever ideal or perfect; sometimes teams must make do and mend. Even substitutes have played their part. There was Syd Copley, who crucially caught Stan McCabe at Trent Bridge in 1930; Robin Sims, who adeptly caught Allan Border at long leg in the 1989 Lord's Test; there was Gary Pratt, whose dead-eye aim caught Ricky Ponting short at Trent Bridge in 2005; all of them, frankly, now eclipsed by Marnus Labuschagne who arrived at Lord's four years ago and hasn't been dislodged since.

The shape of the Ashes of the future seems increasingly

likely to be dictated by the intermediate and the exogenous. It already is. Where the Ashes of 2019 was pushed into late summer by the World Cup, the Ashes of 2023 has been jerked into early summer by The Hundred, with players arriving hotfoot from the Indian Premier League then setting forth afterwards for the World Cup. For the first time in history, there will be no Ashes Test in August. To protect its standard five-Test duration, moreover, the Second and Third Tests, then the Fourth and Fifth, will this summer be played back-to-back. As recently as thirty years ago, Australia played fifteen first-class matches outside the Tests; this summer, they will play none. It barely makes sense to talk of an Ashes tour any more; perhaps a session or streak is closer to the mark.

Since 2021–22, furthermore, the team now led by Stokes and coached by Brendan McCullum has made itself over, not so much in personnel as in ethos, rampaging through Tests against New Zealand, India, South Africa and Pakistan ahead of their appointment with Ashes destiny. As I write this, I'm reminded of that southern summer of 2004–05, when, despite Australia's tight grip on the urn, there were the first stirrings of a new, better, feistier, funner, Flintoffier England. The outcome was perhaps the best Ashes of all, 2005. But treat this less as a prediction than a general commentary on another aspect of Ashes culture, that whatever is either about to happen or in the process of happening automatically reminds you of something that's already happened. This year will mark thirty years since the Ball of the Century, three-quarters of a century since Bradman's Invincibles ran down 404 to win at Headingley, and 150 years since W. G. first visited the Antipodes. And that's just the beginning. From a personal point of view, it will be the ninth Ashes series in England I have attended in the last eleven.

This aspect of the culture is, at the same time, an illusion.

We don't know. We never know. We wouldn't want to know. I remember asking Shane Warne once what kept him playing, in the end, into his forties. He said without prompting that it was his relish for the feeling that as he stepped on the field on any given day anything might happen – it was addictive, and hard to replace. This quality isn't unique to cricket, or even sport. But there seems something about cricket, with all its waiting, with all those gaps and pauses, long and short, loud and quiet, that seems to magnify it. Months out, I have absolutely not the faintest idea what will happen in the Ashes of 2023; by the day before, the possibilities might have narrowed a little, but maybe not that much. Anyway, how great is that?

# Index

NB: Page numbers in **bold** indicate main entries

Aaron, Varun, 370
*ABC Cricket Magazine*, 281
Abel, Bobby, 81
Adcock, Neil, 150
Adelaide Oval Cricket Ground, 33, 38, 315–18, 361
*Age, The*, 170–72, 202, 240, 282
Ahmed, Fawad, 371
AIF (Australian Imperial Force) cricket team, 96–9
AIS Cricket Academy, 226–7
Akhtar, Shoaib, 330
Alcock, Charles, 26
Alcott, Errol, 292
Alderman, Terry, 217, 254–5, 257, 265, **267–9**
Ali, Moeen, 370
Ali, Muhammad, 68
Ali, Wazir, 92
Allen, Gubby, 112
Altham, H. S., 19
amateur status, 80–81
*Amazing Grace* (Tomlinson), 28
Ambrose, Curtly, 133, 150, 324, 327
Amiss, Dennis, 229–30
Anderson, James, 337, 340–41, 344, 358, 363, 365, **376–9**, 389
Andrew, Keith, 176
Archer, Graham, 249
Archer, Jofra, 380–83, 384, 386, 394
Archer, Ken, 160
Archer, Ron, 172, 177
*Argus, The*, 39, 44, 46, 50

Arlott, John, 28, 80, 108, 123, 144, 167, 179, 209, 211, 217
Armstrong, Warwick, 59, 77, **84–8**, 99, 102, 134
Arnold, Geoff, 212, 229
Arnold, Ted, 74
*Art of Cricket, The* (Bradman), 222
*Art of Fast Bowling, The* (Lillee), 222
Ashes, 1–3, 7–10, 285
origin of, 8
Centenary Test (1977), **238–43**, 247
1882, 19–20, 27, 303, 309; 1894–95 series, **35–40**; 1896, 53; 1897–98 series, 41, 43; 1909, 86; 1920–21 series, 99–102; 1930, 110, 132, 394; 1932–33 (Bodyline) series, 120–23, 124; 1936–37 series, 133; 1946–47 series, 118; 1953, 157–8, **164–7**; 1954–55 series, **168–73**, 175–7; 1956, **178–82**; 1961, 186; 1965–66 series, 201–2, 209; 1968, 209; 1970–71 series, 352; 1972, 207, **209–14**; 1977–78 series, 228–30, 233, 246, 394; 1981, 244, **253–7**, 315, 394; 1984, 325; 1985, 260; 1989, 394; 1993, 323; 1995, **277–9**; 1997, **280–83**; 1998–99 series, **284–6**; 2001, **287–9**, **290–92**, **327**; 2005,

**299–303**, **304–7**, **308–11**,
336, 394–5; 2006, **312–14**,
**315–18**, **319–21**, **322–5**;
2009, **337–41**, **342–5**; 2010,
**346–9**; 2011, **350–53**; 2013,
10, **354–9**, **360–67**, 385;
2015, **368–71**, **372–5**;
2017–18, 394; 2019, **380–83**,
**384–7**, 395; 2021, **388–90**,
**391–3**, 394; 2023, 394–5
Ashton, George, 35
asylums, 45–6
Atherton, Michael, 267, 269, 277–9,
333, 353
Austin, Harold, 170
*Australasian, The*, 17, 19, 22, 44
*Australia: Story of a Cricket Country*
(Forster), 203
*Australia's Premier Batsman* (James),
12–14
Australian Cricket Council, 36
Australian Cricket Hall of Fame, 29,
32, 33, 84
Australian Cricketers' Association, 283
Australian Imperial Forces XI, 90
Australian Natives' Association, 44
*Australian Town and Country Journal*,
13
*Australian, The*, 281–3
*Autobiography* (Cardus), 58, 60

*Back to the Mark* (Lillee), 223
*Background of Cricket* (Gordon), 53
Bailey, George, 362
Bailey, Trevor, 165–7, 171
Bairstow, Jonny, 355, 357, 381, 385–6
Baker-Holroyd, John, 1st Earl of
Sheffield, 36
'Ball of the Century', 271
Bancroft, Cam, 368
Bannerman, Charles, 3, 5, **11–15**, 21,
74, 240
Barber, Bob, 231–2
Bardsley, Warren, 99, 126, 288
Barmy Army, 286, 302
Barnes, Alan, 241

Barnes, Sid, 193–4
Barratt, Fred, 125
Barrington, Ken, 195, 231, 234, 316
*Batsmanship* (Fry), 53
*Batter's Castle* (Peebles), 60
Bawden, Mark, 378
Bayliss, Trevor, 374
BBC (British Broadcasting
Corporation), 186–8
Beames, Percy, 170–73
Beattie-Smith, William, 47
Bedi, Bishan, 160, 313
Bedser, Alec, 82, 118, 158, 232
Beldam, George, 62, 64–7, 72, 74
Bell, Ian, 301, 305, 309, 316–17,
355–7, 363, 365–6, 370
Benaud, Daphne, 187
Benaud, Richie, 9, 23, 141, 150,
166–7, 170, 172, 178, **183–9**,
197, 217, 239, 274, 388, 390
Bennett, Chester, 211
Berry, Scyld, 263
*Best I Remember, The* (Porritt), 26
Bevan, Michael, 279
Bird, Jackson, 355
Blackham, Jack, 42
Bligh, Ivo Walter Francis, 8
Board of Control (Australia), 85–6
Bodyline *see* bowling
*Bodyline Autopsy* (Frith), 127
*Bodyline Umpire* (Hele), 128
Bollinger, Doug, 347–8
Bonnell, Max, 89–90
Boon, David, 263, 328
Border, Allan, 245, 254, 256–7,
**261–4**, 323, 325, 375, 390, 394
Botham, Ian, 9, **253–7**, 259
Bowden, Billy, 303, 344
Bowes, Bill, 92, 122, 134
bowling
Bodyline, 9, 77, 92, 120–23,
127–9, 131
fast bowling, 10, 120, 136–7, 141,
221–2, 245
leg-spin, 273
slow bowling, 120, 178, 181

# INDEX

spin bowling, 141, 156, 181, 230, 270–76
swing bowling, 267–9
underarm, 218, 344
Boxing Day Test, 238
Boycott, Geoff, 222, 232, **233–5**, 239, 316
Boyle, Harry, 21, 23
Bradman, Donald, 9, 11, 70–71, 75, 95, 101, 103, **104–9**, 117–18, 123, 127–9, 156–7, 195, 275
Bradman's 254, **110–14**
Bradman's 334, 113, 117, 202
Bradman's 974, 113, 117, 127
Centenary Test, 240, 243
*Daily Mail* and, 165
'Invincibles', 28, 91, 140, 160–61, 395
leg-theory and, 121, 131
*That's Cricket* (movie), 108
Braund, Len, 63
Brearley, Mike, 237, 245, 254, 256–7, 260, 268
Bresnan, Tim, 357–8, 360
Broad, Stuart, 339, 342–3, 345, 354–5, 357–9, 363, 365–6, 370, 374, 377, 389
Brodribb, Gerald, 53
Brooks, Reginald Shirley, 8
Brooks, Tom, 239, 241–2
Brown, Bill, **138–40**, 294, 297
Brown, John, 36, 39
Buchanan, John, 296, 327, 349
Buckle, Frank, 96
Bucknor, Steve, 285, 316, 328
*Bulletin, The*, 36, 43
Buruma, Ian, 51
Butcher, Mark, 291–2
Butler, Keith, 217
Buttler, Jos, 383, 386, 389

*C. B. Fry's Magazine of Action and Outdoor Life*, 66
Caddick, Andrew, 288
Cannadine, David 55
Cannings, Victor, 158

Carberry, Michael, 362, 364–5
Carbine Club, 270
Cardus, Neville, 56, 58–60, 63, 69, 71, 98, 110, 112, 139, 144, 167, 184
Cardwell, Ron, 96
Carr, Arthur, 82, 121, 126–7
Carter, Hanson, 87, 95
Carton, Sydney, 260
Cashman, Richard, 29–31
Cawthray, George, 212
Centenary Test (1977), **238–43**, 247
Chandrasekhar, Bhagwat, 273
Channel 9, Australia *see* Nine Network
Channel Four, UK, 184
Chapman, Percy, 111–13, 132
Chappell, Greg, 33, 162, 210–12, **215–19**, 224, 226, 229, 239–40, 242, 253, 261–2, 325, 332, 390
Chappell, Ian, 33 160–61, 204, 209–13, 218, 225, 228, 332
Chappell, Trevor, 253
Christie, John, 167
*Chronicle and Echo*, 175
*Chronicle of WG* (Webber), 27
Churchill, Winston, 57
Clark, Manning, 107
Clark, Stuart, 325
Clarke, Michael, 301–2, 306, 313–14, 317, 344, 350, 352, 358, 360, 362–3, 365, 368–70, 373–5
Clarke, William, 217
Clifton, Paddy, 192, 195
Cohen, Victor, 32
Collingwood, Paul, 311, 316–17, 320, 339, 344, 348
Collins, Herbie, **89–93**, 97–9
Compton, Denis, 118–19, **143–5**, 166
Conn, Malcolm, 281
Connolly, Alan, 221
Conolly, John, 45
Constantine, Learie, 153
Cook, Alastair, 344–5, **350–53**, 355, 359, 360, 362–5, 369–70, 374, 376, 378
Copley, Syd, 394

Cosier, Gary, 240, 242–3
Cotter, Albert 'Tibby', 87, 100, 240
*Courier-Mail*, 374
Cowans, Norman, 246
Coward, Mike, 281
Cowdrey, Colin, 169, 176, 182, 195, 237
Cowper, Bob, **201–2**
Craig, Ian, 185
Crawley, John, 279
*Cricket* (Cardus), 71
*Cricket* (Hayward), 55
*Cricket* (Jardine), 120, 123
*Cricket and All That* (Compton & Eldrich), 145
*Cricket Captains of England, The* (Gibson), 117
*Cricket Crisis* (Fingleton), 77
*Cricket Crossfire* (Miller), 152
*Cricket Is My Life* (Hutton), 145
*Cricket Reminiscences & Personal Recollections* (Grace), 26
*Cricket Scores and Biographies* (Haygarth), 21
Cricket World Cup, 395
    1979, 251; 1987, 263; 1996, 334; 1999, 295; 2003, 330
*Cricketer, The*, 115, 211, 213
*Cricketing Colossus* (Cashman & Sissons), 29
Crockett, Bob, 85
Crompton, Alan, 225
Crowe, Jeff, 366
Cummins, Pat, 191, 388–90
Cutriss, Albert, 171
Czikszentmihalyi, Mihaly, 218

D'Oliveira, Basil, 237
*Daily Express*, 127
*Daily Mail*, 165, 199
*Daily Mirror* (Sydney), 199
*Daily Telegraph* (London), 171
*Daily Telegraph* (Sydney), 171
Dalpat, Anil, 198
Dar, Aleem, 355, 359
Darling, Joe, 37, 44, 84

Davidson, Alan, 141, 149, 167, 170, 185, **190–96**
Davidson, Betty, 190, 193–5
Davis, Ian, 241
Davis, J. C., 17
Day, Cheryl, 45
Denness, Mike, 228, 234, 245
Devine, Frank, 282
Dharmasena, Kumar, 361, 366
*Diary of a Cricket Season* (Willis), 246
Dilley, Graham, 255, 267
Docker, Cyril, 97
Doctrove, Billy, 339
Doherty, Xavier, 347–8
Doll, Mordaunt, 97
*Don Bradman* (Lindsay), 106
Douglas, Barney, 379
Douglas, Johnny, 99
Dunne, J. W., 137

Edgbaston Cricket Ground, Birmingham, 299–303, 368–71
Edrich, Bill, 135, 144, 171
Edrich, John, **228–32**, 352
Edwards, Ross, 211
Elizabeth II, Queen of the United Kingdom, 241
Ellis, Mat, 50
Emburey, John, 256
Engel, Matthew, 80
*English Eccentrics* (Sitwell), 236
Erasmus, Ray, 363, 366
*Escaping Club, The* (Evans), 102
Esson, Louis, 88
Evans, A. J., 102, 172
Evans, Richard, 273
*Evening News*, 14, 54

*Famous Cricketers and Cricket Grounds* (Alcock), 64
*Farewell to Cricket* (Bradman), 111
Farmer, Paul, 48–9
Farnes, Ken, 77, 132, **134–7**
Fender, Percy, 81, 240
Ferguson, Bill, 97
*Fifty Years of Cricket* (Hutton), 177

# INDEX

Fingleton, Jack, 77, 165, 180, 186
*Finnegan's Wake* (Joyce), 54
Fishwick, Herbert, 69–70
Flack, Bert, 180
Flanagan, Andy, 157
Flanders, 34
Flegg, Susanna, 30
Fleming, Damien, 277
Fletcher, Duncan, 333
Flintoff, Andrew, 9, 297, 300–303,
    306, 313, 315, 317, 336, 339,
    343–4
Foot, David, 115–16
Forster, Henry, 1st Baron Forster, 82
Forster, Robert, 203
Foster, Reginald Erskine 'Tip', 5,
    **73–5**, 113
*Four Feathers, The* (Korda), 57
Frank Worrell Trophy, 264
Fraser, Angus, 278–9, 285
Freeman, Cathy, 293
Frith, David, 30, 35, 101, 127
Fry, C. B., 28, 52–3, 55, 59, 65–6

Gabba (Brisbane) Cricket Ground,
    388–90
gambling, 92–3
*Game's The Thing, The* (Noble), 58,
    165
Gatting, Mike, **258–60**, 270, 279
Gavaskar, Sunil, 251
Geary, George, 134
*George Giffen* (Whimpress), 33–4
George V, King of the United
    Kingdom, 111
George, Peter, 377
Gibson, Alan, 117
Gibson, Jack, 192–3
Giffen, George, **33–4**, 36–9, 42
Gilchrist, Adam, 138, 288, 291, 295,
    297, 302, 310, **312–14**, 321, 328,
    **333–6**
Giles, Ashley, 302, 311, 315, 317
Gillespie, Jason, 282, 300
Gilligan, Arthur, 81, 135
Gilmour, Gary, 239

*Gitanjali* (Tagore), 137
Gleeson, Johnny, 230
Gooch, Graham, **258–60**, 279
Gordon, Sir Home, 53, 55
Gough, Darren, 278, 284
Gover, Alf, 173
Gower, David, **258–60**, 370
Grace, W. G., 22, 23, **25–8**, 43, 51,
    **134**
Graham, Harry, 44
Graveney, Tom, 165
*Great Australian Cricket Pictures*, 61–2
*Great Batsmen: Their Methods at a
    Glance* (Beldam & Fry), 62, 66–7
*Great Bowlers and Fielders* (Beldam &
    Fry), 66, 68
Green, Cameron, 389
Greenidge, Gordon, 251
Gregory, A. H., 17
Gregory, Dave, 25
Gregory, Jack, 77, 88, 92, **94–103**
Gregory, Syd, 37, 39
Greig, Tony, 210, 229, 235, 239,
    240–41, 242, 267
Griffith, Charlie, 150, 199
Grimmett, Clarrie, 33, 92, 132, 149,
    309
Grout, Wally, 185, 195
*Guardian, The*, 211
Guareschi, Valerie, 115
Guy, Joe, 217

Haddin, Brad, 299, 344–5, 358,
    362–3, 366, 371, 374
Hadlee, Richard, 223
Hall, Wes, 150, 221
Hameed, Haseeb, 389–90
Hammond, Sybil, 115
Hammond, Walter, 70, 102, **115–19**,
    153
Hardstaff, Joe, 125
Harmison, Steve, 300, 302–3, 321,
    343
Harper, Daryl, 285
Harris, George, 4th Baron Harris, 14,
    81, 83

Harris, Marcus, 386, 390
Harris, Ryan, 355–8, 363–5
Hart-Davis, Rupert, 60
Harvey, Neil, **160–63**, 170, 172, 180, 185–6, 195, 209
Hassett, Lindsay, 148, 158–9, 164, 166, 194
Hauritz, Nathan, 339, 341
Hawke, Bob, 293
Hawke, Hazel, 293
Hawke, Martin, 7th Baron Hawke, 81
Hawke, Neil, 221
Hayden, Matthew, 202, 300, 302, 309, 327–8, **329–32**, 334
Haygarth, Arthur, 21
Hayward, Tom, 55, 81
Hazlewood, Josh, 370, 385, 387, 389
Headingley Cricket Ground, Leeds, 212, 384–7
Headley, Dean, 285
Healy, Ian, 263, 276, 295, 334, 375
Hedley, Harry, 17
Heine, Peter, 150
Hele, George, 128
Hemmings, Eddie, 246
Hendren, Patsy, 102
Hendrick, Mike, 229, 248
Hendry, Stork, 91, 394
*Herald Sun*, 281–3
Hick, Graeme, 277–9
Hilfenhaus, Ben, 338, 340
Hill, Clem, 33, 67, 87
Hill, Tony, 355, 359, 363
Hirst, John, 43
*History of Cricket, A* (Altham), 19
Hobbs, Ada, 83
Hobbs, Jack, 77, **79–83**, 99, 125
Hoggard, Matthew, 313, 317
Holding, Michael, 294, 332
Hole, Graeme, 167, 172
Hookes, David, 227, 239, 241, 312
Horan, Tom 'Felix', 5, **16–20**, 21, 22, 27, 34
Horne, Donald, 72
House, Jack, 168–71, 173

*How We Recovered the Ashes* (Warner), 8, 74
Howard, John, 295–6, 314, 327
Hoy, Col, 171
Hughes, Kim, 253–4, 256, 261–2, 325
Hughes, Margaret, 171
Hughes, Merv, 323
Hughes, Phillip, 189, 246, 381
Hundred, The, 395
Hussain, Nasser, 288–9, 291–2, 297, 330, 390
Hussey, Mike, 313–14, 317, 342–3, 347
Hutton, Len, 75, 82, 118–19, 133, 136, 141, **143–5**, 148, 164–5, 171–2, 176, 202, 390

ICC Code of Conduct, 295
Illingworth, Ray, 210–12, 214, 237, 260
*In Quest of the Ashes* (Jardine), 121
*In Quest of the Ashes* (Mackay), 201
*In The Eye of the Typhoon* (Tyson), 174–6
India, 1, 51–2, 55
*Ins and Outs* (O'Neill), 199
International Cricket Council, 329
International Cup Cricket, 226
'Invincibles', 28, 91, 140, 160–61, 395
Iredale, Frank, 43
Irish, Ronald, 199
Irving, Henry, 58

*Jack Hobbs* (Arlott), 80
Jackson, Arthur, 246
Jackson, F. S., 52, 67
James, Alfred, 12–14
James, C. L. R., 105
Jardine, Douglas, 9–10, 77, **120–23**, 126, 131, 260, 351
Jayasuriya, Sanath, 334
Jenner, Terry, 245, 270, 273, 275
Johns, Alf, 49
Johnson, Ian, 148, 169–73, 179–80, 184

# INDEX

Johnson, Mitchell, 221, 339–40, 360, 364–6, 368–9, 378
Johnston, Allan, 156
Johnston, Bill, **155–9**, 165–6, 171
Jones, Dean, 263
Jones, Ernie, 100
Jones, Geraint, 300–303, 317
Jones, Sammy, 27
Joyce, James, 54
*Jubilee Book of Cricket* (Ranjitsinhji), 52

Kaluwitharana, Romesh, 334
Kasprowicz, Michael, 299, 302–3
Katich, Simon, 306, 339, 343
Kellaway, Charles, 97
*Ken Farnes* (Thurlow), 134, 136
Keneally, Thomas, 8, 107
Kennedy, Alex, 80
Kew Asylum, Melbourne, 22–3, 44–9
Khan, Imran, 223
Khan, Zaheer, 330
Khawaja, Usman, 354, 358
Kilburn, J. M., 116, 148
Kimber, Jarrod, 63
King, Alana, 276
Kippax, Alan, 90, 113, 128
Knight, Barry, 201
Knight, Donald, 101
Knott, Alan, 212–13, **236–7**
Koertzen, Rudi, 301, 310, 321, 335, 343
Korda, Alexander, 57
Kyle, Jim, 87

Labuschagne, Marnus, 386, 390, 394
Laker, Jim, 141, **178–82**
*Laker* (Mosey), 182
Lane, Tim, 327
Langer, Justin, 285, 301, 320, **326–8**, 331, 381
Lap, Phar, 175
Lara, Brian, 75, 133, 202, 294
Larwood, Harold, 9, 92, 95, 101, 103, 121–3, **124–9**, 131, 240, 377
*Larwood Story, The* (Larwood), 125

*Last Invincible, The* (Harvey), 161
Laumen, Louis, 72
Laver, Frank, 87
Lawry, Bill, 161, 203, 210, 232
Lawson, Geoff, 218
Leach, Jack, 381
Leckie, David, 282
Ledward, Jack, 156, 171
Lee, Brett, 291, 300, 302–3, 309, 311
leg-theory, 121, 127, 131
Lehmann, Darren, 372, 375
Leifer, Neil, 68
Lever, John, 269
Leyland, Maurice, 122
*Life Worth Living* (Fry), 28
Lillee, Dennis, 207, 210–11, 213, 218, **220–23**, 224, 227–9, 239–40, 242, 254–7, 262, 268, 325
Lindsay, Philip, 106
Lindwall, Ray, 141, **146–50**, 158, 165–6, 170, 177, 377
Loader, Peter, 176
Lock, Tony, 178–80, 232
Lockwood, Bill, 36
Lord, John, 51
Lord's Cricket Ground, 164–7, 380–83
Loxton, Sam, 161
*Lucky: The Life of H. L. 'Bert' Collins* (Bonnell), 89
Lyon, Nathan, 276, 355, 357, 359, 364, 366, 383, 385–7, 389, 391, 393
Lyttleton, George, 60

Macartney, Charlie, 93, 96, 99
MacGill, Stuart, 274, 284
Mackay, Ken, 201
MacLaren, Archie, 36–9, **57–60**, 80
Maddocks, Len, 169
*Magnificence, Misery and Madness* (Day), 45
*Maharajahs, The* (Lord), 51
Mahony, Richard, 30
Mailey, Arthur, 85, 99, 122
Major, John, 252
Malan, Dawid, 390, 392–3

Malcolm, Devon, 278–9
Mallett, Ashley, 160–61, 227
*Manchester Guardian*, 59, 69, 112, 167
Mandle, Bill, 41
Mankad, 'Vinoo', 85, 139–40
Marsh, Geoff, 263
Marsh, Rod, 207, 210–11, 213, **224–7**
Marsh, Rod, 218, 239, 241–3, 248,
    254–6, 262, 325, 374
Marsh, Shaun, 371, 373
Martindale, Manny, 130
Martyn, Damien, 301, 302, 326
Marylebone Cricket Club (MCC), 8,
    53
Mason, Ronald, 101
Massie, Bob, 210–11, 213, 269
Masters, John, 51
May, Peter, 165, 179–80, 182, 185
May, Tim, 277–8
McCabe, Stan, 294, 394
McCabe, Steve, 340
McClelland, William, 171
McConnon, Jim, 170, 176
McCool, Colin, 230
McCosker, Rick, 239–40, 242, 250
McCullum, Brendan, 395
McDermott, Craig, 263, 278, 323
McDonald, Colin, 180
McDonald, Donald, 17
McDonald, Ted, 77, 88, **89–93**,
    100–102
McDonnell, Percy, 42
McEnroe, John, 273
McGilvray, Alan, 28
McGrath, Glenn, 226, 274, 282, 291,
    299–300, 309, 311, 321, **322–5**,
    375
McGregor, Adrian, 217
McInnes, Mel, 171
McKenzie, Graham 'Garth', 210, 221
McKinnon, Donald, 50
McLaughlan, Lizzie, 22
McLeod, Bob, 49
McMahon, John, 144
Mead, Walter, 63
Meckiff, Ian, 141, 221

Melbourne Cricket Club (MCC), 49,
    85–7, 157, **168–73**, 285
Melbourne Cricket Ground (MCG),
    19, 38–9, 202, 239–42, 247–9,
    270, 275, 319–21
*Melbourne Punch*, 32, 39
Menzies, Robert, 39–40, 151, 159, 172
Mickle, William Julius, 23
Midwinter, William 'Billy', 5, **21–4**
Millard, Percy, 158
Miller, Andrew, 93
Miller, Keith Ross, 141, 148, 150,
    **151–4**, 155, 158, 165–7, 169–70,
    180, 185, 239
Mitchell, Tommy, 122
Modi, Lalit, 341
Mohammad, Hanif, 202
Moody, Clarence, 33
Moore, Maggie, 23
Morris, Arthur, 170–71
Mosey, Don, 182
Moyes, Johnny, 185
Mullally, Alan, 285
Mullins, Pat, 18
Mundine, Anthony, 293
Muralitharan, Muttiah, 323
Murdoch, Billy, 14, 27–8, **29–32**
Murdoch, Gilbert, 30–31
Murray, John, 237
*My Life Story* (Hobbs), 82
*My World of Cricket* (Harvey), 160–61

Ned, Gregory, 39
Nel, Jack, 158
Nelson Cricket Club, 91, 93
*New Immortality, The* (Dunne), 137
*New York Times*, 105
*News of the World*, 187
*Next Man In* (Brodribb), 53
Nine Network, 187–8, 218, 282–3,
    354
Noble, Monty, 58, 84, 165
Noblet, Geff, 164
North, Marcus, 340
Ntini, Makhaya, 305

O'Connell, Max, 238–9, 241–2
O'Keeffe, Kerry, 243
O'Neill, Gwen, 199
O'Neill, Norman, **197–200**
O'Reilly, Bill, 17, 147, 154, 294, 351
*Old Man, The* (1948), 28
Old Trafford Cricket Ground,
    Manchester, 58, 180–81
Old, Chris, 229, 242, 255
Oldfield, Bert, 97–8, 101
*On Top Down Under* (Robinson), 388
*On Tour with Bradman* (Flanagan), 157
one-day cricket, 241, 285, 293, 299,
    334
*Ornamentalism: How The British Saw
    Their Empire* (Cannadine), 55
*Out of My Comfort Zone* (Waugh), 295
The Oval Cricket Ground, 82,
    308–11, 342–5
*Over to Me* (Laker), 182

*Pace Bowling* (Willis), 246
Packer, Kerry, 71, 187, 207, 243, 282,
    309
Paine, Tim, 381, 385, 387
Palmer, Vance, 88, 107
Panesar, Monty, 182, 312, 314, 321,
    337, 340, 360, 361–3, 365–6
Pant, Rishabh, 160
Parish, Bob, 241
Parker, Grahame, 22
Parkin, Cecil, 81, 100
Parkinson, Michael, 109
Parks, Jim, 237
Parore, Adam, 324
Parris, Matthew, 354
*Passing Tests* (Chappell), 204
Pawle, Gerald, 133
Peebles, Ian, 60, 198
Peel, Bobby, 36–7
Pellew, Clarence, 97
*Perfect Batsman, The* (MacLaren), 80
Perkins, Kevin, 125, 127
Perkins, Kieren, 282
Phillips, A. A., 71–2
Philpott, Percy, 230

photography, 64–8, 72, 94–5
Piccadilly Grill Room, 126
Pickworth, Ossie, 170
Pietersen, Kevin, 300–301, 306,
    310–11, 317, 321, 338–9, **346–9**,
    354–7, 364, 366
*Playing the Game* (Buruma), 51
Pollard, Kieron, 352
Pollock, Graeme, 162
Pollock, Peter, 231
Ponsford, Bill, 111
Ponting, Ricky, 226, **287–9**, 300–301,
    315, 317, 320, 327–9, 335, 337,
    340, 347–8, 394
Pope, Ollie, 390
Porritt, Arthur, 26
Porter, John, 26
Pratt, Gary, 343, 394
Pringle, Derek, 246
Prior, Matt, 339, 344, 355, 357, 366
professional status, 80–82, 86
Provident Fund, 243
Pyke, Frank, 221–2

Qadir, Abdul, 273
Qasim, Iqbal, 246

*R. E. S. Wyatt: Fighting Cricketer*
    (Pawle), 133
radio, 107
Rae, Simon, 27
Ramadhin, Sonny, 158
Ramprakash, Mark, 285, 287, 324
Ramsey, Michael, 124
Randall, Derek, 239, 242–3, **247–52**
Ranjitsinhji, Kumar Shri, 43, **51–6**,
    65–7, 74
Ransford, Vernon, 87, 168–9, 171,
    173
*Ravi Lancers, The* (1972), 51
Ray, Mark, 283
Read, Chris, 321
*Reasons Why, The* (Foot), 116
Redpath, Ian, 229
Reed, Ron, 281
*Referee, The*, 43, 95

Reliance Mobile ICC Rankings, 329, 332
Reynolds, Tom, 282
Rhodes, Dusty, 390
Rhodes, Jonty, 251
Richards, Viv, 294, 313, 380–81
Richardson, Arthur, 103
Richardson, Henry Handel, 107
Richardson, Nick, 89, 91
Richardson, Tom, 36, 39
Richardson, Victor, 39, 210
Ring, Doug, 157, 165–7
Ringwood, John, 149
Ritchie, Greg, 283
Riverside Cricket Ground, Durham, 355
Roberts, Tom, 36, 151
Robertson-Glasgow, R. C., 9, 116, 134, 152
Robertson, Austin, 243
Robins, Walter, 112
Robinson, Ollie, 389
Robinson, Ray, 94, 147, 156, 158, 186, 225, 388
Rogers, Billy, 192
Rogers, Chris, 355–6, 358, 361, 365, 373, 378
Root, Joe, 3, 362, 364, 366, 370, 388–90, **391–3**
Ross, Alan, 53, 144, 258
Rothmans of Pall Mall, 199–200
Rouse, Steve, 300, 303
Rowe, Lawrence, 226
Royal Television Society, 183
Rudolph, Jacques, 75
Russell, Jack, 353
Ryder, Jack, 156, 240

Sabina Park, Jamaica, 130
Saheb, Jam, 56
*Seeing the Sunrise* (Langer), 331
Seitz, Arnold, 172
*Sentimental Nation* (Hirst), 43
Shafayat, Bilal, 340
Shea, Murray, 157
Sheahan, Paul, 213

Sheffield Shield, 86–7, 153, 156
Sheffield, Lord *see* Baker-Holroyd, John, 1st Earl of Sheffield
Sheppard, David, 144
Shrewsbury, Arthur, 5, 27, 81, 234
Siddle, Peter, 191, 340, 348, 359, 364, 366, 371
*Silk Express: The Story of E. A. 'Ted' McDonald, The* (Richardson), 89
Simpson, Bob, 71, 186, 201, 203, 262–3, 281
Simpson, Reg, 249
Sims, Robin, 394
Singh, Harbhajan, 289
*Singleton Argus*, 23
Sissons, Ric, 29, 31
Sitwell, Edith, 236
Slater, Michael, 327, 331, 375
slow batting, 234, 316
Smith, Alan, 237
Smith, Hayden, 126
Smith, Keith and Ross, 152
Smith, Robin, 267–9
Smith, Steve, 366, 368–9, 373, 375–6, 380–84, 389
Smith, Syd, 101
Smith, Tiger, 126
Snow, John, 210–11, 245
Sobers, Garry, 249–50, 291, 312
Sophia Gardens Cricket Ground, Cardiff, 337–41
South Africa, 32, 136
South Melbourne Cricket Club, 42, 50
Spofforth, Fred, 30, 100, 309
*Sporting Globe*, 100
*Sporting Times*, 8
*Sports Illustrated*, 68
Stackpole, Keith, 211, 213
Stakhanov, Alexei, 373
Standing, Percy Cross, 54
Stanlake, Billy, 377
Staples, Sam, 125
Starc, Mitchell, 389, 393
Statham, Brian, 150, 172, 176–7
Steele, Ray, 213

# INDEX

Stoddart, Andrew 'Drewy', 5, 35–9, 43
*Stoddy's Mission* (Frith), 35
Stokes, Ben, 2, 202, 360, 363, 366, 382–3, 384–7, 390, 394
*Strand, The*, 54
Strauss, Andrew, 58, 122, 227, 300–301, 306–7, 320, 337, 339, 344
*Stroke of Genius* (Haigh), 61n, 63, 72
*Summer Game, The* (Haigh), 162
*Sun* (Sydney), 185–6
*Sun, The* (UK), 309
*Sun News-Pictorial*, 242
*Sunday Age*, 283
*Sunday Herald Sun*, 281
*Sunday Times*, 198
Surrey Cricket Club, 80–81
Sutcliffe, Herbert, 122, 132, 164
Swann, Graeme, 227, 339–40, 342–5, 356–8, 361, 363–6
Swanton, E. W., 167, 197
Swanton, Jim, 134
Sydney Cricket Ground (SCG) , 37, 95, 351, 277–9, 326
    riot (1879), 14, 25
*Sydney Mail*, 13, 69–70
*Sydney Morning Herald*, 13, 173, 245

T20 cricket, 271, 299, 336, 352
Tagore, Rabindranath, 137
'Tailenders' (podcast), 379
Tait, Shaun, 311
Tate, Maurice, 112
Tavare, Chris, 256
Tayler, Albert Chevallier, 74–5
Taylor, Johnny, 97
Taylor, Mark, 277–9, 280–83, 328, 331, 334
Taylor, Ross, 73
Tendulkar, Sachin, 104, 294, 393
*Test Cricket: The Unauthorized Biography* (Kimber), 63
Test matches
    1877, 11, 16; 1878, 25; 1880, 25–6, 30; 1899, 28; 1945, 152–3; 1968, 291

*That's Cricket* (movie), 108
Thomson, Jeff, 213, 229
Thorpe, Graham, 277–8, 323
*Three Straight Sticks* (Wyatt), 132
*Three Weeks in the Kew Lunatic Asylum* (Farmer), 48
Thurlow, David, 134, 136
*Tigers Among The Lions* (Ian Chappell), 212
*Times, The*, 353
Titmus, Fred, 229
Tomlinson, Richard, 28
*Tours and Tests* (Farnes), 136
Tremlett, Chris, 360
Trenerry, Bill, 97
Trent Bridge Cricket Ground, Nottingham, 372–5
Trescothick, Marcus, 300, 305, 309–10
Trott, Adolphus, 42
Trott, Albert, 38
Trott, Harry, 5, **41–50**
Trott, Jonathan, 297, 355, 358, 360, 392
Trueman, Fred, 141, 150, 198
Trumble, Hugh, 43
Trumper, Victor, 5, 17–18, **61–72**, 86–7, 240, 334
Tufnell, Phil, 279
Tuke, Henry Scott, 54, 67
Turner, Charlie, 30, 38
Tyldesley, Ernest, 102
Tyldesley, Johnny, 74, 81
Tyson, Frank, 136, 141, 150, 172, **174–7**, 239

umpires, 241
Underwood, Derek, 212–13, 229, 237

van der Bijl, Peter, 135
Vanthoff, Bill, 168, 170–71, 173
Vaughan, Michael, 122, 300–302, 305, 309, 338
Verity, Hedley, 122, 128
Victoria, Queen of the United Kingdom, 35

Victorian Cricket Association, 85–7
Victory Tests (1945), 152–3
Voce, Bill, 121, 125–7, 131
Voges, Adam, 373–4

*W. G. Grace: A Life* (Rae), 27
Wagner, Neil, 382
Walker, Max, 213, 239
Walsh, Courtney, 324, 327, 376
Walters, Doug, **203–5**, 241
Ward, Alan, 245
Wardill, Ben, 49
Wardle, Johnny, 171
Wareham, Georgia, 276
Warne, Shane, 9, 92–3, 178, 258, 265,
    **270–76**, 277, 295, 298, 315–18,
    349, 375, 376, 396
Warner, David, 13, 163, 358, 361,
    364–5, 369–70, 385
Warner, Pelham, 8, 74, 79, 96, 111,
    117–18, 122, 153
*Warriors* (documentary), 379
Watson, John Boyd, 31
Watson, Shane, 343, 348, 350, 356,
    358, 361–2, 365, 371
Watson, Willy, 165–7
Watt, Bill, 240
Waugh, Mark, 281, 289, 334
Waugh, Steve, 79, 83, 138, 263, 284,
    288, 291, **293–8**, 331, 334, 351
Webber, Joe, 27
Webster, Rudi, 217
*Weekly Dispatch*, 81
Wellington, Amanda-Jane, 276

Wells, H. G., 137
Whimpress, Bernard, 33–3
White, Felix, 378
White, Jack 'Farmer', 111–12
Whitington, Dick, 169
Whitington, R. S., 245
Whysall, Dodge, 125
*Wicked-Keeper, The* (Parore), 324
Wilde, Simon, 52
Williamson, J. C., 23
Willis, Bob, 204, 229, 238–9, **244–6**,
    255
*Willow Patterns* (Benaud), 187
Wilson, Joel, 385
Windsor, Ted, 84
*Winning Ways* (Webster), 217
*Wisden*, 21, 43, 98, 307
    Cricketer of the Year, 135
    Five Cricketers of the Century, 79
    Five Cricketers of the Year, 199
Woakes, Chris, 382, 389
Woodcock, John, 211, 213
*Woodend Star*, 44
Woodfull, Bill, 108, 111–12, 132
Woolley, Frank, 100, 240
World Series Cricket, 71, 187, 207,
    218, 243, 245, 261
World War I, 96
World War II, 152
Worrall, Jack, 12, 86
Worrell, Frank, 186
Wyatt, Bob, 118, **130–33**

Yallop, Graham, 160, 256, 390